(signature)

BLACK WATER
Tales from the Cloquet River
By Mark Munger

Cloquet River Press
www.cloquetriverpress.com
Stories from the Lake Superior Basin

First Edition
Copyright 2013 © Mark Munger

ISBN 978-0-9792175-4-8

Published by:

Cloquet River Press
5353 Knudsen Road
Duluth, Minnesota 55803
(218) 721-3213

Visit the publisher at: www.cloquetriverpress.com
Email the author at: cloquetriverpress@yahoo.com

Printed in the United States
Cover Photo by Mark Munger
Author Photo by Dave Michelson

Acknowledgments

I'm indebted to Marla Ahlgren, Creative Writing Instructor at Fond du Lac Tribal and Community College, Cloquet, Minnesota, for her many hours of dedicated proofreading of the manuscript for this collection.

A special thanks to Charlie Wilkins from Thunder Bay, Ontario, a great writer who took the time to listen to me when things weren't going so well.

Lastly, to my wife René and my four sons: Thanks for putting up with this old man's dream. It hasn't been easy but I know you understand.

Mark Munger
Duluth, Minnesota
2013

For René and the boys…

Table of Contents

A Word from the Author

Most of these essays first appeared in the *Hermantown Star* newspaper as columns over an eight-year period from the mid-1990s to the early 21st century. The various editors of the *Star* gave me my first "paying gig" as a writer and for that, I am forever grateful. Four new essays are included in this collection: "The Boys Are Back", "Ashley, ND 2010", "Caribou", and "Katherine Lake". These essays have been previously published online: "Boys", "Ashley", and "Caribou" on my own website (www.cloquetriverpress.com); and "Katherine" on the 1000 Friends of Minnesota site (www.1000fom.org), where the essay was selected as a contest winner from submissions sent in from around the State of Minnesota celebrating Minnesota's lakes and rivers.

The other essays in this collection also appeared in previously released Cloquet River Press books. The earliest stories were collected in *River Stories*, the first book published by my modest little press in 2002. The others appeared in *Doc the Bunny and Other Short Tales* published in 2005. Many essays that I no longer believe "cut the mustard" have been discarded, trimming the ultimate batch of essays for this compilation to what I consider to be "the best of the best". A few stories were also excluded due to subject matter: Essays dealing with my upbringing in the Piedmont Heights neighborhood of Duluth, Minnesota (my hometown) have been culled with an eye towards including them in a memoir.

Enjoy these reflections on a life lived along the banks of one of Minnesota's great rivers.

Mark Munger
2013

A House for Minnie Williams

It was getting on towards autumn when she finally settled on the house she wanted. Model 7016 in the 1921 *Sears Modern Homes* catalog. The price was $1200.00 for a four bedroom, one bath, pre-cut home; the "Glendale." For her money, she was to get: framing, interior walls, yellow pine trim and floors, a brick chimney, asphalt shingles, exterior siding, exterior doors, windows, two porches, all paint, nails, varnish and hardware.

Minnie Williams tilted her head and viewed a calendar on the wall. September 1, 1921. Her eyes glanced around the dirty interior of the place. Oily smoke curled up from a kerosene lamp on the table. The lamp's dim light allowed her to see only a portion of the room she occupied.

Richard had promised (when he brought her from Des Moines, Iowa to Fredenberg Township, Minnesota) that she would not have to raise her children in a log cabin. That promise had been made five years and two babies ago. She sighed. Richard always kept his word...eventually. The door opened behind her.

"Good evening, Richard."

Minnie smiled at her husband as he walked into the light. He was short, no more than five-foot-five, and slight of build. His eyes caught the lamplight, reflecting blue. His black hair was shoulder length and greasy from a hard day's work. His face was rough and bearded.

"Evening, Minnie. What's for supper?"

She rose slowly and pushed herself away from the table. She stopped, pausing to rub her swollen belly. She massaged the fabric of her dress, working a cramp deep within her womb.

"Anything wrong?" her husband said as he reached around her engorged waist.

"No, just a spell. It'll pass. There's chicken and dumplings on the stove and milk in the ice box."

Richard eased her into the only other room on the main floor. The room held their rough-sawn bed, a leather chair, a

9

chest of drawers and a small end table. "Sit yourself down in the good chair. I'll fix myself a plate."

Richard filled a tin plate with food before sitting down at the table. He studied the open catalog as he ate.

"This the one? 'The Glendale?'"

"That's it. We need the four bedrooms. Can't cram another child into this cabin."

Minnie tilted her head back in the chair, hoping the pain would subside.

"We got $500.00 from Great Northern Dam and Improvement Company for the flowage rights a' front of this place. That plus the money I got from the white pine I cut should be enough for your Sears house."

Richard gingerly lifted a piece of boiled chicken from his plate with his knife and slid the food into his mouth. White grease and gravy dripped onto the worn surface of the pine floor.

Minnie smiled and leaned back in the chair. Long blond hair spilled out from beneath her scarf. At thirty, she was two years older than Richard. Plain featured and of modest figure, she stood four or five inches taller than her husband.

The couples' two boys slept soundly in the darkness of the loft above her. The boys slept together on a thick homemade mattress stuffed with straw warmed by the rising heat of the cook stove; though much of the stove's heat escaped the cabin through countless gaps in the log walls.

"Maybe we oughta ride over to Taft and catch the train to Duluth. You can go in and see Doc Smith. We'll order the house from town."

"I'd like that."

It was easier than she had expected.

Imagine, she thought to herself as she mailed off a cashier's check and order form to Sears during their visit to Duluth, *imagine a world where you can look in a magazine and order your home lock, stock, and barrel.*

On October 30, 1921, two months after Minnie had ordered the home from Sears, four large bundles of building materials were shipped from Homan Avenue, Chicago, on the Chicago &

Northwestern Railroad, bound for Taft Station. In Duluth, the flatcar carrying the Williams home was switched to the Duluth, Winnipeg, & Pacific line. The same day, Richard Williams and five men from the township met the train at Taft. It took a come-along and the strength of all six men to load the bundles on separate wagons for the final eight miles of the journey.

Minnie Williams and the other wives stood outside the cabin. November was unusually warm. There was no snow on the ground. The route towards the new home site sliced through an empty land. Great white pine stumps bore mute witness to a vanquished forest.

Off in the distance, the draft team pulling Richard Williams' wagon came into view. The horses trod with steady power on uneven ground. At the edge of the west bank of the Cloquet River, the farmer motioned for the parade of wagons to halt. The cantilever bridge that would eventually connect the two ends of the Taft Road had not yet been built. The main road over the Island Lake Dam was closed for reconstruction. There was only one way to get Minnie's new house to the other side of the river.

Williams urged his two Percherons down the loose soil of the hillside. The horses snorted and stomped. Their great ebony flanks shivered in excitement. For a brief moment, Minnie feared that the animals would turn away from the black water. But Richard knew his horses. He coaxed them into the steady current of the river. The other drivers watched quietly as Williams' team advanced to the far shore. The other wagons entered the stream only when the lead wagon was safely across.

The aroma of hot food and coffee greeted Richard as his wagon crested the eastern bank of the river. Once on the level, his eyes fell upon a white cross singularly positioned in short brown grass. He slid out of the wagon seat. The tails of the horses twitched though there were no flies.

Richard's first wife, Cora, was buried in the cold earth before him. She had died at twenty. Minnie was her older sister. A gentle hand touched his shoulder. He turned and met Minnie face to face.

"Cora loved this place."

Minnie's voice was subdued as she handed him a cup of coffee. Her eyes floated over his face like clouds blown by the wind.

"This is no time for cuddlin'," another voice declared. "We best get this house together before the snow flies."

Emmett Johnson strode towards the couple as he spoke. Johnson was a carpenter. Short and rotund for a Norwegian, his brown hair and beard were speckled with gray.

"Got the plans right here, Emmett. Let's take a look."

Williams pulled the blueprints out of his coveralls and handed them to his neighbor. Johnson stared at the documents. Each piece of lumber was pre-cut, labeled, and corresponded to the numerical scheme of the blueprints.

Johnson whistled.

"That's the way to build a house. What are we waitin' for?"

Richard nodded in agreement. It was time to build Minnie Williams a new home.

I can't tell you what happened to the Williams family. I don't know whether their third child survived the winter or whether the couple lived a long and happy life. What I can tell you is that, on this January night, as a bitter northwest wind assaults our seventy-five-year-old Sears home, the love of Minnie and Richard Williams can still be felt here.

Beneath the Canopy

There is not much primeval forest left on the one hundred and thirty-two acres of land in northeastern Minnesota that I call home. Progress has disturbed nearly every inch of my farm along the banks of the Cloquet River. If you came for a visit, you wouldn't think this to be the case. Sentinel white and red pines tower over second growth forest. Deer, wolves, bear, eagles, osprey and assorted lesser creatures remain abundant despite the intrusion of humans. Notwithstanding the plethora of animal life, these woods are not the same as they were a century ago, before Europeans arrived to log the forest and till the soil. The one exception to this is a delicate labyrinth of swamp occupying a small corner of our property. Beneath the rare cedars of that refuge, little has changed.

Marsh grass grows thick between black alders. A thin ribbon of fresh, cold water ebbs slowly through the bog, sliding gently towards the stream's juncture with the river. Two islands of cedar rise from the tremulous ground, providing a stable platform from which to view the swamp. A scent of cedar, carried by a brisk wind, finds my nostrils, and reminds me of the age when Ojibwe hunted this ground and walked its narrow paths. The unnamed creek meanders between the trunks of trees exposing gnarled roots to cool air. Minnows dart in the shadows seeking protection.

This bog exists in the twilight of wilderness; between the manicured pasture of our old farm and an open gash left by my neighbor's clear-cutting of mature aspen on adjoining land. A line of maples climbs a hogback to the south. Though the steep spine of the ridge provides a marginal barricade against progress, it does not take much imagination to conjure up the specter of skidders crawling through wet peat, crushing the vegetation, deforesting this rarefied garden.

Every day, dozens of vehicles pass this spot. I can hear them now, roaring along the roadway, as I sit within the embrace of cedars. I suspect that the folks driving on the adjacent highway aren't interested in this swamp. Their lives are too hurried, too

13

rushed, to contemplate the secret beauty of this marsh. Perhaps that's for the best.

Strawberries

Jerry Drew warned us. I mean, it's not like he didn't give us plenty of advance notice that they were there. We just didn't understand. How could we? We were from the city.

They were out in the pasture; concealed, silent, growing larger and larger; swelling from the heat and the rain. There was no sign, no fence to mark their territory, to alert us to their presence. It was left for us to discover them.

I remember Jerry's cryptic words as he and his family packed themselves into their station wagon and headed down the driveway the last time. Just before he hit the blacktop, Jerry stopped the car and backed up slowly until the car was right beside René and me.

"Oh, yeah. One more thing."

He smiled and waved his arm toward the pasture.

"You may want to keep an eye on the strawberries. We put in a few plants last year."

My wife and I had nodded, still shell-shocked from the move. We watched mutely as the Drews departed. The strawberries were forgotten. We were eager to get to the business of making the old Sears house our home. The berries would have to wait.

It took my family a few weeks to get settled in, to become accustomed to the bats and field mice that also called our farmhouse their home. It took quite a bit longer to figure out how to connect the mower deck to the ancient Ford garden tractor that came with the place as part of the deal. In the end, I managed to attach the deck using fewer parts than the manual called for. I saved the extra pieces. Just in case. Again, I was far too busy to look for strawberries.

Next on the priority list was the barn. The building was filled with sheep manure and needed attention of the most deliberate sort. It took two weeks of shoveling and wheeling dung before I struck the concrete floor of the old dairy barn. Throughout my labor, the strawberries remained undiscovered.

Towards the end of June, I took two weeks of vacation. I planned to spend my time off reading, tinkering, and finding the best fishing spots on the Cloquet River. I was home, reading an Ursula LeGuin novella, when René finally found them.

"Mark, there must be a ton of strawberries out there."

I wasn't interested. The term "ton" reminded me of sheep manure. The acrid dust of that experience still clung to my nostrils. My shoulders and back ached at the prospect of moving a "ton" of anything.

"Uh-huh," I replied, without looking up, my nose buried in my book.

René would not go away.

"You have to see them for yourself. Come on."

My wife stood there, very pregnant, very sweaty, and very determined. I yielded. I put down the book and followed her out into the field.

"See?"

Outlined in the tall grass, I could make out what looked to be about a quarter acre of green, leafy plants. The plants formed tight, perfect rows, their leaves glistening in the bright summer sunlight.

"What are they?"

"Strawberries. They're loaded with fruit."

"Who'd be crazy enough to plant so many?"

I didn't expect her to respond.

"The Drews."

"I knew that."

She lifted the leaves of one of the plants and forced me to bend down. I studied the fruit. The size of the berries made me rethink my disinterest.

"They're huge! How many have berries like this?"

"All of them."

René stood up triumphantly. I continued to examine the ripe berries. The heavy fruit hung precariously in the still air. I began to dream: strawberry pie, strawberries on ice cream, strawberry jam; the possibilities seemed endless. René's voice called me back to reality.

"They need to be weeded."

"How's that?"

"You heard me. The weeds are choking out the plants."

My wife's arms rose. Her gesture encompassed a vast expanse, which up to that moment had seemed to be a quarter acre of heaven. Until she mentioned the weeds, a quarter acre hardly seemed sufficient for all the plans I was making.

"Really?"

"Really."

I began to perspire. Great beads of sweat formed on my forehead and dripped onto the plants. I thought I detected one of the strawberry plants dance in perverse delight as my body's moisture landed on its leaf. I sensed I was becoming delirious.

That evening, René and I began to hack away at the weeds beneath a cloud of obnoxious mosquitoes. We pulled. We tugged. We strained at the thick-rooted parasites. In addition, we found that there were so many ripe berries we couldn't harvest them all. Hundreds ripened and fell to the dirt before we could salvage them. Every relative, friend, or neighbor we could round up was enlisted to pick. Their efforts hardly dented the crop.

Finally, we placed a sign out on the Taft Road:

Pick Your Own Strawberries. 50 Cents a Pound.

Strangers got their fill. More berries ripened. Like out-of-control chocolates on an assembly line in an old "I Love Lucy" episode, our strawberries continued to ripen faster than we could pick them. And the weeds, despite our best efforts, continued to sprout.

By the end of my vacation, four hundred and fifty pounds of berries had been harvested. Another hundred pounds or so remained in the field. My dreams of strawberry pie and jam had been replaced by the reality of aching knees, a body covered with bug bites, and a realization that, without a gasoline tiller, the weeds would always win.

The following season, the patch produced half as many berries and twice as many weeds. Conceding defeat, I fenced in the pasture and let Nicholas, our horse, eat strawberries, weeds, and grass to his heart's content. I thought I'd seen the last of strawberries on the Munger Farm.

17

But there's something magical about strawberries. Something compels René and I to try to grow them. Maybe we share some sort of primeval hunter-gatherer need that can only be satisfied by growing strawberries. Or maybe we're both just plain stubborn. Whatever the reason, year in and year out, we add new strawberry plants to our vegetable garden. We water them, mulch them, nurture them, and try to weed them, but the weeds always win out.

You'd think we'd learn our lesson. You'd think that we could admit defeat. It would be cheaper and less frustrating to simply drive to town and buy berries at the market. But I'm here to tell you: Dreams of homegrown strawberries die hard.

Winter Geese

They came to live with us on my thirtieth birthday, a gift from three of my high school buddies. I'm now fast approaching fifty so that my memory of things that happened on my thirtieth birthday may or may not be accurate. That disclosure having been made, I think my mind has retained most of the details about the geese.

My pals Larry, John, and Steve gave them to me. Two white farm geese: one male, one female. Being that Larry and John were carpenters at the time and Steve was an engineer, the boys saw to it that the geese came packaged in a well-constructed cage. But the geese were large and the cage was small. It soon became apparent that the birds needed more room.

I don't remember their names. I do remember their voices. Their loud, obnoxious calls still reverberate in my mind. I built them an enclosed pen out next to the barn. The first few weeks we had them, I did my best to keep our golden retriever (Pelly) away from the birds. I tried to keep the geese fed and watered. I wasn't a farmer. I'd never owned poultry. I think the birds took advantage of my ignorance.

That November, the Cloquet River plummeted to the lowest level that it has ever been at since we moved to Fredenberg Township. Normally, because our farm is located only a mile or so below the dam forming Island Lake, the flowage in front of our place stays open all winter. But that year, the Cloquet River froze over. Only a small oval of water surrounded by thin ice remained open in front of our place.

Somehow, I left the door to the goose pen unlatched. When I went out to feed the birds, they were gone. Fresh snow told the tale. I followed goose tracks to the river. Out in the middle of the open water, our geese swam. Even to this city boy, it was obvious that our geese had no intention of returning to their cage on their own.

After a period of contemplation, I envisioned a plan. Pelly was a golden retriever, a bird dog. It would only be natural for me to call upon him to help me retrieve the geese. I yelled to my wife René and asked her to bring the dog down to the water. I didn't really intend for her to get involved in the chase. She was within days of delivering Dylan, our second son, and in no condition to chase elusive geese over slippery ice. But she came, bringing the dog and a steady stream of suggestions as to how we might capture the birds, with her.

Pelly dove eagerly into the water after the geese. His enthusiasm concealed the fact that he was old. Ice formed on his long chest hair as he swam in circles after the panicked fowl. Honks echoed off the frozen banks of the river as the birds dodged the aged dog's attempts to grab their tail feathers.

My wife and I were positioned on opposite edges of the ice. The frozen surface cracked as we scurried back and forth. It seemed improbable that Pelly would catch the birds. I was convinced that either the dog or the geese, if not both, would die of exhaustion before the birds were captured.

Despite my lack of faith, the old dog managed to corner the female goose against the shoreline. As the bird tried to strike the dog on his nose with its bill, Pelly sank his teeth into the bird's tail feathers and plucked the squawking goose out of the water. With an air of restored youth, the dog trotted across the ice holding the bird.

Running towards the dog, I slipped on the ice and landed unceremoniously on the dog and the goose. René howled in laughter.

"I'll give you a six point five for that dive, Mark."

I concentrated on holding the flapping bird under my arm. The bird's head twisted in defiance, tried to break free of my grip, and bite me. I held the goose tight to my body with one arm, clamping my other gloved hand around its bill.

"Very funny, dear. Now what do you propose I do with this goose?"

My question was real. I hadn't considered what we'd do with the captured bird while we stalked its mate.

"You could bring her back to the pen and come back for the other one."

It seemed like a sensible suggestion. Anyone that knows me knows that, during times of crisis, I am usually sensible. For whatever reason, I decided to take a more creative approach.

I trudged up the frozen riverbank with the goose under one arm. My boots slipped on fresh snow. Pelly dashed up the embankment behind me. As I crested the hill, the goose broke free of my grip. Her long white neck coiled. She struck at my gloved hand but she couldn't pierce the leather glove. I reestablished my grip and tucked her head back under my arm. An outbuilding blocked our path. We were not on our land. We were on a neighbor's property. Behind the shed, a small cabin sat tucked into the woods, its windows boarded up for winter. Firewood dusted with fresh snow was stacked neatly in front of the cabin.

I opened the door to the outbuilding and cast the bird into the darkness. Heavy springs automatically closed the portal.

"That should hold her for now, eh Pelly?"

The dog didn't respond. He was headed back down the hill.

Out on the river, René shuffled over ice.

"Where'd you put the goose?"

"In a building by the old cabin."

"What building?"

I didn't answer. Pelly was once again in the water. The dog's pace had slowed. His panting grew labored as he paddled in aimless circles trying to corner the gander. There seemed to be no method to the retriever's approach. The dog appeared to be engaged in a mindless chase, a journey with no beginning and no end. Snow fell. Thick wet flakes settled on the branches of low hanging trees. Muted cries of the captured bird floated down to us from atop the rise.

Suddenly, the dog broke free of the water's grip and launched himself at the gander. A bitter strike from the bird's bill missed the retriever's nose. Pelly's mouth clamped down on the bird's neck. René grabbed the thrashing goose away from the dog. Globs of thick blood fell to the ice.

I took the bird from my wife. The gander struck out at me, narrowly missing my face. My gloved hand pressed the bird's bloodied feathers apart.

21

"He's OK," I advised. "It's just a surface wound."

Climbing the snow-covered hillock to the cabin, the bird squirmed in my grasp. Its chest pounded in fright. Behind me, my wife leaned over to pet the old dog. Her feet gave way, dropping her unceremoniously to her rump. I couldn't resist.

"That's a ten."

René ignored me and continued to stroke the hard-with-ice fur of the retriever from her new position. I climbed the slope with the second bird.

"Mark, where are you putting those geese?"

I didn't answer. My gloved fingers clumsily unlatched the door to the outbuilding. I opened the shed and stuffed the second goose inside before its mate could escape.

"I'll need a hand," I called out. "We can each carry a bird back to the house."

Standing in the gentle vortex of falling snow, I listened to the muffled sounds of the trapped birds and observed that someone had cut the silhouette of a quarter moon into weathered siding above the building's entrance. I smiled and wondered what the geese thought of it all.

The Long Retrieve

The sky was blue and high. There was a chill to the air, a precursor of winter to come; though the sun's strength retained a hint of summer. The leaves were gone; the browns and grays of late autumn having replaced the greens.

On the north bank of the river, we walked an old trail. He remained ten to twenty feet in front of me. The leaves beneath our feet were wet with dew. The ground cover made no sound as we moved. An odor of rotting leaves hung over the path. He kept his nose close to the forest floor despite the fetid smell.

We were hunting grouse. We hadn't encountered any partridge by the time we made Mud Lake. The dog had acted birdy a few times, pacing frantically to and fro in the dense undergrowth on either side of the trail, but hadn't flushed any birds.

Mud Lake was ominous. The pothole's water was stained black, the color of tar. A flock of mallards floated contentedly in the middle of the pond. The retriever lifted his nose to the birds.

"Out of range, boy."

The words weren't important. The tone of my voice was what mattered.

"Let's keep moving. Maybe we'll kick up a partridge or two down the trail."

The dog wagged his tail and went back to working the dense balsam and aspen lining the path. I watched his thick red fur dodge in and out of the trees and sparse grass. Every now and then, I could see his white chest hair as he strained to peer over the undergrowth. The fur of his ears and legs became matted and covered with burrs.

WUMPH.

My heart stuttered when the grouse erupted. The bird took off low and behind me. My .410 side-by-side barked. Once. The bird flew on. Twice. The bird set its wings and sailed unharmed over a stand of sickly birch.

23

Instinctively, the dog chased the departed bird.

"Come, Pelly, come."

The dog didn't heed my calls. He was convinced I'd hit the partridge: I guess it's a retriever's prerogative to have too much faith in his master's abilities.

In time, the dog accepted the fact that I'd missed and came back from his quest. I sat on cool ground and rested against a large balsam. The dog sat at my side. I stroked his soft coat, picking out burrs where I could. He licked salt from my hand. The shade of the tree kept us cool. Pelly's ears twitched. The breeze carried the voices of ducks.

We left our place of contentment in search of prey. As we walked south, the path disappeared into marsh. Box alders and willows formed a nearly impassable thicket. The dog dodged beneath low branches with impunity but it was slow going for his human companion. The dog moved with the energy and vigor of a pup. He was twelve, a sage among golden retrievers. He did not hunt like an old dog that day.

Every now and then I lost sight of him in the bramble. Every so often I heard the thunderous crash of another ruffed grouse fleeing to safety. It was no use. I couldn't see the birds rise. The few shots I managed were made in complete frustration and without aim. After five or six birds escaped, I'd had enough. I was wet and tired. Due to my marksmanship, I was also birdless.

I crossed the Cloquet River downstream from my house. Pelly plunged through the cold water, swimming when he had to, walking when he could. The blue sky was gone. A seamless gray blanket covered the world. A brisk breeze rose from the east, causing whitecaps to exaggerate the current. Exiting the water, the dog bounded up the bank, his nose once more to the ground.

I walked onto our hay field. The grass was short; the hay had long since been put up in the old dairy barn. The dog bounded across yellow stubble, ears trailing behind in the wind. In the distance, our white farmhouse stood stark against a terse sky.

"Here Pelly."

I called the dog back. Five ducks rose behind the old cantilever bridge spanning the river. My glasses were clouded with condensation. I wiped the lenses with my shirtsleeve. The old dog and I stood behind a thin line of aspen on top of the riverbank horizontal to the flight of the birds. The ducks approached. I repositioned my glasses on my nose, the metal frame cold against skin and watched the flock. The ducks were Whistlers.

"Down, boy."

The retriever crouched. I knelt down. We watched the birds: They came in low, with their legs extended, ready to land on the water in front of us.

I'd never fired my .410 at a duck. I had No.8 shot in both barrels. I doubted that the pellets could penetrate the chest feathers of waterfowl. Despite my misgivings, I lifted the gun to my shoulder. My right eye followed the leader. I squeezed the trigger slowly; holding my breath as the Whistlers landed.

Crack.

The leader tumbled headlong into the river. The other ducks accelerated away before I could shoot again. Pelly dove from the bank and landed in the water. He swam out to retrieve the downed bird. The combination of the river's current and the wind kept the duck away from the dog. The dog could not see the bird in the water. He paddled in circles searching for the downed bird, his head held too low to see over the waves.

Whether he did it intentionally or not, I will never know. But as I was ready to give up and call him in, the dog arched his neck and spotted the duck. With speed, Pelly closed the distance to the floating Whistler. Gripping the duck in his mouth, the dog tried to return to me. The current was too strong. The river carried the retriever and the duck downstream. Changing directions, the dog plotted a diagonal course towards the far bank. Pelly looked upstream after exiting the river. Water dripped from his long coat. The retriever shook himself. Water flew but the bird remained in the dog's soft mouth.

I unloaded my shotgun and began to walk home. On the other side of the river, the old dog broke into a trot. He kept a tight hold on the duck. Through the brush lining the riverbank, across the wooden deck of the decaying bridge, the dog carried the dead Whistler. He didn't release the bird until I took it out of his gentle mouth.

Pelly had retrieved a single, seemingly insignificant duck, a full quarter-mile. That was the last time we hunted together. During the winter of that year, a car hit Pelly out on the road. His hip was fractured and he had to be put to sleep.

As I write this, my shotgun leans against a wall across the room. The gun's stock is freshly oiled, ready for another hunting season. Through the window above my desk, I can see our current dogs, Maggie and Sam, running through the yard. They are fine animals and wonderful pets. Though they're not Pelly, I'm consoled by the fact that; whenever the leaves turn brittle and begin to drift to the ground; whenever the geese and ducks gather to take wing; Pelly's last hunt comes back to me. It is then that I know his spirit is still here. In my mind's eye, I can see him trotting slowly through the closeness of the forest, still carrying the Whistler, still making the long retrieve.

A Familiar Place

The boy sat nervously at an old oak desk. His legs were short; they barely touched the oak planks of the floor. He was the sort of boy prone to doodling and daydreaming. The thick lenses of his eyeglasses gave him a studious look but his mind wandered. His eyes were not on the social studies text in front of him. His eyes were focused outside, riveted on the swirling elm leaves and the retiring green of the grass. A city park stood empty across the cracked blacktop of the street next to the school.

"Hope it doesn't rain at the farm."

Jeff's voice called the boy back to the classroom. The words were whispered, in hopes that Miss Hollingsworth, their teacher, would not overhear them. Theirs was not an ordinary class. They were "special"; selected from various elementary schools of the city and thrown together in one classroom. They were the geeks, the brains, the bookworms. Jeff, like the boy who listened to him, looked the part.

Jeff wore glasses too; glasses with black plastic frames. The glasses rode high on Jeff's nose. As Jeff spoke to Wayne, another classmate, the glasses slid down Jeff's nose. Wayne was one of the few in the class who didn't wear glasses: But Wayne was still a nerd.

"Can we drive the car?"

Wayne asked the question under his breath. Jeff's response was just as subdued.

"Sure. The old Ford still runs. We can drive it as long as we don't take it on the road."

The boy was curious. He had never seen the farm. He was new to the class. He had arrived late, in October. He was sent to replace a girl from his school, a girl who could not handle the pressure of being surrounded by genius. Most of the smart kids had been brought together the year before, in fifth grade. But not him. He only knew one girl in the "special" class when he arrived. The other kids were complete strangers. He didn't know Jeff or Wayne. He dared not ask about the farm.

In his mind, he saw an old white farmhouse standing alone, surrounded by uncut hay. He was certain that a lake cut through the property. Cold, October water danced in that lake. He wanted to go there, to run and play with the other boys on the shores of that unnamed water. But he was an outsider. He was not invited. His vision of the place faded as Miss Hollingsworth walked by.

Eventually, the others in the class came to accept him as one of their own. He and Jeff became friends. Years passed. They played football and basketball together. One day, because of their friendship, he was finally invited to the farm.

He'd never stopped thinking of the place. From the very first, his mind revised and reshaped his vision of what the farm looked like. When he finally visited the old homestead, he found that the farmhouse was indeed white. Square logs, fashioned in the old way, the Finnish way, remained hidden behind pine lap siding. The timbers were as solid and remarkable as he thought they would be.

But there was no lake. The only water on the place turned out to be a shallow creek. The lack of a lake did not diminish the beauty of the farm in the boy's eyes. He loved history. The farm's past whispered to him as he stood in the pasture contemplating mounds of stones that had been piled there. Despite being only in his teens, he was old enough to appreciate the sweat and toil that built the place. The spirit of the immigrant men, women, and children who had farmed and died there touched him. His eyes scanned the landscape with possessive angst. He sensed that the farm could only be owned by those who had created it.

Years later, on the backside of the farm's woodlot, the boys built a ramshackle cabin of aspen. They used aspen because there were no longer any large fir trees remaining on the land with which to build.

Through the summer's heat, the incessant bites of black flies, and the buzzing of mosquitoes, the boys worked the woods. Their toil reminded the kid of the terrible price the immigrants must have paid to live there. Though the cabin was a mere shed compared to the intricate dovetailed buildings the Finns constructed nearly a century before, he felt a connection to the land when the shanty was finished.

As insignificant as it seemed, the tiny cabin was a refuge. It was a place to hunt, to ski, to play cards. It was isolated by time and distance from real life. In some small way, the cabin made the boys a part of the farm's history.

They grew older; the boys became men; they married, found jobs, and fought the battles of adult life. The cabin stood empty. After several harsh winters, the roof fell in, the logs rotted, and the walls collapsed.

This night finds him back at the farm. Above him, the sky stands clear and dark. A kerosene lantern flickers in the wind. The shadows of giant spruce trees sway, dancing in time to the evening breeze.

Bang.

Bang.

The screen door to the front porch of the farmhouse announces the entry or departure of each guest. The man, now in his forties, an age which seems to confuse and annoy him, sits before the warmth of a bonfire.

"Dad, have you seen Dylan? He and Evan are hiding on me."

Chris, the man's third son, casts the question out into the night where it echoes off the weathered walls of a failing shed. There is no glass left in the windows of the outbuildings. The barn has long since disintegrated. Its lumber fuels the fire. He was here when the barn fell. How long ago was it? Five years? Ten? The man can't remember.

It's October. Jeff and his wife have invited their friends and relatives to celebrate the coming of the harvest. Everyone knows that there is nothing to harvest at the farm. These fields haven't known crops or cows, or the bite of a tiller, for forty years. It's not the promise of harvest but the promise of old memories, which draws them back.

Jeff sits cross-legged before the fire. He plays a timeless Crosby, Stills, Nash, and Young song on his twelve-string guitar. His fingers remember notes he has not played in two decades.

29

Though the guitarist no longer wears the glasses of his youth, Jeff's wire-rimmed frames ride low on his nose as he concentrates on the song.

Children pull boards off the shed. The adults don't complain. Older boys slide the seasoned pine planks into the fire. Sparks swirl up into the night and turn to ash as they climb.

The man thinks back to their old school, their old classroom, where he first heard Jeff talk about Grandpa's farm. He closes his eyes. The fire's warmth, the music, the darkness, allow him to come to a very familiar place. He sits quietly next to his wife, listening to the wind, the trees, the soft chords of a forgotten melody from an old friend's guitar and deep within himself, the man hears the lap of waves against a shoreline, a shoreline that exists only in the dreams of youth.

The Lemonade Stand

Above the slow current of the river, the span of an old bridge stood. Rust stained the bridge's iron frame. Gaping holes in the timbers exposed the frailty of its deck. Noisy crows circled the tenuous arch of the cantilever, once delicate and ornate, now bowed and frail with age.

Two boys sat near the span at the end of a long gravel driveway. Workers milled around the bridge. A dry wind captured dust. Shards of flying sand pummeled the boys. The sun's heat stung their exposed necks and arms, their skin white and tender after the long winter. A young hand darted across the card table and removed the glass pitcher full of lemonade in advance of the squall. The smaller boy, his dark hair hanging loose around his head in very straight, even rows, joined his blond-haired cousin under the card table with the pitcher. Despite the heat and the thirsty crew of construction workers busily dismantling the bridge, they sold no lemonade.

At nine, the boys' experience in commerce was limited to begging their parents for money to buy He-Man toys. But they'd watched enough television to understand the concept of selling retail: You need a product that someone wants.

"Greggy, no one's buyin' our stuff."

Matt sat cross-legged in the dirt, protecting the mouth of the pitcher from the swirling dust devils with his hands.

"Ya. Maybe ten cents a glass is too much."

"Maybe. But if we charge five cents, that's only..."

The younger cousin's brow knitted as he tried to do long division in his head.

"...Two and a half cents apiece for each glass. We'll be here all year trying to get enough to buy a Skeletor Slime Pit," Greggy blurted out.

A worker walked by the table, glancing at the crude sign:

Lemonade, 10 Scents a Glass.

31

"Hey mister, wanna glass?"

Matt, never at a loss for a question, poked his head out from under the card table as he spoke.

"No thanks, kid. Got a thermos full of coffee. A little too early for lemonade. Catch me after lunch."

The wind stopped. The boys stood up and dusted off their blue jeans. It was Greggy, his blue eyes peering at the workmen, who stated the obvious.

"You know what we need?"

"What?"

"Somethin' else."

"Like what?"

"I dunno."

Questions. More questions for Matt to ponder. Suddenly, it came to him. His round face beamed in triumph.

"Come on. I got an idea."

Leaving the open pitcher to the swirling dirt, the boys bolted for the house.

Sometime later that day my wife René searched the cupboards for macaroni and cheese. She hadn't seen the boys since early in the morning when they asked her permission to set up their stand. They would be hungry. There's nothing better than macaroni and cheese to satisfy nine-year-old boys. Having just completed the grocery shopping for the week, René knew there were several family-sized boxes on the shelves. But when she opened the cupboard doors, the boxes, along with several cans of vegetables, and Campbell's soup had inexplicably vanished.

René put on her tennis shoes and went outside. The wind had died and the sun stood unusually high for late spring. Calm heat hung over the valley. At the end of the driveway, she could see the boys sitting behind a table. Walking down the dirt drive, she noticed that the cantilever of the old bridge had been removed.

"Hi, Mom. We're doing really good," Matt yelled, his small voice projecting broadly.

"Yeah, Auntie Nay, we've just about sold a whole pitcher."

Greggy's voice trailed after his cousin's, its pitch a bit deeper, the words slightly less excited.

Across the road, the construction crew rested in the shade of trees. Crumpled Styrofoam cups littered the ground near the men.

René approached the boys and caught a glimpse of their promotional sign. Freshly amended, it now read:

Lemonade, 10 Scents a glass. Free Pryze.

The boys sat on folding chairs, eyes concealed by cheap sunglasses. Matt wore his Minnesota North Stars cap pulled down hard upon his head causing his ears to protrude. Greggy's Oakland A's cap sat loosely atop his yellow hair, his head clearly too big for the cap.

"Do you boys know anything about the missing cans of vegetables, soup, and boxes of macaroni and cheese from the kitchen?" my wife asked.

From the fresh marker on the boys' sign, and the three cans of peas stacked neatly on the table, René guessed what had happened to her canned goods. Looking intently at the boys, she poured herself a cup of lemonade. Waiting for a response, she took a long drink.

"Ugh. Didn't you put any sugar in this?"

The tartness caught her off guard. She expected a slight twist of lemon, followed by the sweetness of sugar. Instead, she tasted only lemon.

"Sugar?"

Matt looked at Greggy. Smiles flowed across their sun-reddened faces.

"So that's why they spit the stuff out."

Greggy's voice was quiet as he spoke. Matt tried to contain a giggle.

"What about the soup, the vegetables, and the mac and cheese?"

Gathering his wits about him, Matt removed his sunglasses and looked up at his mother with gentle brown eyes.

"That's what we used for prizes, mom. See, Greggy and I figured that we'd do just like McDonald's does with a Happy Meal: Give them a surprise with every glass."

"How many cans and boxes did you give away?" René asked in as stern a voice as she could muster. She was having trouble keeping a straight face as she listened to the boy's marketing scheme.

"'Bout ten cans of soup and three boxes of mac and cheese."

A heavy sigh escaped from René as she picked up the three remaining cans of peas.

"No one seems to want the peas," Greg added.

"I think the lemonade stand is closed for today," René said curtly. "Let's have some lunch."

"Sure, mom. Besides, we sold twenty glasses. That's..."

Again, Matt did the math in his head as they walked down the dry dirt of the drive towards the house.

"...A buck apiece," his cousin responded. "If we do this every day for a week, we'll have enough to buy a Skeletor Slime Pit."

My wife turned her head and looked at the boys.

"I think we better have a talk about economics. Your lemonade stand will likely cost Uncle Mark and me more than we can afford."

The two boys looked at each other. They were puzzled by my wife's remark. Without much effort, and at no cost to them, they were each a dollar richer than they'd been when they woke up that morning.

A Christmas Carol

Sure, you can go buy a Christmas tree from a nursery, from some Boy Scout lot, or from some dubious looking stranger lurking in an alley. But what fun would that be?

When I was in law school, René and I didn't have a lot of money. Naturally, we bought our first few Christmas trees. Now that I'm relatively successful, we don't buy our trees. We chop them down in the woods. We don't have to pay anything for the privilege because the trees are harvested from our own land. But the Munger Christmas tree, though free of charge, is never without cost.

I'm sure you've seen those Currier and Ives etchings. You know, the ones showing the kids all bundled up in the sleigh with dad and mom gliding through the snow behind the family horse, a picture-perfect Christmas tree in tow. Sort of reminds you of Dr. Zhivago, now doesn't it? It's a scene that my family aspires to year in and year out. We have yet (after many winters of trial) to achieve anything close to such serenity and bliss during our annual Christmas tree ordeal.

My wife and I start our annual tree trek with distinctly different values. René, being an artist, seeks to find the cosmetically perfect Christmas tree. I, on the other hand, simply want to find one that is tall, green, and absent bird droppings. I'll always head for the lowly balsams, of which our land has thousands. René will always migrate to the Norway pines, which are more difficult to find. And in separate parts of the forest, we will both locate what we believe to be a suitable tree.

Year after year, if you're out and about in Fredenberg around the holidays, you can hear the discussion from the woods. It's unchanging, as constant as the star over Bethlehem.

"Mark, that is the ugliest Christmas tree I've ever seen."

"What's wrong with it? It's green, isn't it? It's straight, isn't it? Come on René, we could be out here all day and not find a better tree."

"I found one."

"What, another one of those spindly Norway's you always pick out? Get real."

You get the picture. Ultimately, as the kids disappear into the forest to avoid taking sides, the debate rages on. And always, exhausted by my wife's persistence, I yield and shuffle back to the house with her selected Norway.

Some years we use Cisco (my wife's thirty-year-old mare) to pull the tree back to the house on a plastic slider. Some years (when I'm too lazy to harness the horse) I pull the tree with our Skidoo. Usually, the Skidoo quits, in which case I end up pulling the snow machine and the tree back to the house with my International 606 tractor. But each slow, painful retreat from the woods finds me muttering under my breath.

"My tree was better."

But no one listens.

There was one year when René was too busy to look for a tree. The kids and I picked out a dandy balsam; tall, supple and fresh, with no bird poop. You could tell by Old Cisco's jaunty gait, as she labored to pull the tree home, that even she knew we had a winner. With great care, the kids and I trimmed the tree with a minimum of arguing. We decorated the balsam to the sounds of George Bailey's angst echoing in the background in an attempt to surprise mom. The surprise was on us.

"That's the ugliest tree I've ever seen," René said as she stood in the enclosed front porch of our house.

"What? You've gotta be kidding, dear. I mean, just look at how green it is, how straight and..."

"I know, Mark, no bird poop. But look at all the bare spots. You can't hide bare spots like that."

"Sure you can. That's why God invented lights."

"You've already got too many lights in the bare spots. Look at the boughs. They're bent to the floor under the weight of the lights."

"We'll get some wire and tie the boughs to the wall."

"You're ruining Christmas. That tree is a disgrace."

Dylan, our second son defended me.

"But mom, we like it. It's a neat tree."

36

René didn't reply.

The tree spent the night fully decorated in the front porch; proudly proclaiming to all that bald can be beautiful.

In the morning, I made sure my path to the truck took me past the tree. The balsam was, to my way of thinking, perfect in every way. I kissed my wife on the cheek as I left for work.

"Lighten up, dear. It's just a tree. Besides, it kind of grows on you."

There was only silence as I departed.

Coming home from work that evening, I drove past the front porch. Through frosted windows, I saw bright bulbs, tinsel, and lights adorning the firm, unyielding boughs of an upstart Norway pine. Walking up the back steps, I noted another curiosity: Where, that very morning, there'd been a lovely eight foot high pine standing guard over a slumbering poppy bed, only a stump remained. As my eyes adjusted to the fading daylight, I discovered, nestled in the snow hugging the rear porch, the discarded balsam that had once been our Yuletide tree.

"Merry Christmas, Mark," my wife called out as I opened the back door and entered the warmth of the kitchen.

Ice Fishing

"**Dad**, don't you think we should just park the car at the top of the hill and walk to the lake?"

I asked that question several years ago when my father, the quintessential fisherman, invited my eldest son Matt and I to go late-season ice fishing with him.

We drove up US Highway 2 to a small, nameless lake near Brookston, Minnesota to fish for "monster" crappies and bluegills. Dad assured us that we'd catch fish. After all, the lake we were going to was one of Dr. Leppo's favorites. Everyone knew that Dr. Leppo, next to being the best pediatrician in town, was also the best ice fisherman in northeastern Minnesota. With an endorsement like that, I figured there was no room for error.

Dad has always been the kind of guy to challenge his vehicles. Back in the 1960's, he took some pals to Canada goose hunting. Somewhere in the middle of the prairie, Grandpa decided his Jeep Wagoneer could do just about anything. He saw no reason to heed signs that read: "Road Ends". It took three bulldozers and a farm tractor to pull the Wagoneer out of the swamp at the end of that road.

"Don't worry. This car has posi-traction. We'll be fine."

Before I could protest further, the Cadillac rolled down the snow-covered boat landing and out onto the ice. Matt, six or seven years old at the time, looked at me. Even he realized that Grandpa was once again pushing the limits of mechanized travel.

It was a gorgeous March day. A white sun rose high above us as Dad started the power auger and drilled three perfect holes through the frozen surface of the lake. Despite the warmth of the day the ice was thick and hard.

"Matt, get me a couple of minnows, will you?"

"Sure Grandpa."

Wet up to his elbows from reaching into the minnow bucket, Matt triumphantly marched to Grandpa with two small Crappie minnows crushed between his choppers.

"Thanks."

After half-an-hour without a bite, I wandered away from my fishing rod in search of wood for a fire. Grandpa continued to stare intently into the cold water as if trying to will the fish into biting.

I scanned the lake as I walked. We were the only ones fishing. I pondered the reasons this could be. I kept my thoughts to myself as I gathered dry maple branches from the shoreline and trudged back to make a fire.

I drew a match across my belt buckle. The sulfur caught. I touched the delicate flame to a dry piece of birch bark wedged under wood.

"Any luck?" I asked, keeping one eye on the rising flames.

"Just a couple of nibbles. Perch, I think," Dad replied.

"What do we have to eat?" Matt asked.

"Hot-dogs, chips, and candy bars," Dad responded.

"Goodie."

My son managed to drop several hotdogs into the fire before he successfully cooked one. We sat on overturned plastic buckets, eating lunch, catching no fish and not really caring too much about it.

By four in the afternoon, Grandpa had seen enough of Dr. Leppo's secret lake. We'd pulled out two tiny perch. Both fish weighed less than the minnows used to catch them. Matt ate four hotdogs, two candy bars, and drank two cans of Coke. He was hungry again.

The Cadillac started without incident. Dad looked at me with a confident "I told you so" smirk. Things appeared to be fine until we left the level surface of the lake and tried to make it back up the hill. Posi-traction could not overcome the intentions of the car's designers: A luxury automobile is meant to be driven on clear, dry pavement; not out onto an ice-covered lake. We were stuck.

I tried to help. I found pieces of discarded plywood and placed them under the rear wheels of the car. The Cadillac took offense and spat the boards at me. I pushed. I shoveled until I was blue in the face. Nothing could make that low slung, heavily armored tank move uphill in loose snow.

We left the lake without any fish and without our car. Walking down an unnamed dirt road in the middle of nowhere, my six-year-old complained about his need for another meal. When he complained that his legs were tired, I hoisted him onto my shoulders and carried him through snow-covered silence. We stopped at each cabin or home we passed. We knocked on door after door. There was no one home on the lake.

"They're probably somewhere else, catching fish," I muttered.

Grandpa scowled.

As the sun went down, we came to a house occupied by a nice old couple. The husband gave us a ride to a tavern out on the highway.

"Hi, René. It's Mark. We're gonna be a little late. The car's stuck on the lake. We're trying to find someone to pull it out."

The call to my wife was not an easy one. She was fully aware of my father's propensity to turn an ordinary day into an adventure.

"Stuck? How?"

"It's a long story. We're waiting for a kid with a truck to pull us out. Then we'll be home."

Outside the tavern, the sky was black and the wind was cold. We sat at the bar eating greasy cheeseburgers and watching Austin City Limits. An old man behind the counter wearing a ribbed undershirt and a two-day-old beard scratched himself impolitely and read the paper. We were his only customers. He seemed annoyed that we were even in the place.

Grandpa inhaled a cheeseburger and left with a local farm boy who had offered to pull the Caddie up the hill for twenty bucks. The closest wrecker was forty miles away and the guy wanted a hundred and fifty dollars to drive out to our location. Given the circumstances, the kid's offer was a bargain.

"Be back soon," Dad promised.

I nodded and slid a couple of quarters into the pool table. Emmy Lou Harris sang softly from a Wurlitzer. Matt munched on French fries. Time passed as I knocked pool balls noisily around the table.

A loud rumble shook the tavern. Bright headlights intruded into the bleak, dusty interior of the bar.

"Looks like they're back," the old man remarked, nodding in the general direction of the noise.

I pulled out my wallet. Matt jumped down from his stool and darted for the door.

"Thanks for the burgers," I said.

The bartender grunted. I slid money across the lacquered surface of the bar and walked out of the place. It was ten o'clock.

We drove home in quiet. Matt was curled up in the back seat fast asleep. Somewhere near Pike Lake, Dad finally spoke.

"Sorry about this, Mark. But you wanna know something funny?"

"What?"

"That kid who pulled me out? He was only fourteen. Doesn't even have a farm permit."

"Really?"

"Yup. Nice kid. I paid him an extra twenty bucks."

That was a few years back. Somewhere near Brookston, Minnesota there's a dairy farmer in his twenties who tells the story of two attorneys and a little kid from the city who tried to go four wheeling in a Cadillac.

The Fireman's Ducks

"**A** friend of mine from the fire department has a problem."

Larry, one of my high school buddies, was on the phone. His call found me at my law office during a moment of confusion. A trial loomed ahead of me. I was preoccupied.

"What's wrong?"

"Nothing's wrong. How'd you like some ducks?"

"Ducks? What kind of ducks?"

"I think they're mallards."

I paused. I already had custody of farm geese given to me by Larry and two other "friends" on my thirtieth birthday. A cow was too expensive a gift: a goat, too destructive. So they'd given me geese. Two geese, which had, of course, turned into four geese. Four geese, which were in danger of becoming eight geese.

Did I really need more poultry wandering about the place, leaving their "packages" on our sidewalk?

"Why is he getting rid of them?"

My voice held no trace of enthusiasm. My mind was busy drafting jury instructions. I was vulnerable to suggestion because I wanted to get back to my work.

"The guy's pond is freezing up. He wants to butcher them but his wife and kid won't let him. I said you might want 'em."

There was really no thought behind my answer.

"Sure. The boys would like that. But what am I gonna keep them in? My pen is too small."

"Just put 'em in the pasture and let them use the barn at night. They can't fly."

Two days later, a gunnysack full of quacking birds came home with me from work. By the light of the November moon, I untied the string securing the neck of a burlap bag and dumped a mass of feathers and bills onto frozen ground. Eleven fairly normal-looking mallards; some male, some female; and one very odd looking black and white Muscovy duck struggled free of the tangle.

As the ducks scurried around the enclosed pasture, I filled a feeder with corn. Hearing the feed fall against the metal skin of the feeder, the ducks rushed in unison towards the sound. Our geese, much larger and more aggressive than their smaller cousins, puffed out their chests and blocked the ducks' access to the food. Intimidated, the mallards and the Muscovy veered away. Darting uncontrollably across the grass, they collided headlong into the wire fencing while the geese triumphantly pecked grain.

Matt rose with me the next morning to do chores. We dressed for dawn's chill before venturing outside to see how the ducks had fared. We found the geese nestled quietly in a corner of the barn. The pasture appeared empty. We walked through the hayfield, searching the tall grass for the ducks. They were nowhere to be found. As we approached the river, we heard the muted voices of waterfowl.

A light snow was falling. Snowflakes speckled the drab morning air with white. We found our ducks, bobbing in unison, suspended in the slow current of the Cloquet River, partially hidden by the fragile yellow marsh grass of the far shore. The Muscovy sat in the middle of the raft of waterfowl, appearing foreign and obvious. We stared at the birds. We were at a loss as to how they'd escaped. The pasture gate was secured. There were no gaps in the fence. The ducks could not fly. And yet, they were free.

I placed a tray of corn on the ground near water's edge. We stepped back, giving the birds space but the bait didn't work. All winter long, our ducks floated in front of the farm, laughing in their duck voices at the city boy. As spring ascended, as their wing feathers grew, the mallards attempted short, experimental flights up and down the river but the Muscovy never left the surface of the water.

By Easter, the mallards were extending their flights. Each day at dawn, the flock would rise and fly off. The Muscovy tried to follow by paddling frantically up and down the river.

Each night at dusk, the mallards came back, settling gently around their flightless friend, surrounding it with their number.

One day, the mallards didn't return. The Muscovy drifted up and down the Cloquet River; its plaintive quack a lonely, singular voice. Wild ducks reclaimed the river as their own. The migrants didn't tolerate the Muscovy's attempts at kinship. Whenever it approached, the Whistlers would dash in unison after him, driving him off.

Summer came and went. Autumn arrived. Wild mallards gathering for the great migration were more kind to the Muscovy. They allowed the domestic duck to float amongst them on the river. In October of that second year, just hours ahead of the first snow, the wild mallards took wing. After their departure, I didn't see the Muscovy.

A year later, I was walking towards our barn, intent on shoveling horse manure. Entering the dark confines of the old log building, the smell of horse heavy in the air, I was greeted by a ruckus. As my eyes became accustomed to the muted atmosphere of the place, I discovered the source of the noise.

Our cat was frantically chasing a duck between the well-muscled legs of our horses. Feathers flew as the feline pounced after the bird, clawing frantically at the duck's tail. Short, desperate "quacks" resounded from the timbered walls as the bird scurried beneath the bellies of the livestock. The horses ignored the perturbation. They were content to chew fresh hay; unmoved by the tragic dance swirling around them.

I kicked blindly at the cat with a leather boot, sending the animal racing up a wooden ladder into the hayloft. The duck appeared exhausted as it adjusted its plumage and sat on soiled oat straw. I could hear its panicked breathing as it cowered under the manger. I tossed my fatigue jacket on top of the shivering bird, pinning it to the ground. I retrieved the jacket and duck. The Muscovy struggled against my embrace. Its head peaked out of the jacket. I studied the creature's milky eyes and wondered about nature, about chance.

Is this the same bird?

Whether it was or wasn't, I knew there was no point in trying to reclaim something that hadn't been mine: At least that's what I told myself as I knelt on the soft gravel of the riverbank and watched the Muscovy paddle off in search of companionship.

The Deer Hunters

For most of my forty plus years on this earth, I've been a hunter, and a deer hunter at that. But despite my personal connection to hunting, there's something different about living at ground zero each November when deer hunters take to the woods.

When my wife and I moved to Fredenberg Township just north of Duluth, it was the fulfillment of our dream. Well, at least my dream. I'd always, and I mean always, wanted a hobby farm. Not that I knew anything about farming. It was the concept of land, of space, that captured my attention. A place out in the woods and field, one that I could call my own, was what I craved. My love of the land had little to do with hunting or fishing, though I'd done plenty of both growing up.

Not long after our return to Duluth, the city we both call home, René and I started looking at country houses: dozens of houses. Many of them were the same bungalows from Hades that we'd looked at before we bought our house in town. Four years passed before we found our farm. We moved to the country in 1984, on the eve of my first Grandma's Marathon. But that, as they say, is another story.

Our first summer living out, we learned a great many things about country life. Things like: What do you do when you discover you now own a quarter acre of ripe strawberries? And: What do you do with a barn full of sheep manure?

That first year living out, when the green grass of summer gave way to the yellow hay of autumn, it dawned on us that hunting season was just around the corner. Soon there'd be legions of deer hunters, fellows we didn't know, marching across the countryside with high-powered rifles. They'd surround us. Engulf us. Hold us prisoner and confine us while war raged 'round us in the forest and across the fields. How could we cope? How could we protect our son Matthew?

Our first October on the place, René and I bought every item of orange clothing that the Fredenberg Minno-ette, (our local bait, tackle and convenience store) had in stock. Gloves, hats, pants, sweatshirts: We bought it all. Then we hit Target and K-Mart in town for backup. During the weeks before Halloween, we began indoctrinating Matt to put on his war gear before venturing outside. We were ready. Ready for the onslaught.

My first deer season in the country, I joined the hunters. I wanted to hunt the thousands of acres of Minnesota Power land abutting our place. Uncharacteristically diligent, I went out in early September to build new deer stands for the season. By the beginning of November, I had several new hunting platforms ready for use. On opening day, other guys found my stands first. One guy was brazen enough to drive his pickup truck across a Minnesota Power pasture so he could park right underneath one of my new stands. I discovered the man's boldness after I marched across the cold, snow-covered hayfield before the break of day and found his brand new Ford pickup parked directly beneath my stand. The next year I remedied the situation: I bought the land from Minnesota Power and posted it "No Trespassing".

Even with our best precautions, the hunters still came. They read our signs and stopped at the house to ask if they could hunt our land. Mostly, I let them. As the years passed, my own interest in hunting faded. Too many hunters; too many folks I didn't know wandering the woods with guns. Hunting, at least hunting around others, requires a certain degree of trust. The other guy is ambulating through the forest on an adrenaline high with a loaded weapon. You best know who the other guy is before you enter the woods. That was one reason my urge to hunt declined.

Then there was the fact that my boys, at least the three older ones, were involved in sports, flying kites, playing fort, or just plain goofing off on our land. I began to tell the people knocking on my door: "Sorry, our place is closed to hunting."

I found you can't say "no" to your neighbors quite so easily. I cross-country ski and horseback ride on my neighbor's property. They want to be able to hunt on mine. My neighbors Al and Earl deer hunt. They walk my ski trails each November hoping to find a big buck. More often than not, they shoot something less. Sometimes, to fill out their licenses, they shoot a spike buck or a doe. I understand that this is part of the equation, part of deer hunting.

One Sunday the kids and I were climbing into our mini-van, getting ready to leave for church. It was a warm morning. Deer season was open but I hadn't heard any gunfire.

I knew something was up when I saw Earl (he's the father) and Al (he's the son) climbing over my electric fence. They were wearing the orange uniform of deer season. They carried their rifles loosely in their hands.

"Hit a doe, Mark. She ran through the pasture by the horses," Al advised.

"No way Al."

"Yep. She's down the bank, next to the river, in front of your house."

The three of us (the father and son smelling of artificial doe urine, and me smelling of Old Spice) walked over to the riverbank. The stricken doe had severed both strands of wire to our electric fence as she sought escape across the Cloquet.

"There she is," Earl said.

The doe was neck deep in the current, hugging land, totally still, and partially hidden by a thicket. Standing above the animal, I watched the doe's nostrils flare as she labored to breathe. The pupils of her eyes were dilated, whether from shock or fear, I couldn't say. She remained motionless in an attempt to become invisible.

Crack.

Al's .30-30 barked. I heard René cry out in alarm from inside our house. The doe's head jerked. Then she was still, her brown body floating lifelessly in dark water.

My third son Chris and his buddy Spencer came running up to watch as we pulled the deer up the steep incline. Dylan, the second of my four boys, arrived at the edge of the bank just as the animal came to rest upon our lawn.

"Cool," Dylan whispered, poking the dead deer with a stick.

Matt, our eldest, a child who has long expressed doubts as to the wisdom of hunting, remained in the background. He was curious enough to leave the protection of the van but not inquisitive enough to venture too close.

René arrived. She watched with measured disgust as Al and Earl gutted the doe in our front yard.

"They shot her back on Earl's field," I said, "and she ran through our fence. She made the river but couldn't swim across. Al had to finish her off."

My wife nodded. She'd lived in the country as long as I had. She knew better than to instigate a debate about the morals of deer hunting with our neighbors. In the country, hunting just is; it's ingrained in the fabric of rural life.

"Time for church," I announced, turning my back to the other men.

René and I sat in the front seats of the Pontiac and closed the doors. I felt sadness and understanding in equal measure as I put the vehicle in gear.

Under a Catfish Moon

I was raised like every other Minnesotan. In Minnesota, you're a walleye fisherman, a trout fisherman, or a little of both. I grew up convinced that folks who fish, at least those worth talking to, do not try to catch fish bearing whiskers.

Before we moved to the country, I thought catfish were slightly behind rock bass and marginally ahead of carp on the desirability scale. That all changed when I learned the secrets of fishing under a catfish moon.

Our hobby farm has a small creek running through it. The creek is short. It measures only a mile or so in total length. This rivulet is nameless. It lacks significance when you look for it on a map. But like so many small waters, its importance to the natural order of things cannot be measured by its size. In its tiny watershed, deer hide beneath the occasional grove of cedar; herons lurk in the yellow marsh grass defining its swampy course. Leopard frogs, salamanders, and assorted peepers thrive in its slowly emptying pools. The frogs provide an early spring chorus that tells us that the creek, for now, is healthy and running clean.

For the first few years we lived in the country, I watched city folk fish from the cantilever bridge that used to cross the Cloquet River in front of our house. These interlopers fished at night, by the light of a campfire, a gas lantern or, on rare occasion, by the light of a full moon. These tourists were after channel cats.

Sometime before the county demolished the old bridge and replaced it with an ugly concrete structure of little character and even less integrity, my wife decided to take up catfishing. I can still remember the night.

I was late coming home from work. When I pulled into our driveway the summer skies were filled with the brilliance of the Milky Way. It was late. A full moon stood over our house. I parked my pickup truck and began to walk across the lawn towards the kitchen door dodging various toys and a kid's wading pool. When my shadow passed over the pool, the water erupted. Startled, I bent down and looked into the pool. Despite the lack of light, I was able to make out the silhouette of the largest catfish I'd ever seen. The fish remained attached to my son Dylan's Snoopy rod by nearly invisible line. With my bare hands, I hoisted the fish out of the pool by monofilament.

Croak.

I'd never known fish to speak. The voice of a fish protesting its capture was intriguing.

Perhaps, I thought, *I've underestimated the ranking of the catfish in God's aquatic hierarchy.*

The commotion in the yard drew my wife out of the house.

"Who caught this monster?" I asked.

My voice was excited. The size and weight of the channel cat was impressive. Even in the darkness, I could see the extent of my wife's smile. It was one of those "I'm-a-better-fisherman-than-you-are" smiles. It's the smile you see when you're in a boat with a woman who's caught all the fish for the day.

"I did."

"Must go eight pounds or more."

I had no experience in gauging the weight of channel catfish but my estimate seemed accurate.

"I'd say at least ten," she corrected.

I felt the need to burst her bubble. The tone in her voice was beginning to cross the line from mere pride to boastfulness.

"Maybe nine."

She didn't show any concern that I'd diminished the import of her catch.

"I think we should let him go," she offered out of the blue.

"What?"

"He's so big. He's probably the father of all the catfish around here. Put him back. We can always catch him again."

I didn't have enough energy to tell my wife that, given the creature's size; it was more likely a "she" than a "he".

"OK," I agreed. "I don't feel much like cleaning fish anyway."

I picked up the rod with my free hand and bit down on the monofilament line with my teeth. It took several bites to sever the eight-pound test. As I held the fish aloft by a short piece of line, I noted that the flanks of the animal were a beautiful steel blue; that the body was lean and long; that its whiskers were graceful and tipped in black. Unlike its ugly cousin, the brown bullhead, the channel cat looked like a game fish.

The big cat swung heavily from the line as I walked across the front lawn. The heft of the fish forced the line into the exposed skin of my palm. I ignored the pain. I was convinced that René was right. We should let her go. I knelt precariously on the slick earth of the riverbank as I slid the fish into black water.

Since that evening, my family has made catfishing a ritual. Four or five times a summer we collect down on the point, where the little creek meets the river, to sit around a campfire and fish. By gathering together, we remind ourselves that we're a family. We reclaim something foreign in this rushed, panicked world. We watch clouds parade around stars; we study the night sky as evening gathers. And, incidental to all else, we fish, hoping to hook into that big one I returned to the Cloquet River.

By now, she'd be approaching the twenty-pound range. If we ever latch onto her with our cheap equipment, it'll be a fight to remember. But catching her isn't what catfishing is about. It's about slowing down, about taking the time to sit and stare out at the depths of the woods or follow the path of a falling star as it speeds earthward. It's about listening to the slap of a beaver's tail against the still night waters of a pond, or understanding the poetry contained within the rustle of the pasture grass when an evening breeze kicks up.

It's about our boys, Matt, Dylan, Christian, and now Jack, sitting around the campfire, toasting s'mores, telling ghost stories. It's about their friends, Kristi, Jake, Ian, Spencer, Tim, Brian, Dominick and all the rest catching whatever the river offers up on any given night; or about being content, on many nights, with catching nothing at all.

It's about my wife René, the woman who introduced me to fishing under a catfish moon, the woman who still holds the Munger Farm record for the biggest catfish we've ever caught. I keep watching her to find out her secret. If I figure it out, I'll pass it along.

Blue-Bottomed Ladies

There's something about the mystery of a blueberry bog that does not translate between the genders. I know of only one or two men who, with gusto, enter bogs in search of blueberries. Nine times out of ten, it's the women who do the picking.

I've tried it. My wife René has coaxed, begged, and pleaded with me so many times and with such determination that I've given in a time or two. The last time I followed her through the dense clouds of stinging, biting insects into a blueberry bog was a few weeks ago. In truth, it wasn't half-bad. I got to eat a few berries while I picked. I saw the sun rise over the tamaracks and cedars. And I filled a gallon ice cream pail with berries; clearly establishing that I can, if motivated, pick as many berries in two hours as my wife can.

"See how many I picked? Bet you don't have as many as I do," I insisted.

I walked over to René, proudly holding my pail. She could see the level of berries in my bucket through the plastic because the sun was at my back.

"Almost as many as me, Mark."

I stopped next to her and looked into her pail. My view of the contents of our respective buckets didn't square with hers.

"Mine's almost full. You're a little short, dear," I replied.

I smiled and stuck my hand in her pail, picked out the biggest berry I could find, and popped it into my mouth. The wild fruit's flavor was strong and sweet.

"Mark, your pail is full of green berries, sticks, bugs, and other stuff that won't taste too good in a pie."

She reached into my pail and pulled out a stem with four green berries clinging to it.

"See?"

I frowned and stared into her bucket. My eyes searched for a hint of brown or green. There was nothing save the velvet blue of ripe berries to be found. I retreated without saying another word: I was determined to fill my pail with splendid examples of berrydom if it took all day. Ten minutes later, my hands blue and swollen from berries and mosquitoes, I walked by René on my way to the truck, a defeated man.

What is it about blueberry picking that's so inherently female? Is it patience, the same virtue that allows mothers to keep their voices low in the face of the escapades of young children? Or is it simple stubbornness: a woman's best defense in any argument with her mate?

My wife claims her need to pick berries, particularly blueberries, is simply part of the natural order. She says she has an unconscious need to enter the bog, to pick berries, no matter the conditions, no matter the berry crop. René claims that only her January dreams of another blueberry season allow her to survive the depths of winter in northeastern Minnesota. Whatever the motivation, I don't understand it. I understand bugs. I understand wet feet. I understand canned fruit.

As June fades to July in the country, cars and trucks slow as they pass by the bogs. Our women are looking for signs, signs that the berries will be thick and full. You can hear them talking in the checkout lines in grocery stores or over coffee.

"Gonna be a real good year this year. Lots of water, lots of sun."

"Where do you pick, René?"

"I can't tell you. If I told you, you'd tell someone else, and soon, the whole darn countryside would be there picking."

Folks, this is not brook trout fishing, where time honored tradition between men makes it impolite, if not impertinent, to ask where someone caught their trout. Trout are hard to come by: They are a resource of limited quantity, easily over-harvested. Blueberries should not be considered in the same light. There are billions of blueberries in Minnesota. Nothing about blueberries justifies such a level of secrecy.

When the berries are ripe, you begin to notice women crouched alongside the roads, squatting in wet grass. You can tell them by their uniform: Gray sweatpants, the pant legs tucked tightly into knee-high rubber boots, the sort of boots farmers wear when they muck out the barn. They wear their hair tucked beneath a ball cap, unwashed because there is no time to shower when the blueberries are ripe. They wear no perfume. The sweet delicacy of Opium or Este Lauder is replaced with the industrial pungency of "Deep Woods Off". Makeup and lipstick are forgotten. In the zeal to dive into the bog, to wade through fetid water and pick precious treasure, there is no need for finery.

You can tell the real die-hards, the ones like my wife and her friend Ronda. The butts of their sweatpants are stained a deep, resonant blue from hours of sitting on berries, berries they should have picked instead of squashed with their behinds.

Every once and awhile, you'll find a man who has this same need, this same unquenchable desire to harvest. In fact, if you're observant, you may see a man sitting in René's blueberry patch picking to his heart's content. Make no mistake about it. That man isn't me. It's my friend Ron.

Ron sits on his hind end and picks blueberries just like René, Ron's wife Nancy, and all the other Blue-Bottomed Ladies. But Ronald's trousers are never stained by the task. His secret? He wears blue jeans. René calls that cheating. I call it common sense.

The Ride of the Cat

I am not a huge fan of cats. Oh, I'll grant you that when you live in the country, even the most dog-loving scoundrel eventually comes to recognize that some felines, those that actually mouse, have value. Still, after all is said and done, cats are cats. They're not dogs, to state the obvious.

Matt, my eldest son, was just starting hockey. I was in my early thirties, still trying to reclaim, or more truthfully, find for the first time, some modicum of athleticism. That year, I'd taken up both league bowling and league broomball. I didn't know it then (though I have come to realize it since) that having a child in youth hockey in Minnesota isn't being involved in a sport; it's being involved in a lifestyle and a hockey parent's personal recreational activities cannot be sustained in the face of that reality.

"You're gonna come with me and watch my broomball game at the Beacon. Then we'll head over to the rink for your practice."

"OK."

Matt and I were bouncing along in my metallic blue Datsun pickup truck as we spoke. I enjoyed early Saturday morning broomball games. Due to the hour, you weren't seduced into drinking beer. It was a good way to start the weekend. I'd played a lot of ball hockey growing up and always wanted to play ice hockey. Broomball seemed like a natural progression for a thirty-something who couldn't skate.

"How's hockey going?"

"Great. I really like my coach."

"How about your team?"

"They're OK too."

My eldest son stared out from underneath an oversized Vikings stocking cap as the little four-by-four lurched its way into Hermantown. Matt's deep brown eyes, eyes inherited from his mother, danced as he spoke. There was no question he had caught my enthusiasm for the sport of hockey. A clean white

Hermantown Hawks sweatshirt covered his shoulder and elbow pads. The practice jersey hung below his waist like a nightshirt as he sat low in the bucket seat. Blue and white hockey socks, held in place by garters, concealed shin pads and disappeared into the depths of blue breezers. All of the equipment save the pants was brand new. The breezers were weary and tired, having been passed down from generation to generation of Hawk Squirt D players.

I drove the truck in thickly cushioned broomball shoes. The padded soles of the shoes made it difficult to feel the action of the clutch and caused me to grind the gears more than once on the trip in. A light snow fell as we made a left hand turn onto the Hermantown Road, the front wheels locked in four-wheel-drive.

Matt was quiet as we pulled into the parking lot of the Beacon Inn. As I opened the driver's door, sounds of a game already in progress greeted me. Shouts of amusement, of encouragement, of disparagement, slid across the wet atmosphere, enticing me to watch the conclusion of a broomball contest in progress.

"Hurry up, Matt."

"I'm comin' as fast as I can, Dad," the child responded in a defensive tone.

I don't recall much about my game. I could make up some stuff about scoring the winning goal, having the team's only hat trick, or the like. But truthfully, after so many years, the games I played that year have merged into one memory: The cat.

From time to time on our farm, we've had cats. Generally, they come and go as they please, living contently in our garage or in the old barn. I've had to remind the kids (at that time, Matt, then later, both Dylan and Chris as they grew into the job) to change the kitty litter and feed the cats. But in truth, cats are a lot less effort than dogs. That's probably why they give you a lot less in return.

When the broomball game was over, we had time to kill. Matt sipped a Coke and I had a cup of coffee while reliving the

58

excitement of the contest with my teammates. There was no reason to rush. My son's hockey practice didn't start until noon.

At the time, we had a cat; a yellow striped tabby named Snickers. Admittedly, Snickers was one of the better cats we owned over the years. He was friendly to the point of being nearly canine. He stayed out of trouble and kept out of my hair, which endeared him to me.

My son and I left the bar. As we walked across the frozen gravel of the Beacon Inn parking lot, I heard the faint cry of a cat. Nothing really unusual about that in Hermantown, a rural town with probably hundreds, if not thousands, of cats living within its borders. But the cat's voice seemed vaguely familiar.

Meow.

The cry grew louder as we approached the Datsun. It wouldn't have been surprising to find a stray cat, or even a cat that lived at the bar, seeking shelter beneath the chassis of a truck parked in a parking lot.

"Where's that coming from?" Matt asked.

"I think it's coming from under our truck."

"It sounds like Snickers."

"Matt, all cats sound the same."

"Dad, I can tell Snicker's meow."

Dubious, I knelt to the ground and searched under my truck for the source of the sound.

Meow.

"I'm sure that's Snickers."

Opening the driver's door, I pulled the hood release. Metal creaked in the frigid air.

Meow.

I walked to the front of the Datsun. My gloved hands found another lever. Cold steel creaked again as a second latch released. Standing over the engine compartment in my sweat pants and broomball jersey, "Radford and Company" stenciled across the chest, I raised the hood.

There (perched comfortably on the cold four-cylinder engine) was Snickers. Other than a little grease and oil on his fur, the cat appeared unaffected by his twenty-mile ride into Hermantown.

The Perfect Ski

Opaque ice had formed around small boulders in the river's current. Away from the protection of the rocks, the root beer colored water remained open. The skier, wearing outdated cross-country skis and boots, pushed his middle-aged body through eight inches of new snow and stopped at the water's edge.

In his early adulthood, he would have glanced quickly at the river as he made the turn from swamp to riverbank. He wouldn't have slowed his pace to watch the gentle flow of water. His objective in cross-country skiing for most of his adult life had been physical exercise, not the contemplative study of nature. His change in attitude hadn't happened out of the blue: Over time, he'd been persuaded that the purpose of skiing was something more than mere exertion.

His stays were not long; he didn't linger idly at the places that tugged at his inner self. The stops lasted a moment or two, unless an eagle was overhead or a whitetail stood silently watching him. A brief respite was all his new philosophy demanded.

Fierce snowflakes pelted his face. He was warm from the work of moving through new snow. Swirling clouds of saucer-sized flakes rose and fell. As it settled, the snow lost its luster and merged with dirtier snow piled on the ground. He could not see the tops of the maples and birch. The crowns of the trees were lost in storm. After wiping his nose on an old paper towel he found in the pocket of his wind pants, he pushed off.

Wumph. Wumph.

The skis labored through heavy snow: He trudged along. The grace and economy of a traditional Nordic glide were denied him by the weight of the snowfall. Other than the sound of the skier's progress, the forest was silent. The skier did not hear the legions of snowmobiles he knew were out on Fish Lake a half mile to the south. He was enveloped in the sort of solitude that one normally finds in wilderness though he'd started this journey from his own back door.

Despite the heavy snow, he began to develop a pattern to his stride. He was able to make near-normal progress beneath a protective canopy of balsam and spruce. The interwoven branches of the evergreens insulated the trail from the full impact of the storm.

Sweat formed beneath his stocking cap as he tried to maintain his pace. Fog clouded the lenses of his glasses, making it impossible to see. He folded the glasses and slid them into a pocket.

Moving through the woods with marginal vision, he climbed a slight rise. Five Norway pines stood together on a hillock overlooking a big swamp. Thick undergrowth forced him to guess at the perimeter of the marsh and the forest's demarcation. He looked up at the pines and wondered about their age. Though they were not old growth, they were large; 70-80 feet tall he guessed, considerably older and larger than the aspen forest around them.

I wonder why I have ample time to contemplate the life of old trees but find so little time to hear the things my kids tell me.

He asked the question of himself knowing he'd never really know the answer.

The River Trail joined Old Man Farley's Trail. A few feet along Old Man Farley's Trial, the Ridge Trail cut in. He skied to the intersection and studied the snow cover on the Ridge Trail. The path hadn't been skied in weeks. He felt worn out, too tired to ski through knee-deep snow. Something forced him to accept the challenge. He plunged ahead.

The skier had to stop every three or four hundred feet. His heartbeat was audible as he strained to climb the grade. Normally, he would have herringboned up the incline. But he was spent; he could not pull the tips of his skis out of the thick snow as he climbed. He turned parallel to the contour of the slope and inched his way up the ridge.

He stopped at the summit. There was nothing of significance to see from the top of the hill. His need for rest was born of exhaustion, not scenery. His breathing was labored. His low back burned from the strain of lifting his skis. Leaning on his ski poles, he bent at the waist and tried to flex the overused muscles of his spine. Snowflakes, their edges sharpened like shards of glass, propelled by an unceasing wind, stung his unprotected eyes. He skied on.

Fatigue caused the skier to pull himself along by his arms. His legs were merely the means by which his body remained connected to the ground. He anticipated a downhill glide through balsams. Normally, the decent was at breakneck speed. Due to thickness of the new snow, he knew the thrill would be modest. As it turned out, it was nonexistent: He had to push with his ski poles to keep moving downhill.

Climbing the last portion of the trail, he came upon fresh deer tracks. There was little doubt that the animal had heard him sliding through the snow and bounded away. The skier thought about the whitetail, thought about the steady accumulation of snow, and acknowledged the certainty that many deer would not survive the winter. They were safe from hunters but not safe from nature.

Thrupppp.

Snow exploded beneath a dying spruce. The suddenness of the event caught the skier in studied reflection. A partridge flew low, barely visible in the dim light, pelted by snow as it set its wings. Another bird burst through the thick needles of the same sickly tree. Then another. And another. In all, five ruffed grouse rose from beneath a single spruce. The skier thought he could have hit the last partridge had it been hunting season and had he been carrying a shotgun. He also had to admit to himself that he might have missed the bird.

The trail looped back. In summer, the path forced horses and riders to revisit ground they'd previously covered. In winter, the loop allowed the skier to ski out on a trail already broken.

Over time, his arms and legs regained strength. Gliding on snow previously compacted by his own toil, the skier searched within himself and located the cadence he'd learned skiing the banks of Miller Creek as a child. His skis sliced through the storm's residue. He no longer felt forty-two. He no longer felt winded. He no longer felt a need to contemplate or gauge the world. He was a bird soaring to the sun; a dolphin diving to the depths; a stallion racing the wind. He sprinted for home.

Beneath the eves of his garage the man stepped out of his ski bindings. Absolute quiet embraced the farm. The wind started and stopped in an endless shifting of effort. The skier walked slowly towards the old farmhouse. He moved his arms in circles to loosen tired shoulder joints. As he reached for the door handle, he stopped. Watching the wind's affect on falling snow, he realized that, while he would never live to see a perfect world, he had at least lived to experience the perfect ski.

Magical Cat

Those of you that live in the country-and I'm talking about real country now, out beyond cable television, away from the lights of the city, know that you cannot live in the country without a cat.

I've always had dogs. Big dogs. Labradors and golden retrievers. But since my family moved to our farm, the feline kingdom and I have reached an uneasy truce. At any given time, I allow one or two cats to reside in our garage or barn. In return for food and lodging, the cats patrol the tall grass, preventing mice, voles, and shrews from invading our home.

After decades of careful study, I must admit that cats do have their place in God's scheme of things (though I'm not certain that God has a better handle on cats than you or I do). Any way, the thing about outdoor cats is that they don't hang around too long. Since we've lived in the country, I think we've gone through a jillion or so. There have been so many; I can't remember all of their names. I do know that the first few were named after candy. That was Matt, our oldest son's doing. We had, as I recall, and in no particular order, M&M, Snickers, Licorice, and Baby Ruth. The last one also answered to "Baby Luth" an alternative given it by our second son Dylan, a child born with perpetually swollen tonsils. Baby Ruth was a sweet white and brown fur ball who performed mousing duties with quiet determination. She wasn't overly affectionate or particularly aloof. She accepted human attention but didn't relish it.

It was a hot summer. Dylan was four years old. In the country, it's not uncommon for a cat to go missing. Country cats usually turn up alive and well after such absences, though often disheveled and marred by adventure. Baby Ruth, despite her neat appearance and well-intentioned grooming, was no exception to this general feline propensity to wander. But as a day's absence turned into several days and nights with no sign of her, even I, the reluctant cat-lover, began to fear the worst. Out where we live, there's no end to the misfortune that can befall a cat. Owls, eagles, and hawks prey upon them from the sky. Dogs, fox, wolves, and coyotes snatch them on the ground.

Dylan is the sort of a child who looks at the world with a sense of wonder. He's always been that way. Thus it wasn't unusual when, in response to my wife's inquiry about Baby Ruth, the following exchange took place.

"Dylan, have you seen Baby Ruth?"

"Baby Luth 'isappeared."

"What do you mean she 'isappeared'?"

There was a lengthy pause as Dylan's blue eyes searched an overcast sky. Mother and son were walking from the garage to the house dodging rain as they conversed.

"She's a magical cat," Dylan offered.

"Magical? How is she magical?" René asked.

Adjusting his Duluth Dukes baseball cap, my son turned his head so that he looked at his mother. His eyes were diverted. He didn't meet her gaze directly. Still, René detected an element of mischief within the boy's smile. In a soft voice, Dylan offered:

"She can 'isappear."

Visions of old horror films ran through my wife's mind as she sought to understand the cat's fate. By what terrible means had our son dispatched our family pet? Her voice grew stern.

"Dylan Munger, where is the cat?"

The child left his mother's side and walked towards the garage. My wife followed. Once inside the building, Dylan stopped in front of an old barrel stove.

"She's in there."

"Oh, my God," René whispered.

My spouse grasped the handle of the firebox door, offered a silent prayer for the cat, and pulled on the door. Hinges creaked eerily as ash trickled onto the floor.

"Meow."

Sounds of life escaped the metal chamber. René bent down and peered into the rusty barrel. Despite the lack of light, she was able to see the outline of Baby Ruth cowering against the far wall of her prison. My wife liberated the animal. Free of its sooty confinement, the cat shook its fur, releasing a cloud of wood ash into the air.

"Why did you put the cat in the stove?"

René resisted an urge to smile. The sight of the dirty cat and the look on our son's face proved to be too much. She covered her face with one hand as she waited for a response.

"She was bugging me. She wouldn't listen so I made her 'isappear."

With a single bound, Baby Ruth escaped my wife's grasp and landed on top of my workbench where the famished cat immediately went to work on a dish of cat chow.

"Please don't make her 'isappear' anymore, OK?" my wife implored through a tightly restrained smile.

Dylan approached the feline and stroked its fur. The boy's face showed that he was considering the admonition.

"But she's a magical cat."

"I know. Just don't lock her in the stove."

"OK."

My wife and son walked out of the garage and into the summer night. Sometime later that autumn, Baby Ruth 'isappeared' for good. Since her departure, a succession of replacement cats has lived with us only to ultimately vanish with similar regularity. Their departures no longer concern me. I have ceased trying to determine what makes them come, what makes them go.

I've come to understand that Baby Ruth was no exception. She was the rule. Cats are made of magic. They don't abide by rules or logic. My son knew this. He also was smart enough to realize that you can't negotiate with a cat.

Christmas Town

White snow folds over the streets of the town like a quilt. The sky above the town is dark save for the blinking of distant stars. No wind touches the frozen limbs of the trees lining the town square. It's Christmas Eve.

Children and parents skate on Hanson's Pond; their movements choreographed like the gentle motions of ballet dancers. The children don't seem to tire. They don't seem to complain. Their parents don't argue or bicker about Christmas bills, relatives, or whether or not the Christmas trees that stand in their living rooms dignify the holiday that's upon them.

A boy stands atop a small rise, the white beneath him smooth as silk. He holds a sled; the old-fashioned kind with wood slats and rusted steel runners. It seems he cannot make up his mind. He gazes at the bottom of the hill, contemplating gravity. There are no other children with him, which gives his circumstance a lonely, forlorn aspect.

Here and there, passenger cars are parked upon the street. They don't move. Their engines are quiet. Looking closely, you can see the cars are empty. There are no footprints in the matted white on the ground to suggest where the owners of the vehicles have gone. The air is free of exhaust and soot. From the scene, you would expect to smell maple burning in someone's fireplace but there is no odor save for the sweet scent of spruce.

Sharp light from the town's street lamps illuminates the sidewalks and buildings. The town seems well watched and safe. A single police cruiser sits parked in front of the town hall. Like the other vehicles on the street, the squad car is from a different time. The cruiser has not moved for days. There is no crime to speak of in the town. No one living there can remember an unkind act being perpetrated by anyone for as long as the town has existed.

Adult residents of the town stand quietly on the sidewalks. If they are engaged in conversation, it's in low, imperceptible tones. They don't appear to be caught up in the infinite hurry of Christmas. They seem calm, collected, and without worry. All the town's folk appear well fed and without obvious need or infirmity.

Though the buildings lining the square appear modest, they are constructed to last. The paint and trim on each is immaculate. Among their number, there is a bank, the town hall, a hotel, a tavern, a train depot, and several homes. Even though it's near midnight, bright lights shine from the windows. No noise emanates from the structures. If work is being done, or arguments are taking place, or love is being made in any of the buildings, those things are being accomplished in relative quiet.

A lonesome whistle interrupts the silence. From behind the whitened hillside, the single light of an ancient steam locomotive casts a beam. Pulling a coal tender, two passenger cars, and a caboose, the train speeds into town. The "clack clack" of wheels against ties seems to be the only disturbance. No one rushes to the depot as the train passes by. No one moves to board the passenger cars. The train rolls on.

Music breaks out in the hotel: Evidently the guests are still awake and feel like ringing in Christmas with song.

Hark the Herald Angels sing, glory to the newborn king...

The tune is clear. The organist makes no errors in timing or keystrokes. The voices of the hotel guests cannot be distinguished due to the bellicose volume of the organ.

It's a place of utter calm, prosperity, peace, and love; the perfect Christmas town. Though it appears to be old and out of touch, its borders expand every year with new buildings, new residents, new improvements of every imaginable sort.

In truth, the Christmas town of this story came to our house in boxes. It sits upon our floor, beneath our Christmas tree, beneath a myriad of lights and ornaments. Year after year we've added to the display, making it grander, more perfect. Ours is but one in a dazzling collection of such towns that are for sale, not just at Christmas time, but throughout the year.

As I sit and watch the model train chug its way around the ceramic figures and buildings, I wonder what it is that drives us to seek perfection beneath our Christmas trees. Is it a feeling of powerlessness given the breadth of the problems that we face everyday? A feeling of having lost the simple life we knew as children? A need to create a world over which we have absolute control?

I look out our front room window as I contemplate the Christmas town. Across our snow-covered front lawn lies the open water of the Cloquet River.

It seems to me that many of the reasons that lead us to build imaginary worlds beneath our Christmas trees also leads us to move to the country. We feel we'll have more control of our lives, of our children's safety, of our time together, if we can just escape to another place, a place far away from the city.

But in today's world, we cannot move away from each other and create another reality, just as we cannot make a wish and join the porcelain figures of the Christmas town in their seemingly perfect world.

Jesus said: "Love your neighbor as yourselves."

Whether you are Christian, Jew, Moslem, or claim no faith at all, these words ring true.

Watching the temperate flow of the river, I vow to live by Christ's words this Christmas season. I ask that you consider doing the same. Perhaps, if we're successful, we may even crack a few smiles on the ceramic faces of the people living under our Christmas trees.

Beware of Toxic Tuesday

In September of 1990, I was in the process of recovering from back surgery when my wife voiced the notion that I should write the great American novel. When my wounds healed sufficiently to allow me to begin long walks, I started to daydream. Plot themes and characters sprang to life during these sojourns. Winter came. My walks gave way to swimming in the local YMCA pool. As my time in the water increased, I re-worked an emerging story. Late at night, in the quiet of our eighty-five-year-old Sears farmhouse, I transferred words from yellow legal pads into our old Tandy computer's memory.

Christmas of that year, René gave me Jeff Herman's book, *Writer's Guide to Book Editors, Publishers and Literary Agents*. I was heartened that my better half thought enough of my writing to steer me towards publication. Thoughts of life as a famous writer began to seduce me. I was tired of being a trial lawyer. Writing looked to be a way out. John Grisham was a lawyer once, wasn't he? So were Scott Turow and Barry Reed.

I put Herman's volume on the shelf. I was not ready to market my book. I knew that my manuscript, *November One*, would require months to complete. But life got in the way of writing. Daily tasks made the moments available to work on the book scarce. Another winter was upon me before the novel was ready for professional scrutiny. I pulled Herman's tome from its resting-place and jotted down the names and addresses of literary agents who seemed appropriate for my book. I began to query agents; five at a time.

On May 5, 1992, the first query letters were mailed. Within days, I heard back from the agents. All declined to take a look at my work. I struggled to understand why no one thought my manuscript was worthy of at least a cursory read.

On May 20th five new names were added to my list of potential agents. Three agencies responded with resounding "no thanks" but their rejection letters were at least polite. I never heard back from the other two. Self-doubt began to cloud my good humor. But on May 28, 1992, jubilation! Ms. Roslyn Targ asked for the first 50 pages of my manuscript. I sent the requested excerpt the next day. By June 10, I was reading the following:

I have now had an opportunity to read your manuscript and unfortunately I do not feel enthusiastic enough to take on its representation. Hopefully another agent will feel otherwise.

Good luck,

R. Targ.

My tenacity (remember; I was a trial lawyer!) compelled me to keep trying. Natasha Kern, Ruth Wreschner, Judith Berg (remember that name) and two other noted agents were targeted. My attitude improved considerably when I received word that both Ms. Kern and Ms. Wreschner wanted to read portions of the manuscript.

A few weeks later, I was reading the following:

I have the feeling that you are a very nice person and probably also a good lawyer, just the person I would love to number among my clients...

I sensed such an introduction could only be followed by a big fat "but..."

Ms. Wreschner was kind but unimpressed.

Do ask another agent since opinions differ but I don't think I would be successful for you. It might also help to read some books on fiction writing... or take some fiction writing courses. Best of luck to you. If your book gets published, I'll be the loser!

In retrospect, my sensitivity was misplaced. My writing needed guidance. However, with thoughts of "book of the month club" fame dancing before me, an agent's critique of my literary abilities was the last thing I wanted to consider.

A week later, I was on top of the world again.

"Mark," my wife yelled to me as I was tilling our vegetable garden, "there's a Ms. Kern on the telephone for you."

"Hello," I offered when I picked up the telephone receiver, "this is Mark."

"Mr. Munger, Natasha Kern. I've read the first few chapters of your book. While the writing needs some work, I like the plot. I want you to consider working with an editor to smooth out the rough edges. They charge by the page but I think that it would be worth a try. If you like, I can send you a list of reputable editors and you can pick the one you want to work with," she said.

71

Ms. Kern laid it on the line. There were some problems, yes, but they could be overcome.

"I'm willing to give it a try," I responded meekly.

"I want to see the finished product," Ms. Kern added.

Ms. Kern sent me a list of editors. I selected Ms. Lesley Payne to work with. I wrote to Ms. Payne. She called me back. We came to an agreement. It looked like things were finally going my way.

The citizenry of Duluth, Minnesota (my home) will always remember June 30, 1992 as "Toxic Tuesday". On that date, a Burlington Northern freight train derailed, toppling a tanker full of benzene into the Nemadji River. The mixture of benzene and water created a poisonous cloud. I was one of tens of thousands of Duluthians who left town as part of a mass evacuation of the Twin Ports of Duluth and Superior, Wisconsin. June 30, 1992 stands out for me personally, not because of my escape from benzene hell, but because of another telephone call.

"Mark, there's someone on the phone calling about your book," René related as I filled the tank of our riding lawn mower with gasoline.

Once again I went inside the house to talk to a stranger over the telephone about my novel.

"Mr. Munger, Brice Harding from the Judith Berg Agency. Ms. Berg asked that I give you a call. We're interested in your book."

There it was. Further confirmation that what I had written was worthy of consideration. Two days later, I received the Berg Agency's submission guidelines. Within the week, the first 100 pages of *November One* were en route to Ms. Berg. I felt caught in a heady whirlwind of excitement. Two agents wanted my work! I had two professionals ready, willing, and able to go to war in the trenches of the New York publishing industry on my behalf.

On September 2, I called Judith Berg. The agent made it clear that she wanted to represent *November One*.

"René," I said to my wife as we sat on a swing on the front porch of our farmhouse sometime after I spoke with Ms.

Berg, "I don't know what to do. Natasha Kern thinks that the book has merit but wants me to work with an editor."

"Yes…"

"On the other hand, Ms. Berg will take the book as is."

"Sounds like you have a decision to make."

A few days later, I signed a contract with Ms. Berg. I was feeling on top of the world.

By January of 1993, Ms. Berg was satisfied that the book had reached a sufficient level of integrity to submit it to prospective publishers. I began to receive memoranda from the agency listing the names of publishers being provided with *November One*. That same month I also received a contract from my agent regarding the potential sale of the electronic rights of my book. I was on a roll. Just a few short months after entering into the publishing arena, people were lining up to offer me contracts. I signed and returned the E-rights agreement as fast as I could.

By early June, all of the publishers contacted by Ms. Berg had rejected *November One*. Confused, I wrote to Judith (we were on a first name basis by then). I implored her to advise me whether (as other agents had opined) the book needed major rehabilitation. I received no response.

A year passed. By March of 1994, I was getting concerned that Ms. Berg and I were "barking up the wrong tree". I again asked for any comments or concerns that the agency (or any of the contacted publishers) might have regarding the manuscript. The agent provided a rejection letter from Tor books.

Although the subject matter intrigued me and the plot maintained my interest, I found the writing to be slightly awkward at times. Often, the dialogue was forced and unnatural. Therefore, I'm going to pass on this one.

(Letter from N. Montemarano of Tor Books dated 5/12/93).

Mr. Montemarano's comments were startling. I began to believe that the other agent's observations about *November One* had been on the mark. I called the agency and set up an appointment to speak with Ms. Berg. We talked. I stayed put. She was confident a publisher would be found.

On October 19, 1994, I received a proposed contract from Northwest Publishing (NPI) in Utah. My agent's cover letter indicated that, while she was unable to obtain an advance from NPI for my work, she had negotiated an agreement on my behalf.

However, I did speak with acquisitions and with publishing regarding the value of your book and we were able to negotiate some cooperative terms.

(Letter of 10/19/94)

I'm a lawyer. I'm able to understand legalese. As I read through the proposed agreement, I noted that I was expected to "front" NPI the sum of $6,125.00. Even though I was new to the book publishing world, the proposal sounded an awful lot like vanity publishing, something I was not interested in.

I called my agent. I had a number of questions, not the least of which was: "Is NPI a reputable company?"

Ms. Berg assured me that NPI was a solvent regional publisher marketing 100-150 titles per year through industry giants Barnes and Noble and Baker and Taylor. After our conversation, I felt immeasurably better. I was convinced that "cooperative publishing", where NPI agreed to pay the majority of the cost associated with printing 10,000 copies of the book in trade paperback and agreed to provide nationwide marketing support, was not such a bad deal after all. On December 2, 1994, I received an amended agreement directly from Mr. James Van Treese, the owner of NPI. My cash contribution to the cooperative effort had been reduced to $3,062.50. All of the other terms and conditions of the deal remained in place.

Enthused by the notion that my long path towards literary glamour was but a few short steps away, I implored my wife to let me send Mr. Van Treese a check.

"Look at it this way," I argued. "If everything goes sour, we're only out a few thousand bucks."

Confident that NPI would deliver the goods, having been assured as to the publisher's reputation, and having been provided with a copy of NPI's catalog (as well as a sample of one of their books), I convinced my wife to let me send the cash.

A month later, I received a publication schedule from NPI. In July of 1995, Mr. Van Treese requested a three-month extension of the book's release date. I agreed to the modification at the behest of my agent.

September 1995. Ms. Berg wrote and explained that Mr. Van Treese was seeking an additional extension. The language of the letter caught my attention.

Should Mr. Van Treese/NPI fail to publish according to the schedule and fail to return your money, we will discuss a legal recourse at that time. It is my hope that I am just being an alarmist... but I feel it's best to be prepared in the event that NPI defaults.

(Letter of 9/22/95).

I sensed trouble. Embarrassed, I said nothing to my wife. It became more difficult to fend off the inquiries of friends, family, and neighbors regarding the book.

"How's your novel coming?" my friend Jan asked whenever she saw me.

"Slowly," was my patterned reply.

An edited galley of the book arrived in March of 1996. I supplied NPI with revisions and a color photograph taken by my wife, which seemed perfect for the book's cover. I convinced myself that Ms. Berg had sounded a false alarm until NPI sent me the following handwritten note.

Enclosed is a copy of what the art director has come up with despite the situation here at Northwest. At this time, I don't know how long this will take to be printed. If you have any questions concerning this copy, or if I can be of any further help at this time, please call me at...

The note wasn't written on NPI stationary. I tried to call NPI. The company's toll free number had been disconnected. I dialed direct. I was told by the person who answered that NPI had filed for bankruptcy. I dialed my agent and left several intense messages for Ms. Berg. She didn't return my calls.

As I clung to shreds of faith that NPI would come back into the picture, I began to receive legal papers from the bankruptcy court and my greatest fears were confirmed.

The trustee filed a complaint against James Van Treese and Jason Van Treese on February 13, 1997. The complaint seeks recovery from these two individuals of at least $10,500,000.00 based upon defendants' corporate mismanagement of NPI...

(Court Notice dated 4/14/97)

As Paul Simon said, I felt things "slip-sliding away." NPI still held the corrected galleys, the computer disks, and my wife's original photograph for the book's cover. I, along with many others who had been bilked, hired a third party service to scour

75

NPI's files in hopes of salvaging my intellectual property. The service was unable to retrieve anything from NPI related to my book.

Disgruntled but undeterred, I pressed onward. Ms. Berg lined up another publisher, Caramoor Press. Exhausted by the NPI debacle, I agreed to work with Caramoor. I began to rewrite my novel, relieved that I wasn't expected to send Caramoor any money. Shortly after signing a contract with Caramoor, I received a gushing letter from Ms. Berg.

Congratulations on your publishing contract with Caramoor. They have informed me that they will soon be able to announce your release date.
(Letter of 3/19/97).

Nearly five years after my first contact with the Berg Agency, things seemed poised to come to some sort of conclusion. Whether I became rich, famous, or critically acclaimed mattered little. Positive closure for my work, for my sweat and toil, was all that mattered.

Two weeks later I received the following letter from my agent:

We are now at the point where we are diligently trying to sever all ties with Caramoor...We have requested that all materials belonging to our clients are returned to our office by April 9, 1997...
(Letter of 4/4/97)

My agent went on to urge "us" (this was a form letter) to consider publishing with "Romantic Press", a publishing venture Ms. Berg was just beginning. Enraged at being duped again, I detailed my frustrations to the Berg Agency in writing.

It has been five years since I was first contacted by you regarding the novel and I am in exactly the same situation today as I was then with several major exceptions:
1. *I have lost $3,500.00, give or take a few pennies on the NPI fiasco;*
2. *I have lost five years of time;*
3. *Your agency has presented the work to scores of potential publishers... to no avail, obviously diminishing the chances that I will be able to find another agent to take on the work.*
(Letter dated 7/15/97)

A few months later, I finally terminated my contract with my agent.

To make matter worse, a reporter from a Salt Lake City newspaper requested an interview with me about my dealings with NPI. What could I tell her? That I was greedy for fame? That I was, despite twenty years of formal education, undeniably stupid? After taking a deep breath, I called her back. A few days later, she sent me a copy of the article she'd written. Thankfully, the story didn't quote me by name.

Am I bitter about my fate? I don't think so. During my long and difficult education regarding the world of publishing and literary agents, I came to the realization that my first novel needed help. I hadn't paid my dues. Once I came to this point of recognition, I took a few steps back.

During the winter of 1997 I began to write a weekly essay column for our local paper. Years of receiving personal, heart-warming accolades from readers of those articles have convinced me that I can write: I just needed to find my own voice, my own style. Learning a subject, whether it's law or art, requires study. I've become an enthusiastic reader of *Poets and Writers*, *Glimmer Train*, *Grain*, *Heron Dance*, *The Writer*, *Writer's Journal* and other literary periodicals in the hopes that I can gain an informal education in the craft of writing.

These days, whenever I have a block of free time, I work on short stories and essays, mailing two or three pieces a season to literary magazines, ever hopeful that my writing strikes a chord. And I spend hours reading the stuff I should have read twenty-five years ago in college: Hemingway, Faulkner, O'Connor, Lawrence, Steinbeck.

Who knows? Someday, I might attend a writing workshop or take a stab at writing another novel.

Note: The names associated with the agency that represented me are fictional. The rest, as they say, is nothing but fact.

POSTSCRIPT:
In October of 2000 November One *was re-titled* The Legacy, *published by Savage Press of Superior, Wisconsin, became a regional bestseller, and remains in print through Cloquet River Press. The book was acclaimed by* The Mystery Review Quarterly *(Summer 2001) as a "marvelous first novel."*

Grandpa's Raspberries

He stands in memory. His green work pants hang low on his waist. Gray hair, organized in a flat crew cut, bristles from his scalp. An August sun blazes behind him. The details of his face are lost in shadow. His plaid flannel shirt is rolled up to his elbows: The white and red squares remain vivid in my mind's eye.

It's been nearly forty years since he died. I knew him only briefly. He and Grandma were old when I was born. Grandma became older still, living another twenty-five years without him. I was just a little boy when he passed away. That I remember him at all says something about what kind of man he was. The word "gentle" springs to mind. Why that adjective strikes a chord, I don't know. It just seems to fit.

They lived in Duluth, in Riverside by the railroad tracks. Their house was a modest workingman's home. Grandpa tended a vegetable garden behind that house.

I know that Grandpa had other things growing in his garden: Potatoes. Tomatoes. Carrots. None of those interested a six-year-old. They were all "good for you". They were all vegetables. But the raspberries; they were something quite different. They were worth putting on your Keds and following Grandpa out the back door; worth negotiating the maze of junk Grandma had collected and stored on the back porch; worth wading through the sea of purple thistle that bordered the garden.

When René and I bought our place in the country, it came with raspberries. I think the memory of Grandpa's raspberries convinced me to have a vegetable garden. I know my decision to have a garden wasn't based upon visions of fresh cauliflower.

Bending at the waist, I search the canes for ripe berries. Dew hangs heavy off the fruit and glistens in the early morning sun. Each raspberry wears a veil of moisture and shines like a precious gem. Between the plants, intricate lace spans the stems, the handiwork of spiders. Rainwater suspended on the webs shimmers to my footsteps. I pick only the ripest berries. I'm not picking for jam or for the freezer. I'm picking for myself. I want just enough fruit to fill a bowl to eat with milk and sugar for breakfast.

Insects catch currents in the moist air and fly between plants. Here and there, honeybees glide from fruit to fruit. I see many bumblebees each summer at our place. I rarely see honeybees. This summer there are more of honeybees around. I watch them closely. I've heard they are on the decline; that some sort of mite is killing off their hives. Even commercial honey farms in Iowa, which rely upon domestic honeybees, are losing hives. I say a prayer, a small prayer for a small creature.

Our riding horses snort and blow in the tall weeds of the fenced pasture. I watch them swish their tails, heads bent to the ground, grazing. It's cool. Heavy morning fog is just beginning to burn off. The black flies are absent, though a new hatch of mosquitoes finds me as I pick the last of my berries.

I stand upright, stretching my low back, loosening a kink. The rows of canes remain heavy with ripe berries. We have already picked fifteen quarts of fruit for jam and freezing. We have no more room for them.

Maggie, our female black Labrador, snuffles along next to me. Her nose drags through the sandy loam. Stopping at ripe berries, she inhales the fruit and moves on. Sam, a yellow Labrador who has forgotten how to swim, sits deeply in the loose soil. At nine, he is lazy. I select a purple berry and toss it towards him. The raspberry disappears in the pink and black of his mouth. The dog's tail beats steadily against the ground.

At the end of a row, I stare at the remnants of our unkempt strawberry bed. I spent hours last year building the elevated bed for the spoiled little plants. I added new shoots. I tore out every weed I could find. I lost the battle. Most of the plants didn't survive the winter. The few plants that survived cannot be seen: Weeds the height of a small cow stand silent guard over my now-abandoned effort.

My eyes deceive me. I think I see Grandpa smiling at me from across the garden. Does he know that I'm no longer a little boy, that I'm a man with three kids and another on the way? His

79

thick jowls wiggle up and down as he walks towards me. I perceive he is a ghost, an illusion from childhood. But I listen to him anyway. He speaks in the same ragged voice I last heard forty years ago.

"You didn't see me plant strawberries in my garden, did you, Mark?" he asks.

"No, Grandpa, I didn't."

"Too much work, unpredictable, those strawberries. Stick with raspberries and you'll be fine."

I want to ask him more. You know, big questions like where he is; about whether he and Grandma found each other again; those sorts of things. But he isn't here to answer the mysteries of the ages. He's here, however briefly, to help me with my garden.

Eulogy

We were at dinner. My eldest son Matt and I were sitting with my dad and a group of his cronies. Our table overlooked the ice sheet of the Duluth Curling Club. As we waited for our sandwiches, curlers practiced sliding their rocks across smooth ice in the rink below the dining room windows. As the stones moved effortlessly towards the house (the target) our attention was called back to our table. The waitress stood over us with a tray of beverages.

"Who had the tap beer?" she asked politely.

"Over here," one of the guys said.

The woman placed the beer in front of the man. Effortlessly, he reached into his pocket and removed a money clip. Deftly, the customer peeled off three crisp dollar bills from the roll. The waitress accepted the money and gestured as if to make change.

"Keep the change."

"Thanks."

The rest of us were served our drinks. Matt, nine or ten years old at the time, watched the guy draw the beer to his lips and drink. My son stared incredulously as the beverage disappeared from the glass.

Our food came. The adults began to eat. We talked sports and watched curlers. Matt was slow attending to his cheeseburger. He continued to watch the man in the gray beard and glasses and scrutinize the manner by which our companion brought spoonfuls of hot soup to his lips. When the soup bowl was empty, the man contemplated the burger in front of him.

"Mark, would you open the catsup bottle?"

"Sure."

I twisted the cap off the bottle and handed it to the guy. He poured the red sauce over his fries. With deliberate ease, he took the top of the bun off his burger and sprinkled catsup on the sandwich as well.

"Matt, do you play any sports?" the man asked.

"Hockey," my son replied.

81

"Great sport. What position?"

"Center."

"We call him the 'Junk Yard Dog'," I confided. "He likes to stand in front of the net and wait for easy goals.

"Just like Phil Esposito," the man commented.

"Who?" Matt queried.

"One of the greatest goal scorers of all time," the man replied.

Matt smiled when he understood the compliment.

After dinner, my son and I walked back to our car through a deserted skyway.

"Did you see that man drink beer?" Matt asked.

"What man?" I responded.

"The man with no hands."

"Oh. You mean Bruce," I offered.

"Yeah. It was amazing how he could drink beer without hands."

I studied Matt's face as we walked. I felt my mouth turn upwards into a smile.

"He does a lot more than that, Matt. He golfs. In fact, he beats Grandpa regularly. He also curls. And he's a writer."

"A writer?"

"One of the best sportswriters around."

"How can he write without any fingers?" my son asked in a quiet voice.

"I'm not sure. But he's been doing it for a long time."

Over the years, our paths would occasionally cross. When I'd see Bruce, I'd often remind him of Matt's incredulity. The sportswriter would smile. I think he got a chuckle out of the story even though he'd heard it so many times.

Years later, my GMC Jimmy was being pummeled by a summer storm. As the car rounded a curve, I noticed a man with a dog on a leash making slow progress through heavy weather.

"That looks like Bruce Bennett," I said, slowing the vehicle.

"The sportswriter?" Matt asked from the front passenger seat.

"Yeah. He lives somewhere around here."

I pulled my utility vehicle onto the gravel shoulder, stopped, and rolled down the driver's side window.

"Hi Bruce," I shouted over the noise of the storm.

Bruce blinked as rain found its way around the protective hood of his poncho and into his eyes.

"That you, Mark?"

"Yep," I said, pulling my left arm away from the open window, the fabric of my flannel shirt already damp.

He stopped next to the car and instructed his dog to "sit". The canine tentatively placed its rump on the road's wet pavement.

"You remember my son?"

"Sure do. It's Matt, right?"

My son grinned and gave a slight wave of acknowledgement.

I found it remarkable that a man with so many friends, so many admirers, would remember the name of a boy he'd met only once.

"We're headed up Highway 2 to do some brook trout fishing," I explained.

"You've got the weather for it."

"You're getting wet. You better get home," I suggested.

"Good luck guys," Bruce said.

Tugging gently on the leash, the writer drew his dog close to his side and began to walk away. In my rear-view-mirror, I watched the man's form merge with rain. My attention focused on his uneven gait and I remembered that Bruce's unusual stride was caused by impairment to one of his legs. It also dawned on me that although Bruce Bennett was a man who made his living selecting words to describe the world, he never used the adjective "disabled" to describe himself.

Runaway Child

"**Where's** Christian?" I asked my sons Matt, Dylan, and their friend Timmy.

"I dunno."

"He was right here, right next to me," I said, leaving a "Magnum Force" video game for someone else to play. Panic set in.

"He was over there, by the pinball machines, last I saw him," Dylan, my second eldest advised.

I glanced around the room, a small game room on the main floor of our hotel in Orlando, Florida. Chris was nowhere to be found. It was the morning of Easter Sunday. We'd just come back from sunrise services at Sea World with our friends, the McVeans. René was resting. I was in charge of the boys. I'd blown my assignment.

"Matt, you guys go look around the pool."

"OK."

I watched the three older boys move out quickly, as if despite their ages, they recognized the seriousness of a three-year-old being left on his own in a strange place, full of strange people. On a hunch that my third son might be missing his mother, I went into the hotel and checked the lobby. Nothing. I began climbing the stairway, checking the hallways of each floor. Again, nothing. I knew I had to get René involved. I knew she'd panic, become distraught that her baby was now missing in the middle of a mammoth hotel complex. The place was huge; with two separate towers of five hundred rooms each; several swimming pools; a private pond; and numerous alcoves concealing hot tubs behind native vegetation.

"René, open up, it's Mark."

The hotel room door opened slowly. My wife was dressed to go to one of the local theme parks.

"Where're the boys?"

"There's a little problem."

"What sort of problem?"

"I lost Chris."

Anxiety blossomed across my wife's face.

"You what?"

"He walked away from the video arcade. I've checked the building. He's not here. The boys and the McVeans are looking outside."

We scurried down to the front desk. Soon the entire place was crawling with folks looking for our youngest son.

"Did you find him, Matt?" I asked as I approached my oldest son by the pool.

"Nope. No one's seen him."

My eyes scanned the lush greenery of the grounds.

Help me, God.

The McVeans arrived. Dylan and René joined us. Still no Chris. We split up. The dazzling white exterior of another hotel tower, the companion to the one we were staying in, caught my eye.

Is it possible?

I moved faster; to make it in time; before some unknown person or persons took my child, for whatever reason, away from me. I opened the front door and rushed into the lobby of the adjoining hotel.

"Have you seen a little boy, about this high?" I asked the desk clerk, gesturing. "Big brown eyes, red shirt, and blue shorts, sandy brown hair?"

"You the father?" the man asked.

I nodded affirmatively.

"Security is looking for him right now."

Good, I thought. *The word made it over here as well.*

"Thanks," I replied weakly.

Ding.

The doors of the elevator began opening.

"Come on," I murmured, impatient for the occupants of the car to be revealed.

"You looking for this little guy?" a muscular security guard in full uniform asked, his left arm protected by a plaster cast.

Standing in front of the officer was a three-year-old boy; the object of my distress. I threw my arms around my son's neck as the guard escorted the child out of the elevator.

85

"What were you doing?" I asked Chris through a steady parade of tears.

"I wanted to see Mom," he replied in a matter-of-fact voice.

"You trained him well," the guard interjected. "I asked him if he was Chris Munger. He told me 'I can't talk to strangers'. I thought he was the kid but he refused to tell me anything. He seemed put off by this thing," the man continued, raising his cast.

I examined the earnest face of my son and offered an amendment to our standard parental instruction:

"Chris, it's OK to talk to strangers in uniform."

Spring Dance

Winter's grip has been released early. Last year, spring appeared suddenly; after an early May snow; there was an almost immediate transition from winter to summer. This year is different.

I stand in our front yard, where the neatly clipped lawn of last autumn slopes towards the steep, brambly bank of the river. The rake in my gloved hand props me up as I gaze across yellowed fields and past decaying mounds of horse leavings the retreating snow has exposed in our pasture. This day is the reason I live here; a day offering a glimpse of the summer to come; a day of delight and possibility.

I drop the rake and walk slowly towards the water's edge. At twenty-five, I would never have left my chores unfinished to sit and study the world. At thirty-five, I would have pawed and scraped at the sand and filth collected on the lawn until, exhausted, I completed the task. At forty-two, the river draws me away from the never-ending jobs of our hobby farm. I yield to the water's power.

Sundays are made for such journeys. Fresh from the spiritual fulfillment of church, steadied in faith and grace, and instilled with belief, it's without regret that I allow myself a few minutes to act on impulse, to observe the world around me.

On the point, where the silver flow of an unnamed creek intersects the black water of the Cloquet River, I claim a seat on the trunk of an old willow, which serves as a bench next to our fire ring. My eyes survey the riverbanks. I note evidence of the steady work of resident beaver: Their lodge sits a few yards from my perch. Current swirls around their house. An unruly aspen branch projects from the lodge into the water. The branch keeps time to a song that has no words. A pair of mallards winging overhead accents the openness of the sky. Sunlight warms my face. The glare catches the emerald green of the drake's head as he pulls up to land. His mate drops next to him. The hen's drab color blends in with the grays and browns of the maples occupying the riverbank behind her.

I focus on the distant edge of our pasture. Sharp stubble covers the sandy soil of the field in a uniform carpet of gold. Soon, bumble bees and butterflies will dance above the greening field. The grass and clover will become lush and then turn brittle as the seasons change again. I search for whitetail deer at the far edge of the hayfield. None show themselves in the openness of late afternoon.

Loud, obnoxious voices echo from down river. Two Canada geese settle noisily on the water, suspended in the swiftness of the current, churning their legs to remain in place against the weight of the river. Their cries reverberate up and down the river's enclave as if they are disappointed that there are no others of their kind to share the day with.

The log I sit on remains warm despite the receding day. Dusk is near, though there will be light enough to finish my chores. Somewhere in the woods, a drummer adds another beat to the symphony. The urgency of procreation requires a male ruffed grouse to hasten his song in hopes of securing a mate. The cacophony gains speed, ending in an exhausting crescendo. The woods fall silent.

As I stand up, intent upon returning to my work, a final, amazing waltz originates between clouds that have swung in from the west. Two osprey circle each other, dodging and weaving in vast, intricate patterns. Though I am not expert enough to know which of the birds is the male, which the female, I recognize the promenade. It is as primitive, as emotive, as the first awkward steps young humans take toward romance at a school dance. I close my eyes and recall the hesitant waltzes of my own youth.

I open my eyes. The birds unite in frenzy. Lost in the ritual of creation, they free-fall towards the ground. Then, after no more than an instant together, the fish eagles tear themselves apart and soar separately through indigo. The birds catch the wind and their forms become specks above the horizon.

"That was really something," my wife whispers.

I turn to find René standing next to me, shielding her eyes from the low sun. I was so enthralled with the birds that I never heard her arrive.

"Listen," she says.

Frogs have commenced a welcome to the forthcoming night.

"Peepers," she opines.

I nod in agreement.

"Supper's ready," she offers, her voice soft and respectful.

I take her hand. We walk up the hill towards the house. As we get closer, the sound of our boys playing eclipses the chorus of the frogs. As we pass the piles of dead grass and debris, I have the urge to stop. I want to tell her "I'll be in as soon as I get these cleaned up." But this day, I say nothing. I walk past the work. The chores will be waiting for me tomorrow. For now, I choose to listen to the melody of the season.

Crawdad Boys

"**I** need to go to town and pick up some groceries," the woman tells the boys.

Ian, his blond hair tossed to one side by a light summer breeze, smiles. Dylan, the woman's second son, his hair darker than his friend's, grins as his hand grasps the wooden handle of a landing net. The boys stand unsteadily on hot blacktop. Rubber boots two or three sizes too large end just shy of their knees. A galvanized minnow bucket, the lid secured by a spring latch, sits on the pavement in front of them.

"OK, Mom. Ian and me are just gonna count our crayfish and have something to eat," Dylan replies, casting an eye at his buddy.

"Ian and I," the mother says quietly.

"Ian and I."

"If you make lunch, clean up the kitchen."

Dylan's smile broadens.

"No problem. We're gonna eat outside anyway, right Ian?"

"Anything you say, Dill-pickle."

"Make sure you put all of the dishes in the dishwasher and all the food back in the fridge," the mother warns. "And don't leave those crayfish out in the sun. They'll die and stink like crazy."

The woman climbs into the driver's seat of the family van, closes the door, turns the key, and engages the air conditioning. She doesn't hear Dylan's final words as the vehicle lumbers down the driveway.

"Don't worry about the crayfish, mom. We'll take care of 'em."

It takes the woman two hours to complete her errands. By the time she's on her way home, storm clouds are beginning to roll in from the west. An urgent, new wind lifts the stagnant humidity of the summer afternoon.

As the van turns into the driveway, the woman's eyes are drawn to the river. In the near distance, white smoke rises against approaching weather. Small flames leap and dance within the fire pit on the point. Ian and Dylan sit next to the fire, preoccupied with the unknown tasks of small boys.

The woman parks the van and walks towards the fire. A thick carpet of clover cushions her feet. Black clouds, low and fat with rain, sweep across the sky.

"Hi, Mom," Dylan shouts from his seat on a log.

Ian crouches by the fire, stirring ashes with a willow switch, urging the flames to climb higher. A steel pot rests on a rusted grate above the heat. Bubbles form and burst within the metal container. Steam escapes from the pot and collides with smoke.

"Hi, Mrs. Munger," Ian adds in a raspy voice.

"What are you boys up to?" René asks, peering into the pot of boiling water.

"We're having lunch," Dylan explains between gulps of Coca-Cola. Beads of sweat gather on the Coke can as he chooses his words. "They're really good," he adds.

My wife stands over the boys. Her eyes are drawn to the minnow bucket lying on the ground. Bits of crustacean shell rest in the grass around the boys' feet.

"You've got to be kidding me."

"We each ate ten of 'em," Ian quips as he spits shards of crawdad skeleton into the fire.

Swallowing the last bit of meat, the blond child spreads his thumb and forefinger three inches apart.

"Some of 'em were big, bigger than this," he boasts.

"You're going to get sick," the mother opines.

Dylan grabs a set of metal tongs and reaches into the swirling water.

"Want one?" he asks, displaying a very red and very dead crayfish. "They're great with a little butter and salt."

"No thanks. I think it's time to put out the fire and head on up to the house. It's gonna pour any second."

The boys dump the pot of water onto the fire. Ash and steam ascend. Scattered drops of rain splatter against them as the mother and the boys move towards the house.

"What possessed you to do this?" the woman asks as she quickens their pace.

"My dad told us they were good to eat," Ian replies.

"And you told us not to make a mess in the kitchen," Dylan quickly reminds her.

The mother smiles, remembering the frogs, turtles, and crayfish caught and examined in her youth.

"I hadn't figured on seafood. I was thinking more along the lines of peanut butter and jelly," she remarks under her breath.

"What's that Mom?"

"Never mind."

The woman opens the screen door to the farmhouse and ducks into the kitchen as the sky opens up. Drying her wet hair with a dishtowel, she watches the boys descend into the basement to play.

"I'll have to warn Ian's dad: He needs to be more selective about the recipes he shares with his son," she observes.

Arapaho

The mountain rises above us. Stark rock pierces a blanket of Colorado snow under the steady glare of the sun. A chair lift pulls us resolutely upward.

As a child, I was fortunate enough to accompany my parents on several ski vacations to the Rockies. In those days, you had to drive through Loveland Pass, near the base of Arapaho Basin ski resort, in order to reach Aspen. On this trip, my first to Colorado since my youth, I'm astonished. The mountain has been hollowed out: A freeway tunnel threads through the stone heart of Loveland Pass. It isn't necessary to climb the Pass to cross over. We simply drive under the mountain.

Arapaho does not climb leisurely towards the sky. Impatient, arrogant, and with immediate urgency, Arapaho thrusts its bold crags and precarious steeples towards heaven. The mountain's disdain for the gradual is the secret of its seduction.

My two oldest sons ride the chair lift with me. Below us, nutrient starved spruce and battered pines shelter the base of the peak. As we climb, we leave the trees behind and follow the exposed face of the mountain to enter sky. Skiers and snowboarders dance beneath the chair lift, carving patterns on a canvas of fresh snow. A sharp wind greets us: The breeze battles the high altitude sun for supremacy.

At the top, we slide off the chair and come to a stop.

"Take a look at the back of this run," Matt observes nervously.

A yellow nylon cord ropes off the precipice. A sign indicates that the area is closed to skiers, as if any rational human would attempt to negotiate the stone, ice, and pitch displayed below us. It seems like a million miles to the bottom of the valley. In reality, it's a little over 12,000 feet.

"Don't get too close," I caution, pulling Dylan away from the edge.

My second son smiles. Dark goggles conceal his eyes. Matt stands next to us. His face is pale. The difference between the two boys' expressions has nothing to do with courage and everything to do with age. Matt is thirteen. Dylan is eight. Eight year-old boys know nothing about mortality.

"What are those guys doing over there," Matt asks in a timid voice, pointing a gloved finger at two single file lines of skiers climbing parallel trails hewn into the face of the mountain.

"They're going to ski the bowl," I respond.

We watch as skiers drop from the trails leading to the bowl intent upon leaving personal legacies in virgin snow. As each skier makes his or her decent, a rooster tail of powder sprays behind the skier from the effort. Here and there, intrepid explorers fall and career uncontrollably downward, propelled by the steepness of the run.

"Why don't you try it, Dad?" Dylan asks, his words filled with challenge.

"That's an unpatrolled area. I'm too old to be skiing with those kids."

"Come on Dad, you can do it," Matt urges.

I look across the slope. I look at my kids. For a brief moment, I'm a twelve-year-old boy in a Jeep Wagoneer driving through Loveland Pass with my parents. I remember the awe of seeing this mountain for the first time. It doesn't belong in the Rockies. The Rockies don't have ski hills like this: steep insolent chutes of gleaming powder that cry out to challenge those who pass by.

"All right. I'll give it a try," I say with as much confidence as I can muster.

"Good luck."

My sons pole away in search of an easier path down the hill.

"I'll need it," I mutter.

I release my bindings, shoulder my skis, and begin to walk up the mountain. It does not take long for me to realize how out of shape I am. In the sparse air of high altitude, each breath becomes a gulp, an attempt to suck in every possible molecule of oxygen. I fall in line behind twenty or so young skiers. Their faces show no fear; their voices are filled with the strength and confidence of youth. I envy them.

94

At the entrance to the bowl, I encounter a large yellow and black sign.

Caution: Unpatrolled Area. Expert Skiers Only. Ski At Your Own Risk!

I ignore the warning and continue on. My thighs burn and my heart pounds. Absent-mindedly, I miss the turn for the easier of the two trails and continue to climb towards the highest point of departure. One by one, those in front of me stop and lean against the ice wall rising behind us to put on their skis. Silently, each skier contemplates the landscape falling away from the trail before embracing the powder and carving magnificent paths through untouched beauty.

I find a ledge to my liking and stop. Other skiers walk on by, wishing me luck as they pass. There's that word again: Luck. It's not luck I need but strength and skill. Then it's my turn. There's only one-way to the bottom of Arapaho. My K2s balance on the razor's edge. My mind tells me to stop, to take off my skis, and retreat down the path. My heart tells me I can't turn back; that I've waited twenty-five years to ski this moment.

My first turn in the waist-deep snow is a disaster. I haven't skied mountain powder in two decades. I forget to lean back, to keep the tips my skis free of the snow. I catch a tip and tumble headlong down the slope, thrashing and spinning out of control. I come to rest fifty feet from where I started. I touch my face with my wet glove. I'm lucky. My glasses are still on my nose.

Because it's so steep, I have to press my body against the mountain to remain stationary. Both bindings have released. I search the depths of the snow for my K2s. They haven't gone far. My body prone to grade, I gingerly pull my right ski towards my right boot and snap the binding in place. I repeat the pattern with the left.

There's no one near me as I stand up. I dig the edges of my skis into the icy base. I gain a moment of respite before gravity begins to pull me down the mountain. Leaning back as if I'm sitting in a rocking chair, I shift my weight to the rear. I claim a rhythm: I weave a tapestry in soft snow.

This run is mine and mine alone.

"Did you do it dad?" Matt asks as I glide to a stop at the bottom of the hill.

"Didn't you watch me?"

"Nope. Dyl and I got bored. We took a run."

"Well, you missed one hell of an exhibition of mountain skiing," I brag.

"Did you fall?" Dylan asks, staring at the snow packed inside the collar of my parka.

"Of course not. I'm an expert skier," I fib.

"Are you sure, Dad?" Matt inquires with skepticism.

"OK, maybe the take-off was a little rough," I admit. "But once I got going, it was wonderful."

"Gonna do it again?" Matt prods.

I shake the snow away from my exposed neck.

"Not this trip," I reply.

My eyes focus on the mountain. Though I can't follow the tenuous climb of those seeking to create art in solitude, I know that they are there. And for a brief moment, I shared their muse.

Keystone

At 10,000 feet, the air is sparse and rarefied. Dylan, my eight-year-old son; Matt, his thirteen-year-old brother, and I have arrived at the top of Outback, the last of three contiguous slopes comprising Keystone Ski Area in Colorado. Outback is not only the furthest peak from our rented condo at the base of the hill; it's also the most difficult and serious mountain at the resort.

Above the chairlift's reach, we glide on well-packed snow. This is the first time my boys have skied the West. I want them to feel challenged, to experience the things that I experienced when I came to Colorado as a boy on family ski vacations.

"You want to try some powder skiing on North Bowl?"

I study a large trail map painted on plywood. North Bowl is off to our right, above the tree line. There is no lift in place to carry us to the summit.

Matt ponders the map through the thick plastic lenses of his goggles and leans forward on his ski poles as he mulls over my proposal.

"Are you sure it's OK? It's marked "Expert'. It's a black diamond."

Dylan sways slowly from side to side to fend off the impact of the thin air and the stiff wind as we talk. The few trees at this altitude provide little protection from the cold.

"There's nothing in front of you on a bowl. If you take a header, you just fall until you stop. You'll be fine," I advise.

"How do we get there?"

My eldest son's eyes are riveted on the trail map. I detect a hint of understanding and slight reluctance in his voice.

"We walk."

Groans escape the two boys in unison. Despite the grumbling, I persuade them to follow me. Our breathing is labored and our steps difficult as we leave behind the last vestiges of forest.

"It's a long ways down" Matt says quietly, staring at the bowl falling beneath us,

We're poised on the lip of the slope. The sky extends above us in an uninterrupted pallet of bluebird hue. Carbon dioxide forms small clouds of moisture around each of us as we breathe. I ponder what course we should take down the mountainside. The snow beneath us appears to be soft and delicate. I envision three perfectly sculpted tracks left behind as we float through the powder, exit the bowl, and reclaim the trail through the trees. It doesn't concern me that there are no tracks left by previous skiers marking the hill. That detail eludes me as I silently praise God and ready my spirit for the plunge.

"Here goes."

My skis drop over the cornice, but instead of the soft, lacey embrace of powder, I experience the jolt of hard-packed snow. Before I can warn my sons that the scene before us is a cruel illusion, I'm rushing downhill, my skis trapped inside the icy crust. I'm unable to turn or slow my descent. Being a skier of experience, I'm able to ride out the bowl and coast to a stop on a level plateau several hundred feet below the summit. I watch as Dylan, then Matt, become victims of the ice. I watch them tumble down the pitched surface of the Outback. When the snow finally settles, I realize that my sons are stranded hundreds of feet above me.

"Are you OK?"

Dylan's sobs resound from the cliffs surrounding us.

"I can't find my left ski," Matt responds.

"I'll come up there to help you. Stay put," I urge.

The snow is thigh deep. The slope of the mountain precludes me from herringboning up the snowfield to my sons. I remove my skis. My ski boots sink into the deceptive snow. I reach Matt. Dylan is further up the bowl, a mere speck of blue and gray covered in snow. His sobs have diminished but it's clear he can't move without assistance.

"Nice powder."

I don't respond to Matt's sarcasm. I search the snow around him for his missing ski. I find the ski and hand it to Matt. Using my shoulders to steady his body, the boy locks the wayward ski in place, picks up his poles, and readies himself for another attempt.

"Ski straight down to the flats. Don't try to turn; the snow grabs you so you can't."

"Good thing Mom and Chris aren't here."

He's right. It's a darn good thing my wife and my five-year-old son are contentedly plying intermediate runs far below.

"There's no need to tell Mom about this," I urge.

"Sure," Matt responds, a promise of mischief coloring his words.

Dylan's tears are nearly dry by the time I reach him. Both of his skis are lost in the depths of the snow. I dig into the crusted surface surrounding my son until I locate his skis and retrieve them.

"Walk down to Matt."

Dylan doesn't answer me as he begins working his way through the offending snow in angry silence. After an exhausting walk, I arrive at the plateau and hand Dylan his skis. He snatches them from me without a word. I click on my ski bindings and slip my gloves through the straps of my ski poles. My attention is drawn to the magnificent height of the mountain behind us and, in the shadow of that great peak, I contemplate the magic that might have been.

All Done In

Soft light forms a golden blanket over gently rolling fields. A spring sun hangs just above the poplar and birch trees delineating the far edge of our pasture. Peepers begin a melodic chorus, announcing their presence to others of their kind. I begin the day, a Saturday, by raking piles of gravel. The gravel is misplaced.

Pushing snow with my International 606 in November, I inadvertently removed a few yards of crushed bluestone from our driveway with the bucket of the old tractor. Putting the rocks back where they belong requires hours of hard, physical work. It's not easy to wrestle the gravel free from the stubborn grasp of our lawn. I haul wheelbarrow after wheelbarrow of the stuff. As I strain under each load, I constantly remind myself that a moment of foresight in November would've saved hours of work in May.

I finish raking and begin to sweep the porches of our farmhouse. Winter's dust and debris flies though the cool air with each stoke of the broom. Dylan and Chris, my middle sons, help carry outdoor furniture from the garage. It's the only assistance I receive from the boys. Matt, my eldest boy, is nowhere to be found. He's eighteen years old and capable of disappearing in an instant whenever he hears the word "chores".

Late in the day, I realize I have to drive to town. Our two dogs, possessing the collective wisdom of a hamster, chased Bob the cat under our deck. The pursuers forced their way through the lattice enclosing the underside of the porch. The dogs managed to demolish one panel of lattice on the way in and another on the way out.

My wife René rides with me to the lumberyard. It's a good thing she's along. In my hurry to get home, I misjudge the size of the lattice panels. Lumber occupies the entire interior of our van except the two front seats. With limited commentary, my wife uses her hands to keep wood away from the top of my head as we bounce down the highway.

100

Back on task, I replace the lattice. The barricade restored, I turn my attention to the garage. Inside, I find the cat's litter box overflowing and malodorous. Someone (Christian) has not done his job: He hasn't checked the box in weeks. After replacing the litter and eliminating the overpowering fragrance of cat from the building, I begin to clean the garage.

I empty the building of contents so that I can sweep the floor and scour the shelves. It's not a job for a rainy day since everything in the garage has to be moved outside. With the sun high and bright, I'm able to finish the task in a couple of hours.

Just before dark, I notice that the Munger's Farm sign on our front lawn needs repair. Two chains hang from a wooden frame and sway slightly in the passing breeze. High winds last week tore the sign off its chains and deposited it on the ground.

I kneel on soft grass. With a gloved hand, I brush a clod of dirt away from the face of the sign. My eyes focus on the message.

Munger's Farm Est. 1984.

The painted image of a channel catfish, our family "crest" as it were, remains smooth and shiny though applied more than ten years ago. Standing up, I hold the sign steady and reconnect the chains to eyehooks imbedded deep in wood. A graceful wind causes the sign to sway in slow measure.

My chores completed, I open the back door to our home and enter the kitchen. In our upstairs lavatory, I run myself a bath. Steam rises towards the temptation of an open window. I disrobe, gingerly enter the antique claw-foot tub, and immerse myself. The near-scalding water turns my skin crimson.

Our downstairs bathroom has a Jacuzzi tub. Though the sophisticated pulse of a whirlpool has a certain appeal, I prefer the quiet embrace of the old tub when I'm all done in.

Despite the water's heat, the white porcelain surface of the tub is cold against my back. I remove my eyeglasses and place them on the windowsill. The bottom half of the window is open to the screen. It's quiet outside. The boys are inside the house watching television.

Reaching over the edge of the tub, I palpate the tile floor. My hand searches for the copy of *Cold Mountain* that I'm reading. Fingers curl protectively around the book as I lift the novel through ascending vapor. Opening the novel to the bookmark, I concentrate on the last few pages of a soldier's journey home.

"Time for dinner," René yells up from the kitchen.

"I'll be down in a minute," I reply, annoyed at my wife's intrusion into my space.

"Better make it quick or the food'll be cold," my wife warns.

"Alright."

I want to placate René but I know I'll be more than a minute. I've still got ten pages left to read and I want to find out whether Inman marries the girl.

A Very Grave Story

It was cold outside. A cat cried in protest. In the garden, the last of summer's corn rustled in the breeze. Pumpkins rested on near-frozen earth waiting to be harvested.

Our cat at the time was jet black with angry, yellow eyes. Her name was K-Mart. She was fidgety and unpredictable. She was also pregnant. Her belly was heavy with kittens and dragged on the ground. The pregnant cat gained my attention by climbing a window screen as my family sat down to eat dinner.

"I oughta knock her off that screen with my boot, that's what I oughta do."

My wife scolded me.

"It's not her fault, poor thing. It's cold. Let her in before she rips the screen."

My response was, as I recall, unprintable. It didn't matter. The cat came in.

That evening, in the middle of Matt's bedroom, the cat delivered her litter. The bloodstain on the white carpet is still there. Over the next few weeks, Mickey, Minnie, Darts, Daisy, and their mother occupied Matt's closet.

A few weeks before Halloween, I determined that the cats had to go. Gathering the kittens in an old blanket, dodging K-Mart's claws, I carried them out to our old chicken coop. I deposited the kittens on a thick bed of fresh straw and shut the door to keep the little ones from wandering.

A day or so later, René and I were out in the garden harvesting the last of our garden's squash. A low sun hung in the autumn sky. K-Mart warmed herself on a fencepost. Sam, our yellow Labrador retriever paced excitedly. You could almost see the miniature wheels of his miniscule dog brain spin as he eyed a slender crack at the base of the door to the chicken coop.

Without warning, the dog leaped towards the coop. A kitten squealed. Tossing my hoe to the ground, I reached the dog just as his jaws clamped down.

Meow.

103

K-Mart flew from her perch. Her claws dug hard into the soft nose of the Labrador. I pulled the kitten out of the dog's mouth and booted Sam in the rump, sending both the dog and the mother cat end over end across the grass. The dog regained his balance and tore off after K-Mart, chasing her up the pitch-covered trunk of a spruce tree.

"I think it's dead, René."

My wife pulled off her work gloves and touched the kitten's head. The cat's fur was wet with spit. There was no blood. Its eyes were shut.

"Mickey's okay, he's just sleeping."

Christian, our youngest son at the time, walked over to my side and retrieved the kitten from me.

"He'll wake up, you'll see."

"Bring him up to the house, Chris," René said. "We'll put him on a hot water bottle."

"OK."

Though Mickey survived this first ordeal, his walk was unsteady; there was a hint of palsy about his movements. Two days after his near-death experience, the kitten appeared well enough to rejoin his mother. Christian, dressed in his yellow rain slicker, returned the battered kitten to the chicken coop. I walked with the boy, striving against an awful rain. A penetrating cold front had nestled over the river: It felt like it would snow but all it did was rain.

Heavy October fog greeted me when I went out to check on the cats the following morning. Hoarfrost coated slumbering grass. A shallow pool of rainwater had formed in front of the chicken coop. I discovered Mickey submerged in the puddle, the little cat's fur stiff with ice. The animal was dead.

"What's that, Dad?"

Dylan appeared by my side. I showed him the kitten.

"It's Mickey. Will you take care of him? Chris is too young to see this," I said as I handed the little ball of frozen fur to my son.

"Sure."

I returned to the house for breakfast. Chris and René sat at the kitchen table eating hot cereal. My youngest son's attention was diverted as Dylan entered the room. Dylan's jeans were caked in mud.

"What were you doing?" Chris asked.

"Nothin'." Dylan lied.

"Don't' tell me nothin'. You're all muddy. What were you doing?"

I couldn't bear keeping the truth from Chris.

"Mickey died. He must have been scared by the thunder. He went outside in the cold and rain."

The little boy's eyes widened as if to cry.

"Where is he?"

"Dylan buried him by the barn."

"I made a nice cross for him. Wanna see?"

Chris's reply was barely a whisper.

"Ya."

The boys came back a few minutes later. Chris held the tiny, muddy corpse of a kitten in his hands.

"He dug up the stupid cat. I told him not to. He wouldn't listen."

Chris stood silently in the hallway, tears dripping from his eyes.

"Why did you dig the kitten up?" my wife asked, placing a hand on Chris's shoulder.

The boy trembled.

"I could see him breathing."

"You're kidding, right?" I said, trying not to sound irritated.

Christian's preoccupation with an obviously dead kitten was too much to bear.

"I saw the dirt move."

I stood up. I was prepared to explain the meaning of death, the finality of it all. René stopped me.

"My God, he's right. The kitten *is* alive."

"No way."

"It's still breathing."

I studied the dirty, wet stomach of the kitten. Its respiration's were shallow, almost non-existent, but Christian was right. I'd told Dylan to bury the cat while it was still alive.

"I thought it was dead. I swear."

I'd like to tell you that the kitten recovered and lived happily ever after. That's how Disney movies end but that's not real life.

Mickey died on Halloween night. That particular evening, the moon was high and full, an omnipresent harvest globe of orange. Eerie shadows formed along the ground, lured into motion by the patterned march of clouds. I walked alone searching for a forgotten corner of forest as my children slept soundly in their beds at home. Hidden by darkness, I disposed of Mickey's body. I'll not relate to you the sordid details of the burial or the location of the kitten's unmarked grave. When it comes to the offspring of black cats, I no longer leave anything to chance.

John Muir's Woods

During our vacation, we've toured San Francisco, seen the Golden Gate Bridge, and climbed aboard our share of cable cars. We've attended a local production of *Phantom of the Opera*. Someone (I can't remember who) cautioned us not to miss the redwoods. After the cultural significance of the city by the bay, visiting old trees seems anticlimactic. But we follow the advice.

There are no guardrails. The asphalt disappears at the corners. There is no forgiveness to the two-lane highway. Rose-frosted hills fall away to water as the road climbs into the clouds. Once atop the rise, the road spirals down the other side with equal abandon before becoming lost in the shade of grand old trees. I park the car beside an ancient oak, a tree that would be magnificent in any other setting. In Muir Woods, the oak is but an insignificant weed.

It's cool at the base of majesty. Little of the day's heat penetrates the redwoods. René and I realize we are in a sacred place, a place that contains plants that germinated before the American Revolution. The average age of the trees that surround us, that dwarf us as we walk the valley floor, exceeds eight hundred years.

We stare upward at the straight, thickly armored trees as we enter the forest. Ancestors of these redwoods protected the eggs of dinosaurs before the dawn of mammals on the earth. We spy a tiny doe and her diminutive fawn scratching thin black soil. Elk, cougar, bear, and wolf have vanished from this place. Urban sprawl has invaded the surrounding valleys and hills, spreading out from San Francisco to claim the wild places. A single pair of Spotted Owls, a symbolic rallying cry against loggers, still nests here. We do not see them on our walk.

Despite the closeness of metropolis to our sanctuary, bright clear waters course through the Woods. The main path, covered in asphalt, veers to the left. A dirt trail winds upwards on the right.

"Come on, Nay'," I urge my wife, "let's take the dirt trail."

"Where does it go?" my very pregnant and skeptical spouse asks.

"To a picnic area on the top of the hill."

"How far is it?"

"Looks to be about a mile and a half or so. The trail winds uphill. It should be an easy hike."

I turn around. A shadow of doubt clouds René's face:

"Mark, I don't want to end up walking for half the day."

"You won't. I promise."

My wife accepts my reassurance and we begin our climb.

Redwoods close in, interrupting the trail with their roots. I walk to the edge of a small brook bordering the path. I peer into clean water and watch Pacific steelhead, no more than four or five inches long, dart along the stony bottom. We pass scores of trees nine or ten feet in diameter. The trunks of the redwoods are scarred by fire.

"Must be caused by lightening."

"No, it's from a forest fire that swept through here a hundred and fifty years ago," René corrects. "I overheard a ranger explain it."

"But it looks like it was just burned."

"That's because of the strong bark and the weather conditions. The scars don't fade."

I ponder the fact that the wound on the tree in front of me is nearly the same age as the sentinel white pines remaining on our farm. My mind tries to picture what our place looked like before the majority of the old growth was cut. I try to shrink the height of the redwoods in front of my so as to create a corresponding white pine forest. I try to imagine I am in Minnesota in the 1850s.

We cross the gurgling stream on the trunk of an unlucky redwood. Park workers have nailed rough-sawn lumber to the fallen tree to create the bridge. Shards of white sun infiltrate the canopy and touch my face as we ford the stream. Across the creek, we are once again cloaked in cool shadow. The walk to the picnic area takes longer than it should. Finally, I emerge into daylight.

"Here it is, René."

I pull out a trail map. I discover that the reason it took so long to reach our destination is that I missed a turn. We've added a mile to our trek. I look down the path for my spouse. I don't see her. I weigh the proper course of action.

If I walk back to get her, she'll be mad that I'm treating her like a child. If I don't show concern and go back, she'll think I'm a jerk.

Before I'm forced to make a decision, René comes into view.

"We took a wrong turn," I say quietly when she stops next to me. My wife sits down on a picnic table bench and draws warm water from a plastic bottle in urgent gulps.

"No kidding."

"It's not nearly as far back," I offer. "Plus it's downhill."

"Good."

We sit in the shade of small redwoods; infants in the great scheme of the woods. A large hill rises across the ravine. With a little imagination, I could be standing on Eagle Mountain in northeastern Minnesota. But this is not Minnesota. We are in Muir Woods, one of the last remaining old-growth redwood forests in the world. A man and his wife purchased this land at the turn of the century with the idea that this forest would be logged and the land developed. On their first walk through the forest, the couple realized that the place was holy, that redwoods do not exist to be cut into lumber.

Though the man later became a United States Congressman, his most enduring legacy was not the legislation he drafted as a lawmaker. It was his donation of this forest to the public in the name of John Muir, a California writer and naturalist.

Well-rested, we begin our descent. The crowns of the redwoods obscure our view of the sky. We are cooled by forest older than our culture. Entering the valley floor, I smile. I smile because the congressman who saved Muir Woods from the ax, and the president who championed Muir Woods becoming a national monument in 1908, were both Republicans. Imagine that: The ideological ancestors of Ronald Reagan, Rush Limbaugh, and George W. Bush were tree-huggers, just like me.

Of Little Boys and Comets

Earlier tonight, I stood outside with my wife and my son Christian watching the great astronomical event of 1997. Hale-Bopp, the comet of the moment, flew above us, seemingly stationary against vast twilight containing a blue so perfect and seamless that the depth of its color appeared contrived.

Inside our house sits a cheap telescope, a lesson learned: Never buy anything containing cheap optics, be it a camera, eyeglasses, or a telescope. Our telescope makes a lovely conversation piece and nothing more.

Sometime in the 1960's, I fell in love with space. Maybe it was growing up glued to the old black and white Philco television back in elementary school. I remember watching in awe as John Glenn and other Mercury astronauts flew solo into near-Earth orbit. Everything stopped at school when another rocket took off from Cape Canaveral; everything except the pounding of our hearts as we prayed for the safe return of our astronauts.

Gemini came next, and with Gemini the buddy system arrived in space: two astronauts linked by a common fate in a cramped, claustrophobic capsule. Commander White pushed our envelope of piety and faith by leaving the protection of his space capsule and walking into the inhospitable void of the universe.

Finally, Apollo, with its triumphs and tragedies, brought us to the end of manned space exploration, at least for the 20th century. NASA has not yet, as it once contemplated, sent men and women to Mars, Titan, or anywhere beyond the close confines of our own atmospheric neighborhood.

As each rocket sped away, as all of America's children grew older, the television sets came on less often: the inspiration of space exploration grew less moving. As a nation, we became complacent, even bored, with launch after uneventful launch. Until Challenger.

Challenger proved to the children of the 1950s and

1960s that humankind's exploration of the unknown should never be taken for granted. The tragedy of Challenger was not that accidents take place; but that, in today's world of instant media, horrific accidents take place in front of tens of millions of school children.

But what of comets and little boys? There's a page in one of my picture books from my childhood that comes to mind whenever the approach of a comet is announced. The book contained a timeline of Haley's Comet, which predicted that the comet would be back to visit earth in 1986. I figured I would be thirty-two in 1986. *Thirty-two! Wow, that would be really old: as old as my parents.* I recall wondering, as a little boy sitting on the smooth hardwood floor of my parent's house, whether I would be around to see Haley's spectacular return.

The book said you only get one shot in a lifetime to view Haley's unless you're lucky enough to be four years old or younger when it came around the first time. The odds of being coherent on either side of that equation didn't hold much attraction for me. All I had to do was make sure I was breathing and vertical come 1986 and Haley's would do the rest. Seemed pretty easy at the time. Of course, things always seem easy when you're ten.

After reading about the comet as a child, I spent many nights scanning the Minnesota sky with my hand-held Bausch and Lomb ten-power telescope. The instrument didn't add much in the way of discovery potential to my observations but it did make the process seem scientific. Through that weak lens, I watched falling stars, the moon, and high-flying satellites. I never saw a comet. It didn't bother me: I figured God was saving Haley's for me.

Sometime after junior high my little telescope found a resting place in a drawer at my parent's house. I went to college, chased girls, caught one (or she caught me; still an ongoing source of debate at our house), left for law school, got married, and had kids. Through it all, I never observed a comet in the night sky. Of course, I wasn't really looking. I was waiting for Haley's.

112

Sure, there was Comet Kohoutek back in 1973-my first year in college. I remember the excitement of the twenty or so young men and women that gathered for our Comet Kohoutek party-and the despair we felt when the comet turned out to be a total dud. I mean; twenty college kids, rock and roll, "refreshments" and pizza and no comet. What to do?

1986 finally came but somehow, I forgot about Haley's. I'd waited years for the celestial event of a lifetime and I missed it! I don't know if I was working, engaged in some deep philosophical debate with my wife, or off on a lark during the appointed hour. I just plain blew it.

Once I figured out that Haley's had come and gone, I did some rough figuring. The math depressed me. I'd have to live to be a hundred and eight years old to have another shot at seeing Haley's Comet. Even if I lived that long, the probability that I would remember the year Haley's was due back did not, given my forgetfulness at age thirty-two, seem likely.

Time slipped by. The 1980's slid into the 1990's. A third son came along. For some inexplicable reason, I began to find myself staring more often at the night sky during our long Minnesota winters. As I scanned the heavens I tried to recall why space meant so much to me as a child. Perhaps, I postulated, it was the sky's limitless possibility that attracted me. Perhaps it was the idea that looking into space is looking back in time. Whatever the reasons, as I aged, I became more intent on reclaiming the sense of amazement and wonder that astronomy held for me as a child.

Comet Hyakutake teased my family last winter. We watched the comet's faint light stand vertical above us. We stood in the snow and watched its display during bitter below-zero nights. Even though Hyakutake was only a dim pinprick of light, it was a real comet. But it wasn't spectacular. It wasn't Haley's. It didn't completely erase my sense of loss, my sense of having missed my comet-watching destiny.

When Hale-Bopp burst onto the scene, I shrugged my shoulders.

If it comes, I thought, *it'll be another bust. There's only one real comet and I missed it in 1986.*

In the middle of typing this essay, I leave my notebook computer and walk out the back door. Standing in the warm spring air, looking to the northwest, I realize that I was wrong to prejudge Hale-Bopp. This comet, this bright splash of light, which last came to visit us five thousand years ago, stands triumphant in the sky. Contemplating the history that has passed during this galactic voyager's absence, dusk's mantle fades, revealing an ebony backdrop to God's latest celestial production. Uncountable suns appear as distant points of light, framing the wanderer's path. Against this curtain, Hale-Bopp is amazingly brilliant.

I've never seen anything like it. Watching the comet's show, I realize that God has brought me to this moment. I'm infinitely happy to live in a place where stars dance and little boy's dreams come true.

Cleaning the Barn

Let's be candid. Owning animals means dealing with crap. Owning big animals means dealing with lots of crap. I should have anticipated this truth when I went looking to buy my first horse.

It's Sunday afternoon and spring sunshine is warming the metal skin of our pole barn. Christian and Dylan, ages eleven and fourteen, reluctantly load piles of horse manure into the bucket of my International 606. Chris's buddy Spencer is behind another shovel pushing a mixture of soiled pine shavings and manure towards the other boys.

Our new pole barn may be a modern building but the labor the boys are engaged in is thousands of years old. As I watch them push the waste of three horses across the smooth concrete floor, it's easy to imagine Roman stable hands doing the same task with the same tools centuries ago.

"Hey, make sure you get that stuff in the bucket, Dylan," I call out from deep within another stall.

"Ya, right," my teenaged son responds as he drops nearly a quarter of his load on the cement.

My criticism doesn't seem to improve my son's aim or his ambition.

I'm working on my own, away from the boys, so that I can listen to *A Prairie Home Companion* on the radio. The AM/FM radio that I'm using is the same one that I use to catch Minnesota Twin's games when I'm weeding our vegetable garden. The radio is a reject from my mother-in-law. The black plastic case is misshapen (someone left it next to an electric heater.) Today, it's covered with the fine dust of disintegrating horse apples. Every so often I lose the public radio station I'm listening to, which gives me an excuse to sit down and fiddle with the channel dial.

"Come on Dad," Chris whines. "We'll never finish this if you keep taking rests."

"Shut up Chris," Dylan scolds, his blue eyes flashing. "I want to hear the rest of the show."

115

"Don't say 'shut up', Dyl. Just tell him to be quiet."

I try to decipher what Dylan says to Chris under his breath but I find the station and miss the exchange between my boys. It's a good time to do a thorough spring-cleaning in the barn. The air is cold. The stable flies haven't hatched. Our three very fat and content horses stand outside munching the last of August's hay. I try to remember the last time one of them was ridden. I draw a blank. I know it was before the first snow. Maybe October? Maybe late September?

The bucket on the loader is full. I climb into the seat and push the starter. A comforting "pop". The engine purrs. I pull levers. Water drips from the hydraulic cylinders on either side of the bucket as it elevates. When the bucket is chest high, I ease the tractor into gear and pull away. Rusted tire chains beat against the concrete floor as the tractor advances towards an open door.

"Dyl, unhook the fence," I yell over the din of the tractor's engine.

The teenager runs ahead of the International and reaches cautiously for a plastic handle connected to an electric fence.

"Is it off?"

"Yep."

"Are you sure?"

"I'm sure."

Dylan lifts the insulated handle. The wire disengages. I drive into the pasture. Mud and horse feces are compacted by the tractor's tires: The pasture is a quagmire of slime and pooled water. Our horses scrutinize me as I pull alongside the manure pile. The heap began as a small bump on the landscape. Over thirteen years of owning horses, the mound has grown. One day, our manure pile may challenge Eagle Mountain as the highest point in Minnesota!

I raise the hydraulic arms as high as they will go and slowly tilt the bucket. Waste and shavings fall onto the manure pile. The process is repeated until all of the stalls are clean. Dylan latches the electric fence after my last trip. I park the tractor outside the barn. Mud and filthy water drip from the metal frame of the old International. My tractor will be rinsed

116

clean by the next passing rainstorm. It's done its job since 1962 without much fanfare or fuss. A little mud won't hurt it.

"You guys can take off," I tell the boys. "I'll finish up what's left."

The kids don't wait for me to change my mind. They're long gone by the time Garrison Keillor begins his weekly monologue. I listen to the humorist in the quiet of the barn as I push the remaining bits of pine and horse manure onto a shovel. When the scoop is full, I carry the mess outside and deposit it by hand on the compost pile.

My back aches from heavy lifting. Bone tired, I turn the radio off before the News from Lake Wobegon is over, close the big sliding door, and walk out into tenuous sunshine. I sit on a swing on the barn's covered porch and watch the Cloquet River, its black waters impatient from thaw, rush by our farm. Rocking gently, I wonder whether my boys will ever understand what this place means to me.

Searching for Patrick Roy

Western Ontario's wilderness gave way to rolling farmland. Montreal, Vermont, and Massachusetts came and went like a dream. After ten days traveling by train and rented van, we returned to our home along the banks of the Cloquet River satisfied that we'd seen and done as much as we could during our summer vacation. Only Matthew, fourteen years old at the time, seemed unsatisfied with the trip.

"I never got to go inside the Forum," he lamented. "And I never got to meet Patrick Roy."

Roy (pronounced "wha", as in "what") played goalie at the time for the Montreal Canadians. To Matt, a first year Bantam goalie, Roy was the ideal; the best goaltender in hockey. To my son, not meeting the tender for the Habs was a grating failure. It bothered him to no end that our family had ridden Via Rail from Reditt, Ontario, one hundred and fifty miles north of International Falls, to Montreal and back without ever finding Mr. Roy.

"Sorry about that, Matt. We didn't have time."

"We had time to walk around and look at old churches."

I contemplated a reply: I thought about pointing out how much it cost to take a family of five across Canada, through Vermont, to Boston, and back on a train. I thought of computing the expense in neat rows and presenting the evidence, as I often do in court, to my son. But I knew it would only fuel further debate.

A few days later, I came in the house from weeding our family vegetable garden. I found Matthew studiously writing at the kitchen table. A high summer sun cast intense light on the boy's work.

"Whatcha doin'?"

"Writing to Patrick Roy."

"Sort of a long letter, isn't it?"

"I want to make sure he knows how great I think he is."

"Mr. Roy might be too busy to read such a long letter."

118

Matt ignored me and continued to write. Dylan, nine years old, ambled into the room; his light brown hair bleached blond by the season, his arms and legs tanned deep brown from constant exposure to the sun. Dylan's bluebird eyes peered over the edge of the table.

"Whatcha doin'?"

"Writin' to Patrick Roy. Stop botherin' me."

"Why ya writin' to Patrick Roy?"

"I want him to autograph his rookie hockey card. I'm sending it with the letter."

I drew a cold glass of water from our kitchen tap and feigned disinterest.

"Maybe I'll send one to Gretzky," Dylan observed, canting his head to one side in reflection.

"You're an idiot. Wayne Gretzky doesn't have time to sign cards for every little kid that sends one. He's the greatest hockey player of all time. Get real!"

I wanted to intervene, to tell Dylan to go for it. I wanted to try and massage the hurt I saw creep into the little boy's eyes at his brother's rebuke. There was no need.

"Oh ya?" Well I'm gonna send him a letter 'n a card. You'll see."

"Go ahead. You're still an idiot."

Later that afternoon I came back into the house for a snack and found Dylan occupying the same table, surrounded by crumpled balls of paper, his face gripped by serious thought.

"How's it going," I asked, leaning over to examine his work.

"Great. I got the letter done. I'm doing the outside of the envelope."

I watched my second son cram a very messy, nearly indecipherable letter into an envelope. The complete address of the Los Angeles Kings, Gretzky's team at the time, was scrawled in purple marker across the face of the envelope. The boy tucked a trading card of the Great One into the envelope and licked the flap.

Matt entered the room holding his letter to Patrick Roy in one hand.

"Mail this for Dylan, will you?" I asked, handing him the younger boy's message to his hero.

"Lot's of good it'll do'im. He's wasting a perfectly good card. Gretzky's too busy to worry about some stupid little Squirt hockey player."

Six weeks to the day, I handed Matt a thick manila envelope bearing the return address of the Montreal Canadians. Dylan stood to one side of his big brother as the adolescent ripped open the package. The smaller boy's eyes welled with tears. No similar package from the Kings had arrived.

Inside the manila envelope, Matt found publicity photos of Mr. Roy in various goalie poses, Montreal Canadian bumper stickers, and countless other promotional materials from the team. But there was no letter from Mr. Roy and the rookie trading card had not been returned.

Matt's eyes scanned a form letter from the Canadians. It related how busy Mr. Roy was, how impossible it would be for such a great star to read every fan letter and personally autograph each trading card submitted to him by his legions of admirers.

"At least I got some really cool stuff. See Dyl, I told you that you were wasting your time," the older boy advised, his voice tailing off as he climbed the stairway to his bedroom.

I turned to console my younger son but he was gone.

Four more weeks passed. Labor Day loomed. The letter to Mr. Gretzky was forgotten. A thunderstorm threatened the sky above our farm. Late summer rain pelted my pickup truck as I pulled into the driveway. Dodging dollops of moisture, I covered my head with my briefcase and sprinted across the sidewalk into the back door of our farmhouse.

Inside, the house was quiet. It seemed there was no one around. Then I noticed Dylan watching me as I shook rainwater from my hair onto the finely polished oak floor of the kitchen. The boy stood next to the sink, a broad grin across his face.

"How's it goin', Dyl?"

"Great. See?"

His small hand produced an envelope. *Master Dylan Munger* and our address were carefully typed on the paper. There was no return address.

"Matt's stupid."

"Why do you say that?" I asked, accepting the document from him.

"He doesn't know anything."

The packet was small, smaller than letter size. I carefully withdrew the envelope's contents: a single piece of cardboard undamaged by the rain.

"He signed it, Dad, he really signed it."

Sure enough. Scrawled in thick permanent marker across the face of the trading card was the unmistakable autograph of the Great One.

The Last Hunt

It's quiet in the November forest. I'm ill prepared to be out hunting deer. I didn't plan on hunting. A last minute call from my dad convinced me to buy a license and come up to the old shack to hunt with the guys.

I've been coming to this place, a shanty on the edge of a vast aspen and alder forest, since 1969, the year I turned fifteen. In all those years, I've never taken a deer here. Not that I haven't shot deer. I have. A doe up at my pal Jeff's farm. A couple of spike bucks right out my own back door in Fredenberg. But up here, in the dark confines of the valley of Coolidge Creek, I've had no luck at deer camp.

I arrive late Friday night in my Dodge Dakota pickup. As I bounce over the logging trail towards the shack, tentative light illuminates the battered front door of the place. A biting wind causes a propane lantern hanging above the entrance to sway. I park my truck and shoulder my gear. I don't have a rifle with me. My grandfather's 30-30 Winchester is being repaired. I'm borrowing my dad's twenty-gauge over-and-under shotgun. I've never hunted with slugs before but then my prior history with the place isn't filled with successful encounters with whitetails even when I carry a rifle.

"Hello," I call out as I step inside the crude building. Warm air greets my face as I step over the threshold.

"How you doing, Bro?" my brother Dave asks sipping contentedly from a can of Budweiser.

"How's Mark?" Mr. Red, one of the older hunters and a life-long friend of my father, asks.

"Fine," I respond walking through the kitchen towards the bunkroom.

A steady buzzing, the by-product of fluorescent light echoes off the bare walls of the place. Each wall is constructed of fir doors salvaged from railroad boxcars. Plastic cords lead from the lights and weave in and out of the ceiling supports. The other ends of the cords are secured to the lighter sockets of vehicles parked alongside the shack. This electrical system works but requires a high level of diligence to remember to start the involved vehicles every so often to recharge their batteries.

"Anyone using this upper bunk," I ask, swinging my backpack and sleeping bag onto a vacant platform.

"Nope," I hear Poncho, one of the younger hunters say between chaws of tobacco.

I roll out my nylon bag. The mattress, one my father donated from my childhood bunk bed, is lumpy and smells of mice. A kerosene heater glows orange at the far end of the room. My bunk is constructed in the same primitive style as the rest of the place. The supports for the double-decker bed are rough-hewn 2x4's. The sleeping platform is a single grain door from a boxcar placed horizontally across the supports. I toss my backpack under the bunk.

Jimmy, his father Jim, Poncho, Mr. Red and his son David, my brother Dave, and my father sit around an oval table in the kitchen. An antique LP range and oil stove occupy one wall of the room. The oil stove gives off just enough heat to keep the place bearable. A plywood counter supports a sink: A hole leading to a plastic pail serves as the sink's drain. Water carried from a spring several hundred feet from the cabin stands ready for use in two plastic drywall buckets stored beneath the sink.

Dishes and food occupy elementary shelving. A black and white portable television plugged into my father's Suburban sits on the top shelf. A University of Minnesota-Duluth hockey game blares in the background. Mr. Red, nearing seventy and an expert on the sport, grimaces in disgust as he critiques the game.

"Those Canuck kids don't know the first thing about hockey."

Jimmy once played college hockey at Harvard. He knows how easy it is to bait Mr. Red and he can't resist the temptation.

"I'm sure you could straighten 'em out, eh Mr. Red?"

"Darn right. Those boys need to learn how to take a check and how to give a check."

I settle in next to Jim Senior and open a can of Sprite, my days of over-indulging at the deer camp long behind me. I pull out a stack of quarters and join the poker game in progress.

Unlike most years, the game proceeds with a minimum of arguing.

Dawn comes quickly when you go to bed late, sleep poorly, and come to the woods unprepared. My dad is in the kitchen with Mr. Red frying bacon and eggs. I stumble past them, slip on my hunting boots just far enough to cover the bottoms of my feet and walk outside. It's cold. I refuse to negotiate the twenty frigid steps to the outhouse. I find a spot behind my truck to do what needs doing.

Later that morning, I enter the woods wondering why I'm here. I don't like venison all that much. I forgot my rope for dragging deer. I'm carrying a borrowed shotgun loaded with slugs. I left my hunting knife at home. I don't have a deer stand to sit in that I can call my own. Nothing about this hunt seems right. I walk down the main trail. The sky is high and gray, typical for the Opener. There's a trace of snow on the ground. I find one of my old stands but quickly decide it's no longer safe to sit in. I amble on, alert for sounds of deer on the move. I hear nothing beyond the subtle bend of trees in the light breeze.

I come across a deer stand located a fair distance above the ground in a triangle of birch. There's an old rope hanging from the railing of the platform. It's well after daylight. The stand is in an area my camp traditionally hunts. It's unoccupied. I decide to use it.

Up in the deer stand, I shift my weight on the crude board bench and settle in. My eyes close. I snatch bits of sleep. I've heard no shots and I've seen no deer. My head comes to rest against my shoulder and my thoughts drift off.

My slumber is disturbed by a familiar noise. I control my breathing as I shift my rump on the wooden bench. I lift the edge of my orange stocking cap away from my eyes and place my gloved right index finger on the trigger of the shotgun.

A branch breaks. I stare excitedly into an adjacent spruce swamp. Tan shoulders cautiously emerge from the browns and grays of the winter forest. I steady myself and search for antlers. I don't have a doe permit. I didn't apply for one: I've never applied for one. I shot one doe, one time, on someone else's permit because it was the only deer we saw all season. I'm uncertain if I'll ever shoot a doe again.

124

I count the tines on the animal's rack. He's a healthy six pointer. The buck's black eyes survey the woods between us. I study him as his head dips to smell the ground. The buck's nostrils flare as he detects something.

Me?

I don't wait for an answer. I point the muzzle of the gun at the target's front shoulder and steady my aim.

Boom.

The twenty-gauge barks.

Thwack.

The slug strikes solid muscle, tumbling the animal to the ground. Pulling a Swiss Army knife from my jacket pocket, I cut the old rope free of the stand. I'll need the rope to drag the deer. I know the rope belongs to someone else. I vow to return it after I'm done with my task.

Once on the ground, I realize that the buck isn't dead. I raise my meager blade and contemplate slicing the beast's jugular vein. The thought is fleeting. I can't do it. I raise my dad's gun to my cheek.

Boom.

The deer dies and I begin the unpleasant business of gutting a hundred and forty pound animal with a jackknife. When I finish slitting the animal's belly and removing its entrails, the heart and liver saved in an old plastic bread bag and tossed into the game pocket of my orange hunting jacket, I loop the rope around the buck's rack. Checking my compass, I begin the laborious process of dragging the carcass back to the deer shack.

"Hey, that's the deer I shot."

Startled, I turn and watch another hunter clad in vibrant orange emerge from the underbrush.

"How's that?"

"I'm sure that's the one I hit in the hind end."

I study the guy's face. He's unfamiliar. Given that both of us have weapons and given that his tone is accusatory, I want to placate him if I can.

"He walked out from the trees," I explain. "He didn't seem to be hit."

The other hunter bends over the hindquarters of the animal. His hand brushes through the thick winter fur of the hide until the man seems satisfied.

"How many times did you shoot?"

"Twice. The first one hit his shoulder and knocked him down. I shot him once more in the head to kill him."

"I hit him right here," he says, pointing to a small hole through the left leg.

I look. There's a bullet hole between the tendon and the bone. It doesn't appear that the wound caused any lasting damage to the buck.

"I see it," I admit. "But he wasn't limping when he came out."

"I don't want to get into a hassle over this but I've been tracking him for a long time."

I don't need this.

"If you really want the deer..." I offer half-heartedly.

"No, no. You keep him," the hunter mutters. "What camp you with, anyway?"

"Listons. How about you?"

"Davidsons."

Davidsons is the next camp down the trail from us. We've shared more than one drink with the Davidson Camp over the years.

"Never had this kind of trouble with you guys before," the hunter says, his tone terse and bitter. "You shoot out of that stand back there?"

"Yes."

"That rope come from that stand?"

"Yes."

"Well, that's my stand and my rope. See that you put it back when you're done."

I stare at the upset hunter through guilty eyes as I watch him disappear into the tightly woven fabric of the forest. I take a deep breath, and resume pulling the deer to the road, all the while wondering why I ever accepted my dad's invitation.

Old Horses

We've nearly always had horses since we moved to the country. Our first horse, Nicholas, was a mixed breed stallion given to me as a fee by a client. We had him gelded to calm him down. The surgery did little good. Even the efforts of my neighbor Peg, a dedicated horsewoman, couldn't tame him. In the end, after he tossed me to the frozen ground one cold November day, Nicholas left us: My wife traded him for two saddles.

Barbara, a purebred Appaloosa mare, was the next horse to live with us. White with black leopard spotting, Barbara was the first horse I ever rode extensively. When I bought her, she was being kept over at Earl's place with her daughter, Minnie, because her owner had moved. I paid Earl $500.00 for her. She was a bargain. She was fourteen when I bought her. She was eighteen when I found her dead in the pasture one hot summer day. The vet said it was Lyme's disease.

Having never grown up with horses, I was mystified how a person could love such a stupid animal. Galloping Barbara full tilt across our pasture, wading with her through the river on cool spring days, holding out my hand and having her nuzzle it with her moist snout, I learned the secret of old horses. Obedience and a willingness to trust rewarded my patience. Barbara taught me that in our short time together.

After the Appaloosa died, a succession of ill-tempered mares came to live with us for brief periods of time. Minnie, Barbara's daughter, a beautiful red-roan mare, came to me on approval. That spring, she bucked my sister Ann off in the middle of our hayfield, prompting me to trade horses with Ann. I was determined to re-establish authority over the beast. But during my sister's spill, one of the steel clasps securing the reins broke free. I found out about the defect only after Minnie took off for the trees at full gallop with me clinging to her back. With only one rein, and no control over the horse, I rode her as long as I could, hanging on like a rodeo cowboy as she bucked her way towards the woods. Just before the trees, I rolled off the horse, landing unharmed in soft grass. The mare glanced back at me and, with a flourish of her red mane and tail, trotted home. I walked Minnie back to her owner that same day.

My sister-in-law was a horse lady. She and I drove all over the county looking for a decent horse. On her recommendation, I paid $1,000.00 for a ten-year-old registered quarter horse mare. The horse's name was Pumpkin. She acted like a perfect lady when my sister-in-law test rode her. The mare was toying with us.

The first time a boat and trailer passed Pumpkin on the road by our farm, she reared up on her hind legs and dumped me unceremoniously on the gravel shoulder of the roadway. From there, things only got worse. My sister-in-law vowed that the horse would not best us. She arrived at my farm outfitted in a riding helmet and riding boots ready to square away the mare. My sister-in-law landed on her butt four times before she too finally admitted defeat.

Harry was the next horse to live with us. A young, roan-colored quarter horse gelding of no particular distinction, I traded Pumpkin and two hundred and fifty bucks for him. Harry, despite some stubborn traits and an affinity for biting cats and the hair of small children, was a good companion for my wife's old mare. They've been together for more than seven years.

She stands in the bright sunlight. The ground glistens white around her. Tufts of loose hay interrupt the snow. It's been a hard winter and she's getting ready to die. The old mare looks across our pasture with sad eyes. Her head stays low. A rear leg is held up in pain. We cannot tell if the leg is broken or merely sore. The vet has come and gone, saying only that the mare is old. I don't want to put her down because there's no easy way to bury her. The earth is frozen. I pray she lasts until the thaw, when she can be put to rest with dignity and peace. I don't think she'll make it.

Last week, I found the old mare lying on her side in her stall. She had soiled her tail and could not get up. She was weak. I'd run out of geriatric horse food and had been feeding her straight grain. It wasn't complete enough to provide her nutritional needs. The food was too hard for her to chew. Her big eyes looked at me in sorrow.

With a leather strap under her hindquarters, I tried lifting her to her feet. Even in her condition, she still weighed over 900 pounds. I didn't want her to die in the barn. There would be no way to get her out. Snow blocks the main door to the barn and my tractor is broken. She tried to rise. Her feet slid on the floor, pushing away the bedding. She was weary from the fight, tired of struggling to stand. I was convinced she would never get up. But she did.

She moves across the snow in painful steps. Harry stays close to her. I sense that the gelding realizes that the mare is sick, that she's about to die. Normally, Harry's obnoxious in small doses. During the mare's illness, he's irritable, holding his ears flat against his skull whenever I come to lead him into the barn at night. He's stubborn. He doesn't want to leave the mare, perhaps because he senses that her time is short.

They stand together in the pasture, the old mare and Harry. I think they both know that this will be their last spring together. I feel the need to go out and talk to her, to comfort her, even as I write this story.

The mare has carried my children, my wife, as well as family and friends, and me, upon her sturdy back. Before she came to us, she did the same for other folks. She never complained, never bucked, never bit, never refused to do what was asked of her.

Her name is Cisco, a name she had been given long before she came to live with us, a name she bore long before the movie *Dances with Wolves* was ever made. I bought her for René. She cost a hundred and fifty dollars. It's the best money I ever spent. I fear there will never be another horse like her on the Munger farm.

Looking for Moonlight Graham

Sometimes we are destined to be good, not great.

The Chisholm Ice Arena is loud. Fans scream, urging their respective teams on to victory. My son is in the nets for Hermantown. It's a choice he made some years ago: to be a goalie. I tried to talk him out of it. I tried to make him understand that if he wasn't the very best at the position, his chances of playing high school hockey were nil. But he loves it. He loves the mental part of the game; the pressure; the accolades when his team wins.

At one time during the season, my son's team of ten skaters and a goalie was ranked as high as seventh in the state. That was before a back injury ended Michael's hockey career and before we lost another player to misconduct. We went into district playoffs with eight skaters and a goaltender. We lost to teams we'd licked during the regular season. We lost not because the kids didn't try: We lost because the boys were exhausted, worn out by skating short.

We're in our third overtime period against Proctor. We've been able to stay with the Rails in the championship game of this invitational tournament only because we picked up extra players from other Hermantown teams.

Both goalies are playing fine games. Matt stands tall. He does not know that this will be his last game; that he'll try out for the high school team next year as a sophomore but not make it. Right now, occupying the crease, protecting the tie score for his teammates, focusing on the game in front of him, he's playing one of the best games of his career.

Our defense is tired. A Proctor boy breaks across neutral ice and gets behind the Hermantown defensemen. A pass finds the Rail winger all alone in the Hermantown end, two steps beyond our last man.

Matt bears down. He shifts his position to cover the left pipe. The Proctor player skates in from the boards. He lets fly

130

with a high, hard wrist shot. The puck strikes the goaltender's shoulder and lands in front of the net. A skirmish breaks out as our defense and the Rail player scramble for the puck. Matt moves across the crease, staying low, trying to see. The Proctor forward wins the battle. Another shot is launched towards the opposite side of the net. Matt scrambles but he's too late.

The teams line up to shake hands. My son is nowhere to be found. His goalie stick, helmet, and gloves are scattered across the ice. I know better than to follow him into the locker room.

My wife René and our two other sons at the time, Dylan and Chris, join me to watch the awards ceremony. We applaud lightly as the Proctor team hoists the championship trophy above their heads. The winners, their sweat-streaked hair flowing behind them, circle the rink with their prize. Loyal Proctor fans cheer as their team takes a victory lap. My family exits the ice rink to wait for Matt in the lobby.

One by one the Hawks emerge from the locker room. As the Hermantown players carry their heavy equipment bags and their sticks into the concession area, they ask their parents for money. It's a ritual that's been repeated after every game since the boys were ice mites.

"Where's Matt?" I ask the head coach.

"He left awhile ago."

"He's not in the locker room?"

"Nope. He wasn't too happy. He left before anyone else came off the ice."

"We better go find him," I say to René.

"I'm not pleased with the way he's acting."

"Me neither. But it was a tough loss."

"That doesn't give him the right to be a poor sport."

I gather up Matt's equipment and carry it to our van. It's evening. The March night is wet with the melt of spring. I search the parking lot. My eldest son is nowhere to be found.

I drive through downtown Chisholm, Minnesota. Street lamps cast shadows across cracked asphalt. Only the town's taverns and bars are open. Neon signs crackle. I turn around on the town's main street and head uphill, towards the arena. My child has vanished. There is no trace of him anywhere.

"Where the hell did he go?"

131

Dylan slides between the front bucket seats and points through the windshield.

"There he is."

Matt is walking towards us, his hands shoved deep into his pants pockets, his posture slumped, as if someone has placed the weight of the world on his shoulders.

I pull the van alongside Matt and stop. My son glances up at me. Moisture pools in his brown eyes but tears do not break free. He approaches my side of the vehicle. I push a button. The driver's window slides down. Cold air touches my face.

"What's going on?"

My son stares at me.

"Do you realize we've been driving all over town looking for you?" René asks.

Matt remains mute.

"Did you find him?" I ask

Matt's eyes search my face.

"Find who?"

"Moonlight Graham."

I watch Matt fight a smile. He's unsuccessful. The darkness of the overtime loss fades from his face. He casts a backward glance at the Chisholm Arena and enters the Pontiac from the passenger side. It's a quiet ride home.

Too Many Years

The hills rose behind them enveloping the boy and his father in shadow. A train trestle stood silent against the night sky. Their campfire was meager. Fuel for the fire was limited to a few dry branches stolen from the top of a beaver lodge: The beaver had eaten everything else.

A transistor radio sat on the ground. The radio was not on. A battered tin coffeepot sat upon the steel grate of a camp stove. They sipped coffee from cheap plastic cups, talking in low, respectful tones.

"Twenty-two years ago. That's the last time I was here."

The man didn't look at his son as he talked: He looked upward, off into the distant night, as he spoke.

"I came here with my dad, my Uncle Bob, and my cousin Kevin. We sure caught fish that day."

The son stood up, walked over to the stove, and poured himself another cup of coffee. The heat of the liquid caused the cup to sag, to droop until it nearly released its contents. Noise from a passing train interrupted their peace.

A locomotive emerged from the woods. The diesel labored despite the fact that it pulled an empty train: It faced a steep and difficult climb from the shoreline of Lake Superior to Minnesota's Iron Range. They sat quietly and watched the single headlight of the locomotive. The racket made by empty ore cars passing over ties denied them wilderness. Light from the engine's interior allowed them to see the crew. The man and his son waved at the train. A lonesome whistle replied.

In the morning, they ate cold sweet rolls and drank more coffee. They had no concept of time. The boy pulled on his hip waders and worked the edge of a pond near their camp with a dry fly. The father rigged his fly rod with a barbless hook and a night crawler.

"Got one."

The boy lifted the slender tip of his fly rod and pulled a tiny, silver fish out of the cold waters of the beaver pond. It was not a trout but a shiner no more than three inches long.

"That won't be much good in the fry pan, son."

"At least I caught something."

The boy's reply was curt. He removed the fly from the minnow's mouth and gently placed the shiner back in the water. The fish skipped across the surface of the pond, disappearing to wherever it is that wounded minnows go. The humans moved downstream, testing the ripples of the tiny waterway for brook trout. On his third cast, the father felt what he had come to that place to feel. A series of sharp tugs bent the rod. He set the hook. The fishing rod arched: A trout's spirit had been harnessed.

He pulled the fish out of the water and grasped it in his hand. It was a brook trout, no more than four inches in length. The creature's flanks caught the sun. An explosion of color defined the brookie's skin. The fisherman loosened the hook from the trout's jaw and released the fish.

They fished the creek for two hours but never caught another trout. After eating cups of instant oatmeal, the boy and his father loaded up the truck and left their campsite. The day was still new. The sun had just risen and they had no idea where they were headed.

"I think if we stay on this road, it'll take us to another spot Grandpa Harry and I used to fish."

"Sure Dad. Just keep an eye on the gas gauge, OK?"

They drove for an hour. Descending a steep grade, they came to another creek. The truck slowed as they arrived on the valley floor.

"Want to try this one?"

"Sure. Looks kinda tight, not a lot of room to fly fish, but I'll give it a try," the boy replied.

"You could use worms. It's no sin to use worms."

The boy grinned. The father eased the truck off the road.

"Dad, you're just like that drunk guy with his coffee can full of worms in *A River Runs Through It*. Didn't you learn anything from that movie?"

The father stopped the vehicle at the water's edge, turned in his seat, and smiled.

"We'll see who catches more fish."

They pulled on their waders. The father took off up stream. The water came at him in a steady current. Black alders and maples hung low over the creek, making progress difficult. The boy waded a quiet pool below the culvert. A cloudless morning warmed the day.

It was on that unnamed creek where they learned how to fish. Every set of rapids, every stretch of fast water held trout. Most of the trout were five or six inches long. Only the boy caught fish large enough to keep. At noon, they left the creek in search of larger waters and bigger trout.

"Want to try this spot?"

Dust from the gravel road wafted by them as they skidded to a stop. The truck idled on a concrete bridge. Below them, a wide expanse of clean water cut through stones and undergrowth.

"Isn't this the place we thought about camping last night?" the boy queried.

The father surveyed their location. The boy was right. It was the same spot they'd passed up the night before. They'd made a complete circle, following unnamed roads across unnamed streams, ending up essentially where they'd begun.

"This time you go downstream and I'll go up, Dad."

The father nodded. Baiting his hook with a fresh piece of night crawler, he plunged down the bank, his gait awkward due to the waders, and entered the stream. Concealed by the shadow of the bridge, he watched the boy move away. The father tossed a night crawler into black water. The worm landed by deadfall. The current caught the bait and dragged it beneath the surface. A sharp tug told the fisherman that there were brook trout hiding under the logjam. He tried to set the hook. The line went limp. He retrieved the monofilament line and tossed the worm next to the debris. On the second cast, the trout was not so lucky.

They fished in silence. The rounded peaks of the Sawtooth Range stood to the west, framing the solitude of the place. They learned that the tranquil pools held no trout. The brookies were in the rapids; where the water bubbled and boiled. The father was stubborn: He thought bigger fish were holding in the pools. The stream proved him wrong.

They met at twilight in the middle of the river and compared creels. Though the worms caught more fish, the boy had done what he'd set out to do. He'd fished the day in grace, using only flies to tempt trout. And the father had accomplished what he'd set out to do as well. He'd found and caught brook trout, something he had not done in a very, very long time.

They left the river when the sun slid behind the hills. Standing at a guardrail on the bridge above flowing water, watching the boy walk towards the truck, it occurred to the man that his son was no longer a child.

The Hockey Player

The first thing I noticed about him was his hands: They were large, thick wristed, but soft. Then his nose: His nose plunged between his eyes like an eagle's beak. There was no bone remaining where the bridge of his nose had been. The rest of his face was rose colored and kind. Age lines crossed his forehead. Wisps of hair, neatly combed, rested upon his scalp.

I sat in a restaurant booth with my wife. I was talking quietly to another lawyer. The old man was in the booth in front of us. His head was tilted to the side so that he could hear our conversation.

We were talking hockey, not law. We were in Thunder Bay, Ontario and had just played in the Barrister's Cup Hockey Tournament. The lawyer across from me had fared worse than I had during the games. He was the Ramsey County goaltender. His chin bore seven stitches. The old man listened to us and smiled.

"Hockey players, eh? Who you play for?"

You could see the old man's wife, a cheerfully dressed woman in her early sixties, grimace at the question.

How was I supposed to answer him? Should I admit that the two games I'd played the day before were the first hockey games I'd ever played in my life? To say I "played" hockey didn't ring true. The other attorney responded, sparing me any embarrassment.

"We played in a lawyer's tournament. Minneapolis, Duluth, Thunder Bay, and St. Paul all brought teams. I played for St. Paul."

The other barrister motioned towards me.

"He played for Duluth."

The goalie stood up from the table. The old man stared at the bandage on the tender's face.

"Stick to the chin, eh? Stitches?"

"Puck. Got up under my mask when I was down. Seven stitches."

137

"Used to stitch those up right on the bench. Hurts worse if they poke you with a needle first. Better without anything. Took lots of sticks to the face. Nine broken noses."

The old man's nose vouched for his statement. The attorney from St. Paul grimaced as he stared at the old man's face.

"They used Novocain. It's fine. Something to talk about at the office tomorrow."

The lawyer reached down and plucked his infant daughter out of a high chair.

"Nice to meet all of you. I've got an eight-hour drive home. See Ya."

The old man turned around so that he could talk to me. There was much life, much character in his face. My wife and I stood up, intent upon leaving. On reflex, I extended my hand to the old man and introduced myself. His grip was firm but polite. He didn't try to crush my fingers in his hand. He smiled. His teeth were white and shiny: They weren't original equipment.

"I'm from Port Arthur. Used to play some myself."

I took in the old man's broad shoulders and bowed calves. Age had not diminished his physical presence. I guessed that he'd played more than "some". His wife feigned disgust: Her eyes betrayed a sense of appreciation measured by years of sacrifice.

"Oh, don't get him going. He'll want to show you his trading cards."

"Trading cards?"

My interest grew. *Who was he? When did he play? Who did he play for?*

"I'd like to see them."

The woman's smile broadened. Her hand dug into her purse. She withdrew two cards encased in plastic and handed them to me. René looked over my shoulder.

The cards were ancient. The pictures were black and white photos colorized like a Ted Turner movie. The faces on the portraits were those of a man-child, a young hockey player in the prime of his career. The player's nose was full and smooth, without any evidence of fracture. The young man's hair was thick and youthful.

138

"Played for the Red Wings and the Black Hawks."

His voice was quiet, as if he'd been called back to a different time and place by the mere presence of the cards.

"The Black Hawks card was just re-issued. He still gets four or five fan letters a week because of it," the man's wife observed.

I stared at the trading cards. I wondered if Dennis Rodman, Jack Morris, or Patrick Roy would ever look back at their lives in sports with the same pride the old man seemed to. I knew, at best, he'd probably made a few thousand dollars a year playing hockey. He'd played not for money but for a love of the game.

They'd lived all over the United States and Canada. For parts of three decades, they continually moved their home, following his career. They were often separated by his time on the road. During those lonely winter nights, she would sit next to the radio and listen to the games, cheering whenever his name was mentioned.

Some years, he played for minor league teams. Other years, he made it to the NHL. She showed me the ring he'd won as a member of a team from the 1950s that won the Stanley Cup.

"It's not as fancy as the rings they have now. No diamonds. Just a ring, " she observed.

In my mind, I disagreed with her. I thought the beauty of the ring was that it mirrored the subtle strength and dignity of her husband.

"It was a pleasure to meet you both."

I handed the cards back to the woman. We left the couple to their hot coffee and memories. Retrieving our sons Chris and Dylan from the hotel pool, I felt as if I'd left something unfinished. I convinced René we needed to go back to the restaurant.

The old man was just leaving his booth. Six decades of hockey and life made his ascent from the bench seem labored.

"Mr. Woit, I'd like you to meet my sons Dylan and Christian. Dylan's a hockey player too."

A strong hand reached out to each of the boys in turn. I asked the old man's wife to show the boys the cards. Without

139

hesitation, she produced them from her purse. The boys held the faded cards in their hands. They read the statistics.

With more penalty minutes than points, Benny Woit had never been a goal scorer like Brett Hull or Wayne Gretzky. Until that day, I, like most hockey fans, had never even heard his name. But none of that mattered. Standing next to the old man, it seemed clear that there's more to sports, more to living a life, than mere numbers.

"Mr. Woit is from Thunder Bay. He played hockey for the Red Wings and the Black Hawks. He played back in the days when they didn't wear helmets, when goalies didn't wear masks."

The old man grinned. A long, far-away look enveloped his face. Perhaps, for an instant, as he stood talking to my sons, Benny Woit was once again a young man, with young legs, skating in the Stanley Cup Finals.

The Quest

"**Do** you have any maps of Lake County?" I ask a young woman behind a counter.

"Lots of 'em."

The clerk walks over to the wall and pulls open a large drawer in a filing cabinet.

"Help yourself."

I scan the maps for the place I've heard about, Cloquet Lake, the place where the Cloquet River begins.

"Why are we going to the source of the river?" Matt asks as we leave the Two Harbors Holiday Station behind.

"I've always wanted to see where it starts."

"Why?"

"I dunno. I just like to know where things start, I guess."

"You sure there are brook trout up there?" my son inquires between bites of bread and salami.

No, I admit to myself, *I'm not sure.*

I'd read about brookies being planted in the brackish headwaters of the Cloquet River back in the 1930's: Something about a "fish car"; a rail car that carried tanks of brook trout fry to plant in remote areas. But who had written it? Where had I read it? I don't recall.

"I read somewhere that there are supposed to be oodles of big ones up there. No one fishes 'em," I respond, trying to sound confident.

I glance in my son's direction. His eyes are riveted on the road. Lush forest, painted the vivid green of late summer, rushes by: Intervals of dead birch, their tops rotted by disease stand in contrast to the supple aspen crowding the highway corridor. We leave the blacktop and follow a well-graded gravel road.

"There it is," Matt points to a ribbon of water emerging from a culvert beneath the roadway.

I stop the van.

"Might as well give it a try," I offer.

"You sure about this, Dad?" the boy asks.

"Sure, the book..."

Before I can complete my reply, Matt pulls up his waders and heads into the stream with his rod. The sun sits brutally high as I pack my wader pocket with tackle. Grasshoppers sing in the heat as I climb down the bank. Cool water rushes past my waders. I step into a pool. God has handcrafted the place for brook trout: Gravel bottom; low brush overhanging the edges of the stream. Still, I find no fish.

"What was the name of that book again, dad?" the kid teases as we turn onto a minimum maintenance forest road.

Neither of us prompted trout to rise from the depths of the water. I don't answer. A glance at the map makes it plain that Cloquet Lake is not the headwaters of the river. Katherine Lake is. We drive a primitive road through absent forest. Loggers have claimed any trees of value. Scrub balsam, spruce, and adolescent aspen cover the landscape.

I'd envisioned the source of our river to be a quiet, spring-fed wilderness pond protected by steep, rocky bluffs and towering white pines. In my mind's eye, incredible vistas define the path of the river as it tumbles over glacial boulders. The reality of the place engenders disappointment.

Katherine Lake sits near the center of Lake County, Minnesota, miles from nowhere, surrounded by swamp. The terrain is uninteresting. There is no shoreline to the lake. Swamp grass yields to meager depth, creating an illusion that the lake is a true body of water. In reality, Katherine Lake is but a sad teardrop set amidst miles of desolation.

A cottage occupies the lake's only island. The building is inaccessible by land. A foreign-made station wagon is parked on shore. The car is unlocked, an open invitation to mischief but our location is so far from anywhere, it's obvious the car's owner is playing the odds, odds which are long in his or her favor.

A trickle of water escapes the marsh bordering the southern limit of Katherine Lake. The creek winds and twists through reeds and cattails. An ancient, rusted culvert allows the beginning of the Cloquet River to pass beneath the road. We follow a rutted trail through cedar and spruce. Sunlight breaks through the forest to reveal a small campsite. A public boat launch allows access to Cloquet Lake. We exit the van and walk to the water's edge. The water is calm; the lake's surface is black and haunting.

"Cool," Matt whispers, tossing a stone into the rot-stained water.

Soft, thick clouds float above us. We stand silent, touched by peace.

"Doubt there are fish in here."

I watch the wind gently sway stands of wild rice. The movement of the rice breaks up the monotony of the water.

"Too shallow. Might be good for duck hunting, though," I add.

"It's still pretty neat," Matt says reverently.

We leave the lake. The map indicates the road dead ends soon. The landscape changes. Our van plunges downhill. At the bottom of the slope, a slow moving stream meanders through broad marshlands. I sense that this is the real beginning of the Cloquet River. A primitive urge compels me to stop.

I remove my fly rod from its case and toss a dew worm between lily pads. Matt stands at the rail of a planked bridge and watches. The result is predictable. My son smiles as I break the rod down and put it away. He doesn't say anything as we enter the van and turn around.

We leave our destination, our quest partially fulfilled. Disappointment does not deter my resolve. I know, despite hard evidence to the contrary, that somewhere on the upper Cloquet River, brook trout wait for us.

The Quest: a Reprise

We're parked just off the road. René's van is tucked into a small clearing. I've hooked and landed several dozen minnows in the river next to our campsite. I've also landed two brook trout. The minnows were larger than the trout. Matt is having similar luck.

An earlier trip to the source of the river was marginally successful. We found the headwaters of the Cloquet River. But we'd also hoped to find brook trout of mythical proportions. We found no fish at the headwaters, at Katherine Lake. We found only a sense of desolation, desolation so strong that it forced us back to the North Shore, back to familiar ground.

I'll admit it. I didn't spend sufficient time planning this trip. I didn't bring a tent. Before we left home, I removed the rear and middle seats from the van so that we'd have space for our sleeping bags. Looking at the cargo area as I roll out my bag, it's clear space is at a premium.

Outside, the heat won't abate. I watch perspiration roll off Matt's temple as we try to eat our bratwurst, beans, and chips by the light of a battery-powered lantern. Swarms of insects taunt us.

"Let's hit the rack," I urge, swinging wildly at a cloud of mosquitoes attacking my sweat-streaked hair.

"Sounds good to me."

With military precision, I open the van's sliding door and motion for Matt to jump in. I follow as quickly as my forty-something body permits.

"There are a billion skeeters in here," my son observes, disappearing beneath the fabric of his bedroll.

He buries his head deep in rayon leaving his old man to battle bugs.

"Thanks, Matt. You could've killed a few," I remark, as I go about crushing mosquitoes against window glass.

"Night, Dad."

I kill insects until I can no longer hear them droning in the dark. The air begins to chill. Our breath collects and turns to condensation. Matt's respirations are loud and deep. I climb into the warmth of my sleeping bag and attempt to dream of brilliantly hued trout rising from black water. My son's snoring makes such dreams impossible. Somewhere between rest and deep sleep, I realize my bladder is full. I reach over and search for the door switch.

Tnnkkk.

The lock on the driver's side pops up. The lock on the passenger's door does not move. The lock is stuck in the "open" position but is disconnected from the exterior handle. The passenger side door can only be opened from the inside. I climb over a bucket seat and exit out the driver's door.

"Where ya going?" Matt asks.

"I gotta pee," I reply.

Absent-mindedly, I lock the driver's side door.

I stand outside in my briefs and nothing else admiring the evening. The bugs are gone. Cool air has forced the humidity of the day out of the river bottom. Ground fog cloaks the road. I stand barefoot on gravel. My task complete, I turn towards the van. My eyes adjust to the darkness. I watch as Matt exits the van and shuts the passenger door.

"Matt, don't...."

It's too late.

"What, Dad?"

I point the beam of my flashlight at him.

"You just locked us out of the car."

"No way."

"Yep."

We pull and pry at the doors. The passenger-side door lock remains unlatched but the door can't be coaxed open. The sound of another vehicle approaching causes us to seek the underbrush. I mull over asking for help as I shiver in my BVD's. Pride vetoes the idea. I let the pickup truck pass.

I formulate a plan. Picking up a large rock, I walk over to the van and search for the pane of glass that will be the least expensive to replace.

"Mom'll kill you."

I know he's right. I drop the rock and wedge my fingers between the glass and the window frame on the sliding door. The glass moves.

"I think I can pry it open."

"Don't break it."

"I won't."

I apply force. The latch is on the verge of yielding.

Snap.

Plastic flies past my ear. The window opens, allowing me to reach the door handle.

"What'd you do, dad?"

"It's just a plastic latch. Bring me the light."

Wearing only my underwear, I search for the pin that held the window latch together by crawling on my bare hands and knees across the stony ground.

"Here it is," I exclaim, holding up a small shard of metal between quivering fingers.

My son shakes his head. I thread the pin back into place and close the latch. We climb into the van and go back to sleep confidant in the knowledge that we're secure against the outside world. The next morning we drive home over back-roads.

"What're you going to tell mom?"

The broken window rattles. I pray that the latch holds. I visualize the pane of glass falling onto the road, shattering into a million shards as it strikes pavement.

"Nothing," I answer. "And neither will you."

Matt smiles:

"Anything you say, father."

Matt has been around long enough to know that God allows secrets between a father and a son, secrets that shouldn't be shared with his mother.

A Coach's Tale
(In Memory of Coach Pat Andrews)

He shuffles across the hard ice of an outdoor rink. His black rubber overshoes are unzipped. The uppers of his boots flop with each step. A battered hockey stick, the old kind, the kind made of wood, fits snugly in his chopper-covered hand. He uses the stick to maintain balance.

"Smurf, get up off the ice. Go after the puck," the man says in a gruff voice.

The words flow out from beneath a well-trimmed mustache.

A dozen or so Squirt B hockey players, boys nine and ten years old, skate lazily under the glow of floodlights. Some skate with cautious, wobbly steps. Others, like his son, the one he calls "Smurf", skate with strength. The names of the boys are familiar. Allen. Jason. Patrick. Michael. Matt. Tim. Chris.

He doesn't look like a hockey player. He can't skate. He's short and can't hear well. In fact, he wears a hearing aid. But the kids listen to their coach. Their attention hangs on his every word. They work hard. He's toughest on his own son. The boys see that and don't complain.

Because they are squirts, nearly all of their practices are outside. I stand next to the boards in my Sorels sipping hot coffee. Steam from the Styrofoam cup circles lazily into the February night. I watch the coach stop my son and explain something to him. There's no yelling. There's no chastisement. He is the teacher and the boys are his students.

Tonight, we sit on freshly lacquered benches in the New Barn, the new Cloquet Arena. The Hermantown Hawks have been behind for most of the game. Late in the third period, they tie the score. With only minutes to go in regulation, the possibility of overtime looms large.

I look out across the ice at the young men wearing blue, yellow, and white. Not so long ago, they were squirts learning how to play hockey in the open air of the country. Now they're

147

high school seniors, nearly grown men, playing inside a magnificent new arena for the sectional championship.

With a man advantage, our kids fail to hold the zone. The puck squirts free and rolls. A Proctor forward races to center ice and draws the puck in. He crosses the blue line with one of our defensemen trailing him. The puck explodes towards our goal. It bounces off the goaltender's leg pad and slides harmlessly away. A battle ensues along the boards. A referee's whistle stops play. A penalty is called against the Proctor Rails. There's less than a minute to play.

I don't know if any of the others see him. I don't know if anyone in the crowd recognizes him. Down low, just outside the face-off circle, he stands, big as life. He's wearing his overshoes and his bakery uniform. He holds the old wooden stick in one hand. Its blade rests on the face-off dot. How he got out onto the ice, how he got past the troopers and cops, I don't know.

Thirty seconds to play in regulation. I keep my eye on the man. He doesn't move. I wonder why the officials haven't stopped the game to get him off the ice. The puck goes out to the point. A hard shot deflects off the Proctor goaltender into a corner. A pass finds its way out to the left of the goalie and onto a Hermantown stick. Caught in the middle of the play, the man in the overshoes doesn't move. The distraction caused by the apparition allows the boy to break free of the defense, to find space to set up. The puck glides true across the front of the goal.

"Shoot from the pass," the boy hears his father say. "One-time it," the man whispers.

Thousands of shots over a decade of time have prepared the man's son for this moment. Instinctively, the winger hoists the puck towards an opening. The red light flickers, then comes on. Time expires. The game is won.

From the bench, blue, yellow, and white uniforms cascade onto the ice in celebration. Gloves, helmets, and sticks fly through the air. Coaches smile and pat each other on the back. The Hawk Band breaks out in the school rouser. Fans cheer and clap as the players roll around on the ice in a mass of unbridled joy.

Down in the Proctor zone, defeated players kneel in agony. Their season is over. The Proctor players think victory was in their grasp. They believe they let triumph slip away. They're wrong. Victory didn't escape the Rails. The little coach in the rubber overshoes did them in.

The Miracle of the Red Shoes

I watched his downcast, hound-dog body language as the boy walked away from the soccer field. I followed the slow, heavy-footed progress of his spikes across the muddy turf. I leaned against the hood of my pickup truck and studied my eldest son.

"How was practice?"

"I'm going to quit. Coach hates me," Matt responded, poison coating the words.

"What are you talking about?"

"He doesn't think I work hard enough. I'm doing the best I can but it just isn't good enough. I'm gonna quit."

My son stopped next to me and avoided direct eye contact. Dirt and mud covered the blue and white of his stockings. His burly knees and thighs were bruised from the abuse of playing soccer in October in northern Minnesota. His new shoes, highlighted with red stitching, sank into the grass as Matt nervously shifted his weight.

"That wouldn't be too smart. You're a senior. You've been on the team since tenth grade," I said, trying to instill an importance of commitment without using the word.

"So what? I don't play that much. And when I do, like against East, the next game, I'm back riding the bench."

I thought about talking to his coach. My dad would have done that for me when I was a benchwarmer back in high school on the varsity football team. In fact, he did do it. And I resented the intervention. I hated the fact that, at seventeen, I wasn't given enough credibility by my father to fight my own battles. Would Matt feel any different if I stepped into the fray on his account?

"I hate to see you quit with playoffs coming up. You've put so much time and effort into soccer. Hell, you've done a lot more in soccer than I ever did in football."

It was true. I'd started playing football as a sophomore to get a closer look at the cheerleaders. By the time I was a senior, the cheerleaders were still doing their thing and I was still riding the pine. Matt had been given an opportunity to actually play his

150

chosen sport, albeit not as much as he felt he deserved. He had a leg up on the old man, even if he wasn't in the mood to admit it.

"There's no use in staying on the team. I'm not gonna get to play."

"There are probably reasons why others are playing ahead of you. Speed, ball-handling skills, effort. I'm not the coach so I can't make those calls. But I still think it'd be a mistake for you to give up with the season nearly over, especially in your senior year."

I stared at the boy. He raised his face so that I could see his fierce brown eyes, eyes clearly steeled against my logic. I knew that a direct approach was doomed.

"Why don't you talk to Mack?" I suggested, referring to a long-time friend and assistant coach. "He'll tell it to you straight."

"I'll think about it."

The lights of Corey Veech Field blazed white against the autumn sky. Down on the field the Hermantown Hawks battled the Cloquet Lumberjacks. Despite a disparity in talent, Cloquet clung tenaciously to a 1-1 tie late in the second half of the soccer match. A large crowd occupied the bleachers, urging the hometown Hawks to bear down and put the game away. Mack took the time to talk to me before the game.

"He'll be fine. I think I got him settled down. He's starting tonight," the assistant coach said.

"Thanks," I replied. "I didn't want to see him hang it up."

"I told him to make the most of it. Those new shoes seem to have given him a fresh outlook. He can really nail the ball with those things."

As the game extended, Hermantown pressed but could not score. An upset was in the wind.

A Cloquet defender sent the ball over the end line, preventing a certain goal. The crowd stood and began to exhort the Hawks. Over the public address system, I heard my son's name.

"Number 38, Matt Munger, is lining up to take the corner kick," the announcer proclaimed.

151

Matt never took corner kicks. One of the regular starters, one of the more talented players, was always called upon to do the job, to set the ball down on the corner of the field and loft it towards the opposing goal. I was dumbfounded that my son was being given the honor of taking a corner kick in a crucial playoff game.

I dug my hands into my jacket pockets and prayed. My plea was that my son would kick the ball high, clean, and hard. I knew my prayer was selfish, the kind of petition that God rarely grants. It didn't matter. Only my wife, Mack, and I knew how important the kick was to my eldest son. Years of self-doubt would be magnified or reduced by the simple flight of a leather ball across the October sky.

Matt positioned the ball in the left corner. The fabric of his gold and blue uniform caught the stadium lights and shimmered. He raised his left hand, stepped back, and took aim. Keeping his head down, bearing down hard, he stepped into the sphere and launched it over wet grass.

The Cloquet goalie crowded the near post as the ball ascended. Hawk forwards sped towards the net, jostling with defenders for position as the ball began its decline. There was a suggestion of a hook as the ball sailed above the penalty square. As players fought for space in front of the goal, the ball turned sharply in the air, propelled by a defiant spin. The goalie set up to receive the kick. Offensive players shoved and pushed but could not break through to the net.

There are moments in life when reality slows as if preserved on film. Matt's corner kick is one of those moments. As the tender's gloved hands sought spinning leather, as he stretched to the limits of his height, the unexpected happened. The ball skipped off the goalie's hands and landed smartly in the net.

My son's right fist rose triumphantly in the night air as he ran onto the field and met his teammates in front of the despondent Cloquet defenders. He looked up at the stands and found his parents. His mouth broke into a wide grin as the sweaty arms of his teammates embraced him.

After the game, I walked across the soggy field towards Mack, intent on giving him my thanks. The assistant coach's grin was broader than my son's.

"That was one hell of a kick. Those shoes are really somethin'..."

I stopped my friend in mid-sentence.

"It wasn't the shoes, Mack. It was the heart."

A Country Pond

When we bought the old Drew place, we didn't even know the pond was there.

At first glance, it doesn't look like much. If you're lucky and you lace up your skates in early November, you'll find our pond skateable. But once snow arrives, our pond's surface becomes a challenge for even the most skilled athlete. To the casual observer, our pond, like a lot of things in life, seems flawed.

It's obvious that our pond is the creation of man. Its banks display the scars of a backhoe's handiwork. The creek that winds its way under the Taft Road and through the cedar swamp bordering our land is too lazy, too slow, to carve earth and form a pond on its own. One of the farm's prior owners, maybe Frank Kaneski, maybe Gerald Drew, or maybe someone we don't have any record of, gave the creek a hand. And so, a pond was born.

In some mysterious way, the quiet solitude one experiences when skating the creek bottom nurtures visions of a lost age, the age of the Ojibwe and the fur trade. Time spent on the pond during the deep cold of winter draws out a yearning for something that's past, of dreams left unfulfilled.

When my oldest son Matt was born, the thrill of America's Olympic hockey victory over the USSR and Finland took Minnesota by storm. As I watched the team's victory parade wind through downtown Minneapolis, a world of possibilities seemed to loom: Those were Minnesota boys who won that gold medal. Someday, my son could be one of them.

As soon as Matt could walk, he was on skates. In our first years on the farm, we trudged across the pasture, shovels in hand, to clear the pond of snow. We fought the bitter wind and the unrelenting cold as well as the unpredictable onset of December thaws. Regardless of our efforts, nature inevitably tortured the early ice of November into layers of delicate, fragile crust. Despite imperfect conditions, Matt and I both learned to skate. He was five. I was 29. In time, our other boys also learned to skate on the difficult ice of our farm pond.

154

Not so long ago, beaver moved in and built a dam across the creek. Their flawless engineering amplified the pond. The ice became smoother but it still wasn't perfect. It couldn't match what town had to offer.

When Matt first joined organized hockey, he played and practiced outdoors. Then an arena was built and there was little reason for teams to play outside. Inside the new arena, there was no snow to shovel, no insufferable cold to contend with, the ice was perpetually smooth.

In time, our pond saw fewer and fewer kids skating its ice. The pond's limited size and flawed surface couldn't compare with the manmade ice created by a Zamboni. There were no boards. We only had one net. Pucks sailed off the bumpy ice into the snow never to be found again. Pressure ridges and beaver holes interrupted the pond's surface. You had to be careful where you skated. The creek bottom ceased to echo with laughing voices. The pond sat vacant, waiting patiently for the boys to return. But the kids were in town; at the arena where everything was perfect.

A few weeks ago, hockey ended for our family. Eleven years of playing, running, fighting, arguing, driving, spending, cheering, crying, agonizing, worrying, counseling, and laughing came to a halt. A combination of things caused our involvement in the sport to cease. There was no one cause and no one is to blame.

The other day, reflecting on a winter without hockey, I walked down to our pond and stared out across the flawed ice. I'd come to the place where hockey began in our family. I'd come to question whether I'd done right by my sons. I asked myself whether I had fallen prey to a subtle desire to see my boys achieve something in their youth that I'd never achieved in mine. Had I tried to reshape my own childhood by living through them? I had no answer to my question.

A flock of Whistlers flew in. The birds landed in unison, settling on open water near where the outlet of the creek joins the river. In the distance, the sun dropped behind the horizon. Shadows formed across the layered snow. Watching the sunset, I realized that I'd done the best I could. I realized that, despite my

155

fears, my boys know that as well. They'll be back, with or without hockey, to skate with their dad on the pond.

Leaving Mayo

I shouldn't be here. René is eight and a half months pregnant. I still owe American Express two thousand dollars for a trip to San Francisco I gave my wife for her fortieth birthday. I don't have cancer and I don't think I'm dying, at least not any faster than I should be.

For seven years I've had a mystery disease. Disease is a little strong: A disease is something defined, found, maybe incurable, but at least known. What I have, no one seems to be able to categorize. I guess it can't be called a disease: It really can't even be labeled a condition.

I know it's foolish to envy people with tragic illnesses. I know that, given the slow advance of my symptoms, chances are that whatever I have will not kill me. Maybe that's why I hate being here, being at the Mayo Clinic. I just don't fit in. Everyone else here seems to have a condition or a disease that has a name, a treatment. I have symptoms. Ten years' worth of symptoms. Joint pain. Mouth ulcers. Bleeding. Stomach upset. Inability to sleep. Fatigue. Pain in my eyes that feels like someone poured sand in them while I sleep at night. Slightly elevated CPK, Sed rates, CRPs, Bilirubin. Interesting observations and minor alterations in my body's chemistry. But nothing significant enough or helpful enough to allow any of the twenty or so physicians I've seen to provide me with a diagnosis, let alone a course of treatment.

"How's your stress level?" I've been asked by each of them.

"Fine," I say, "except for the fact I have all these things going on with my forty-three-year-old body and no one can figure out what the hell is wrong with me."

I get up at four-thirty in the morning to drive from Duluth to Rochester. The first time down here, in 1992, I drove. My second visit, in 1994, I took a plane. I'm back to driving.

157

I park in one of the downtown ramps and walk the two blocks to the Mayo Building. A heavy fog cloaks the upper-most floors of the clinic. A bronze statue of a naked guy, his balls shriveled in the cold, his skin turned a nasty green by weather, is fastened to the marble exterior of the building. He's perched directly over the main entrance. I look across the street, trying to see if my church, the Episcopal Church, is still there. It is. Somehow knowing my religion is nearby props me up as I enter the clinic.

I'm late. I was supposed to be here at 8:30 am to register. It's 9:15am. I run excuses over and over in my brain.

I'm sorry I'm late. My wife is expecting and she had false labor.

A lie but at least one based upon fact. After all, my wife is ready to give birth.

I had a flat up near St. Paul.

Another lie with absolutely no basis in reality.

My back was acting up so I pulled over at Hinckley and walked around.

Two parts of this story are true. My back, actually my left hip, is aching. It went out on me, as my joints sometimes do, without any reason, three days ago. I've iced it, pain killered-it, rested it, and put heat on it. I walk with a noticeable limp because of it. And I did get out in Hinckley to use the john. But I'm not late because of it.

I'm actually late because I thought I-35 went to Rochester, Minnesota, when in fact, it does not. It goes to Albert Lea, and then, to Iowa.

"Hi, Mr. Munger. Have a seat. The doctor will be right with you," the receptionist says between smiles. She takes papers from me and never asks why I'm late. I limp to a padded chair in the immense lobby on the fifteenth floor and wait my turn.

I spend an hour with a rheumatologist, a guy with a slight foreign accent. Italian or Spanish, I think. He seems to be about my age. He knows little about my problem, or at least that's what I perceive. He has less than half an inch of my doctor's chart from Duluth. I know the complete chart is more like six inches of narrative and test results.

I want to ask him why it is that doctors can get by reading only part of a patient's file when an attorney, at least any

158

good attorney, feels compelled to read the entirety of a client's file. But I don't ask. I'm hoping this guy has something new to add, some new approach to help me understand why I feel the way I do. Why I can't play softball anymore. Why I bleed into the toilet. Why I'm so tired, despite eight hours of sleep, that I can barely see straight.

He asks the same questions I've been asked twenty or thirty times by other physicians. I try to give the same answers. He zeros in on a previous diagnosis made by one of his partners at Mayo.

"I see here that Dr. Marx thought you had fibromyalgia when he saw you in 1994. Do your remember that?"

"I remember that," I remark quietly. "But given my history since then, the doctors in Duluth don't think that fits what's going on."

He nods. I think I've steered him off that path. I want to. I know from my personal injury practice that patients are given the diagnosis of "fibromyalgia" (muscle pain of unknown etiology or origin) as a diagnosis of last resort. It isn't a disease. It is a description conveniently used to label a cluster of symptoms.

We talk more. He examines me. He pushes and prods my body. Some of my joints are tender. When his fingers probe my left hip, I double in pain. He motions for me to sit on the couch.

"From the looks of things, I'd say we're dealing with fibromyalgia. I'll run some more tests, most of the things you've had before, blood, urine, stool, colonoscopy. But it sure looks like fibromyalgia to me."

I want to scream. I want to tell him:

Don't dump a label on my condition simply so you can push me back out the door. Dig, damn it. Dig deeper into your bag of tests and tricks and medicines and find out what the hell is wrong with me.

But I don't.

"I'll be right back. Dr. Jones wants to look in on you. Don't get dressed yet."

He leaves me in the cold exam room. There is nothing to entertain me in the room except portions of my own medical chart, which I've read and re-read before.

My hip and lower back begin to burn. I stand up and walk over to the mirror. I look at my body. There is more hair on my chest than I remember. Up until my mid-thirties, my chest was essentially hairless. Now there are curls and wisps of dark black hair up and down my chest, all the way to my navel and below. Here and there, a white hair signals my age. I touch the scars on my belly where my gall bladder was removed three years ago. The damn thing didn't have stones. It just stopped doing what it was supposed to do. Luckily, I was able to have it pulled out through a scope. All that remains of the pain are three small scars, each less than a half-inch long.

My right thigh sports a two-inch scar, the result of a deep muscle biopsy. The biopsy revealed nothing but left me with the scar as a nice reminder of medical futility.

"It'll hurt for a day or so. Nothing major. Just don't try to run or roller-blade the next day," a nameless, faceless doctor had cautioned before sending me for the biopsy.

Yeah, right. The doctor who fed me that line was a liar; or had never bothered to ask one of his patients what the biopsy site felt like for the next week. I'm not a baby. I ran two marathons, made it through Marine Corps and Army basic training. After the muscle biopsy, I couldn't walk for a week.

I finger a thick scar on my lower back. It runs from just above the belt line to my butt. Somewhere along the way, I had a low-back fusion. They took out a piece of my hipbone and inserted it between the vertebrae in the spine to stop forward slippage in my lumbar spine. Christian, my third, used to examine the scar when he scratched my back. Maybe he'll be a surgeon someday.

Looking into the mirror, I pat my gut. I'm happy that when the nurse weighed me I'd lost five pounds. And somehow gained 3/4". I've always been five ten. Today I was just a tad under five eleven. Maybe I'll eventually be tall enough to jam a basketball.

Still, I don't like the roll of fat that has crept around my middle. I work hard to keep it off, exercising three or four times a week. But the fatigue makes me pace my exercise. It's tough to work out more than a half-hour at a time.

Dr. Jones surprises me as I'm looking at myself in the glass. He sits down next to me on the couch. He's in a suit. I'm in my briefs. The other guy stands by the window and doesn't say anything. Jones looks younger than I am. I like him. He says things that I want to hear.

"What's the worst problem confronting you right now, in terms of symptoms?" he asks in a genuine voice.

Of course, the voice could simply be very well practiced. Still, I accept it as sincere.

"The eye pain and the fatigue. I'm a lawyer and a writer. I can live with the bleeding. I know it isn't going to kill me. I can live with joint pain. Hell, I've had a back fusion for worse pain than what I'm dealing with now."

"Makes sense. Tell you what. Let's do some more blood work, repeat some things. There are a few autoimmune problems that I can rule out. Lupus is one. You don't have it. But there are others that involve the joints and the digestive tract. They might be more in tune with what's going on. Sound reasonable?"

"I gotta tell you that the word that comes to mind here, doc, is 'frustrating'."

I try to be as candid with him as I can. I sense he wants honesty and that he will return it to me.

"I understand. We'll see what we can put together. Get dressed. Someone will come by with your schedule."

I've been through this part of the routine before. I've taken off three days from work to allow for the extensive work-up that Mayo prides itself on. I also know that, for whatever reason, there is no way the testing and exams will ever be completed in three days. When I get the documents from the front desk, they have me staying in Rochester for five days. I can't afford it. I have a baby on the way. I don't share any of this with the scheduling lady. I simply tell her I have to be back to work in three days.

"I'll see what I can do," she says as she hands me a small folder with seven or eight appointment sheets placed inside it in chronological order.

"Keep these for now. Go to the ones you can. I'll start working on getting the others changed."

"Thanks," I mumble.

Staring at the papers, knowing that they represent thousands of dollars of sophisticated medical care, I'm thankful that I've used up the deductible on my health insurance. I wonder to myself what I would do if I didn't have insurance.

I'd live with it, I tell myself. *I sure as hell wouldn't be here.*

I begin my parade through Mayo's diagnostic maze. I start with a simple blood test. I take the elevator to the basement, the subway level of the clinic. I hand my paperwork to another lady behind another counter and take a seat. I sit a row or two away from two women. One of the women appears to be about fifty, the other, about twenty-five.

"She told me I have to make up my mind today. If both lumps are malignant, she recommends a mastectomy with an immediate implant. If one is benign and one malignant, I have the option of a lumpectomy, though the scarring might be pretty bad."

The older woman is speaking loudly. It is obvious she is anxious. She should be. She has cancer. She has a diagnosis. And it isn't good. I realize I shouldn't be here. I don't have a diagnosis. I don't have a condition, at least one that warrants me wasting the time of the Mayo Clinic. She does. If she doesn't get help, she'll die. If I don't get help, I'll simply grow tired and shit a little more blood. I don't belong here.

"I thought the doctor said you needed radiation," the younger woman whispers.

"That's only if I go with the lumpectomy. If I go with the mastectomy, then I don't need it."

"What about chemotherapy?" her daughter asks.

"Only if the lymph nodes are involved. But the problem is, I'll be out. I need to decide now, before she goes in, whether I want the mastectomy or the lumpectomy. What should I do?"

I think about the woman and the terrible choice she is presented. Without knowing the true nature of her condition, she must decide a course of action from which she cannot retreat. Before I can settle the issue in my own mind, my name is called. I wander off for what is likely my fiftieth blood test in the past ten years.

162

I do my business. I leave urine and stool samples in containers provided to me by the clinic on stainless steel carts parked at intervals on the lower level. As I walk through the tiled corridors of the clinic, I pass Pakistanis, Indians, Arabs, Africans, Asians; a myriad of races and cultures that we never see in my hometown. None of these people are poor. They are foreigners with means. They have come here, to the Mecca of medicine, seeking a cure for whatever ails them.

The Moslem women, their faces tightly wrapped with cloth, provoke my curiosity.

Don't they know that this is America? Don't they know they can rip the fabric from their faces and be free of the oppression of their culture?

I recognize my chauvinism immediately and I remember that our culture is not universal. I walk on.

I pass wheelchair after wheelchair of deserted, pathetic people, their absent eyes staring into space. These people do not seem to know where they are. Maybe it's better that way. Will they die here? That's doubtful. They'll likely make it to rest homes, where they will resume staring until they die. I leave the clinic and walk outside towards my hotel.

An old man in a wheelchair gets on the elevator at the Kahler Hotel with me. His attendant, a middle aged African American woman, smiles widely, exposing beautiful white teeth. The patient has only one leg. A bandaged stump is all that remains of his other lower appendage. I try not to stare at the stump. I try not to wonder how he lost his leg. It could have been diabetes or a farming accident. It's none of my damn business.

In the quiet of my hotel room I open the packet of appointments and study them. I've been through each test before. I've seen the same specialists back home. A thick cloud of guilt seeps under the door and enters my room. I ask myself: If I'm Christian, if I believe in eternal life, why do I fight so hard to find answers? Why can't I accept that there may not be a solution to my problem?

I decide that I've had enough. I call my wife and tell her I'm coming home.

As I talk to her, I glance out the window and watch people come and go from the Mayo as the sun casts its final shadow over the city. I sit in my hotel room and study the darkness consuming Rochester. I fixate on the marble exterior of the clinic. I focus my attention on the statue of the universal man suspended naked above the sidewalk. Hanging up the phone, I leave the Kahler and return to the medical center.

"My wife called. She's going into labor," I say to the receptionist on the fifteenth floor of the clinic, resorting to another lie.

I watch impatiently as the woman begins re-scheduling the remainder of my visit for another day, another time. I walk away without agreeing to anything.

Exiting the Mayo Clinic, I no longer feel overwhelmed. Instead, I feel only freedom and settled satisfaction. Passing the naked man, I pause and examine the details of his emerald body.

I become quietly engaged by the sculptor's art as nightfall's modesty descends over the statue. Despite the onslaught of darkness, the naked man's arms remain open and upraised to heaven but I am unable to decide whether the man is yielding to, or arguing with, the Almighty.

A Very Long Fall

You may or may not know that René and I are once again proud parents. In the aftermath of my wife's fortieth birthday and nearly ten years after the birth of our third son Christian, Jack Bridger Munger was born. Jack is the caboose on our train of four sons.

Matt, our eldest, was entering his senior year at Hermantown High School when Jack came into our lives. Dylan, the next boy in the Munger pecking order, was thirteen. Christian, as I said, was nearly ten. René and I had been in the "discussion" stages of planning to have another child when God decided to make our plans operational.

Even with our past track record of three pregnancies and three healthy births, Jack's arrival proved to be less than optimal. Each of the other boys had arrived through technology. Labor was induced because the stubborn little buggers didn't want to exit the womb.

"When do you want to have the baby?" the doctor would ask.

"As soon as possible," my very large wife would say.

"How about next Tuesday?"

"Sounds good," I'd interject.

With Christian there were a few false alarms. One late-night trip to St. Mary's interrupted a quiet evening at the movies.

"Mark, I'm starting to get labor pains," my wife whispered to me in the inky blackness of the theater.

"Can't you wait until the movie is over?" I asked, intent on catching the conclusion of the film, which just happened to be *Baby Boom* starring Diane Keaton.

"This can't wait," René replied, her voice becoming stern. "We have to leave now."

"Are you sure it's not a false alarm?" I questioned, just a hint of pleading in my voice. "The movie's almost over."

"Now," she said, struggling to rise from the hard plastic of the theater seat. "We have to leave now."

165

Of course I was right. We sat at the hospital, monitors hooked up to my wife, waiting for the miracle of spontaneous birth. It never happened. We made an appointment for Christian to be born by inducement two weeks later.

"Mark..." a nervous voice called out early one morning. "Mark..." The voice pleaded. "It's time."

My eyes were heavy with sleep. I thought I was dreaming. I looked at the clock. It was 6:00 AM. René wasn't in bed. Something was amiss.

"Mark...We've gotta go."

Sure enough, it happened. During my wife's fourth pregnancy, she finally followed the script: Her water broke. I won't share with you my entire bad behavior that morning as I careened around the house, a man out of control. All the logical thinking, all of my maturity was lost as I yelled, screamed, chased our older boys, and generally made a fool of myself. Thankfully my mom came over to take care of getting them off to school.

From the way Jack's story began, I knew I was in trouble. I mean, having lost all common sense the morning of his birth, I figured the rest of the ride was going to be bumpy. But you know what? It hasn't been. Because René and I are older, we have infinitely more patience. At least that was true until last Sunday, up until the Very Long Fall.

I was somewhere in another galaxy when he started to scream. It is incomprehensible how an infant weighing little more than twenty pounds can emit such a loud, piercing, wail. But he can. And he did.

"I'm gonna go get him and bring him to bed with us," René remarked in her most maternal tone.

"Sure," I mumbled, turning my back to her spot in our bed. I listened as her bare feet trod down the hallway. Jack held his breath for what seemed to be a minute or more. I could feel the anticipation of his next scream beating against my temple as the silence extended.

"Lay down, Jack..." my wife admonished, placing the toddler between us.

"All done," Jack whispered. I felt his tiny hands exploring the hair at the base of my neck. His body tossed and turned. His feet pushed hard against my flank, nudging me out of near sleep.

"I'm gonna go downstairs," I hissed, my words edged with annoyance.

Before René could say anything, I threw off the quilt and stumbled out of the bedroom. The hallway was dark. I fumbled for the light switch but couldn't find it. As I descended the stairs, I encountered the landing. As I stepped off the platform halfway down the stairs, my bare feet sank into carpet. Sleep on the couch beckoned. And then, suddenly, I was soaring. Not with the grace of a finely winged eagle caught in a draft. More like a loon flapping and struggling to make altitude before the end of the water. My foot pulsed in pain as it caught something near the bottom of the stairs and propelled me through the night. My arms flailed to either side, reaching for something solid to latch onto.

My left hand raced along the banister, probing, searching, as my body fell. The fingers of my hand circled the large balustrade at the bottom of the railing. With all of my strength, I grasped the smooth wooden ball and dug in. The balustrade came loose, just like the one in *It's a Wonderful Life*. As I flew over the child-gate at the bottom of the stairs, my trailing foot caught the fence. Instead of landing safely on the carpet, my body twisted in mid-air. I came down hard on the last stair. The balustrade smacked me near my right eye, where the fine bones of the eye socket form a ledge. I blacked out for a moment when the wooden ball bounced off my face, grazed the top of my head, and came to rest on the carpet.

"Who in God's name left this !@#* gate on the stairs?" I roared.

"What's wrong, Mark?" René responded evenly from the warmth of our bed.

"I just tripped over the gate," I muttered, sitting in the dark, rubbing my face. I noticed my toes were scraped and bleeding. I couldn't see the blood: I felt it dripping on the carpeting.

"Are you all right?"

"No, I'm not all right," I said. "I'm gonna sleep on the couch."

Then it hit me. I was the last person up the stairs. I'd stepped over the gate on my way to bed and left the offending object in place.

"I wish you people would remember to put things away," I grumbled as I removed a blanket from the downstairs linen closet. But Jack and René were already asleep. I found the couch, reclined, pulled the quilt over my burning cheek, and pondered the question of the moment:

Is a lie still a lie when no one is awake to hear it?

Another Winter

The thermometer on the big spruce tree outside our kitchen window reads nineteen below zero. It's only November and the house is already filled with cold. An early winter snow has drifted over the driveway. Though we can negotiate the residue of the storm in our vehicles, the ruts will freeze if I don't get out and plow soon.

The kids and René are off doing other things. I sit at a pine table staring out an arched window. The table, which was René's grandmother's, has been with us for the duration of our marriage. We spent more money having the table refinished than it will ever be worth. Some folks might smirk at that. But you don't always measure the worth of things, or people for that matter, by what others think.

I should be out shoveling. Instead, because it's Sunday, I listen to my new son Jack's exhalations. He's asleep on a blanket by my feet. While I listen to the delicate pattern of Jack's breathing, I try to work on my novel. It's a book that I started seven years ago. I had a publisher for it. The publisher went bankrupt. Now I'm on my own, fine-tuning the prose, hoping that someone else will become as excited about the book as I am.

The day draws to a close. The light fades and Jack stirs. I pick him up and talk to him. Not silly stuff like René does. My theory is that you should use large words and a deep voice with infants so they'll recognize authority. "Goo goos" and "gee gees" don't cut it. I slip up. I find myself talking gibberish to the baby as René and the boys come in.

"How's it going?" my wife asks, her voice hoarse due to a severe case of laryngitis.

"Fine. I just fed and changed him."

"I can see that. The label on the onesy goes in the back."

My wife pulls out the cotton tab from beneath Jack's chin.

"I don't think he minds," I reply defensively.

"No, but it reflects badly on me if someone sees it."

After dinner, my parenting skills no longer in question, I find a pair of wool socks and pull them over my bare feet. Walking through the house in my long underwear, I pass Christian. He's sitting at the kitchen table complaining he's too full to eat any more. Resisting an urge to remind him about starving kids in Africa, I retreat to the basement.

By the light of a single bulb in our utility room, I step into my blue and white bib overalls. The waist seems a little more snug; the buttons a little more stressed; the denim, a little thinner than last year. I force my arms into the sleeves of my fatigue jacket. Though it's been sixteen years since boot camp, the jacket looks brand new. I cover my head with a rabbit-skin cap and pull the flaps of the hat snugly over my ears. I slide a pair of leather choppers over my hands to complete my stylish outfit.

Our 1962 International 606 is stubborn and refuses to turn over in the frigid air of the barn. Though I hooked a battery charger up to the tractor before it snowed, my efforts to start the engine drain the battery. I re-connect the charger and climb back on the machine. The vinyl seat emits a "crack" as I sit down. All three of our horses clamber into the barn and stare at me from behind a gate. Their large eyes plead for grain. I ignore them and concentrate on the International.

Brmmmmmmmmm..pop..Brmmmmmmmmm...pop....Brm mmmmmm.

The engine starts but dies. It finally catches but runs at too high an idle. I push the accelerator lever forward, finding a comfortable pitch, shove the choke half way in, and climb down. I know that the tractor, like me, is mature. Both of us need a little time to warm up.

The chains of the tractor's big rear tires slap in unison against packed snow as I plow. I watch my ten-year-old son dodge behind the banks I'm creating. I know what will come next. A chunk of snow flies through the night air but falls short of the tractor. The snowball bursts into blue shards.

"Ya missed, me, Chris."

Another chunk leaves a gloved hand.

Splat.

The missile hits my neck. Snow stings bare skin.

"Not this time, dad."

"You must wanna die young, kid," I threaten, turning the tractor away from his barrage.

I leave the artificial light of the house and plow by headlight. Somewhere ahead of me, the open water of the Cloquet River threads its way through whitened ground. The moon is absent. Only the distant cool glimmer of silver stars punctures the evening. The old tractor churns forward, collecting snow in its bucket.

At the intersection of our driveway and the Taft Road, I draw a lever towards me. The bucket. With patience learned from past mistakes, I pull another lever to raise the scoop. Hydraulics groan in the cold.

Engaging in a process that will be repeated over and over until the driveway is free of snow, I manipulate the levers and extend the arms of the loader. The cylinders stretch to maximum reach and dump snow, creating an ever-higher bank for our boys to play on.

After an hour of work, the driveway is clear. As the 606 bounces towards the barn, I sense that my task, my chore, is a link to the real farmers, the real ranchers who inhabit snow country. I envision that somewhere out in western Minnesota, a dairy farmer is counting on an old International or an old John Deere to make it through another winter. As the tractor's chains slap newly cleared asphalt, I wonder whether that farmer has to dodge snowballs when he plows his driveway.

Fishing the Betsy

Brown water catches the embrace of an overhanging cedar bough. The branch dances with the current. I'm standing waist deep in the river's grip protected from the cold by neoprene waders. Along the sandy banks of the stream, dozens of fishermen silently stand. We're all waiting for steelhead, migratory rainbow trout. The fish are supposed to be here by the thousands, seeking gravel beds in the swift water to procreate. Instead, there are only red horse suckers, an undesirable rough fish, swimming the river.

For years I've heard my father speak in reverent tones about the Betsy. I've seen photographs taken over his twenty or more seasons of fishing the river. Every year that he's made the twelve-hour drive to Beulah, Michigan, he's caught fish. Except this year, the year I decided to come with. This year, Grandpa Harry got skunked.

It's a long drive to southern Michigan from northern Minnesota. My father, his pal Bruce, and I packed our gear into my dad's Tahoe and headed out one Saturday morning with hours of road ahead of us. Because it's March, winter in northwestern Wisconsin and the Upper Peninsula of Michigan is clearly on the decline. The snow banks lining the two-lane highway out of Bruce Crossing, a little hamlet located in northern Michigan that offers visitors the choice of driving to Marquette or Houghton, were half their former size.

Our travels took us through the hardwoods of northern Michigan, past the eastern coastline of Lake Superior, until we climbed the massive span of the Mackinaw Bridge, the only physical link between the part of Michigan that cheers for the Green Bay Packers and the rest of the state. Hundreds of feet below, water lapped against concrete supports, reminding me that my wife, a person not given to seeking out heights, would not enjoy crossing the Mackinaw Straights.

To pass the time as we drove, we listened to Walter Cronkite's memoirs on audiotape. It was necessary to supply something to listen to since every radio station along the way seemed to be dedicated to Patsy Cline and Waylon Jennings.

"I don't think I'm going to be able to ice fish this trip," Bruce observed, noting the lack of snow and ice on the Lower Peninsula side of the bridge.

"How's that?" I asked, somewhat puzzled since I wasn't aware we'd be doing anything but steelhead fishing.

"Bruce likes to go perch fishing on the little lakes near the Betsy," my father said. "I'm not quite sure why."

My dad is a rainbow trout fanatic. He'd stand in a river twenty-four hours a day if his seventy-three-year-old legs would let him. There was a hint of sarcasm to his words as he chided his buddy for seeking perch; fish that most Minnesotans toss back when fishing for walleye.

"Harry, they're great eating. Jumbo perch like the ones I catch here aren't easy to come by."

Our destination was a small ma and pa motel standing within a stone's throw of the Betsy River; meager digs when you consider that, as we passed through Traverse City, we marveled at row upon row of million-dollar-plus vacation and retirement homes lining the shoreline of Grand Traverse Bay.

When the alarm went off this morning, I left our cottage just after 6:00am. My dad was already on the river. Bruce slept in.

Negotiating the river, I try spots that look trouty. My task is difficult because the water is low and there are more folks fishing than there are good spots to wet a line. When I do find a place to try my luck, I catch suckers. I never hook a game fish. Each of the ugly rough fish provides a transitory thrill at the instant of attack: A thrill that quickly abates once the steady telltale pull of the sucker's effort is established. But it's a great week to be outside. The sun climbs high. A ceiling of sea-foam blue soars above the valley. Though white clouds sometimes race across the horizon, they never gather to form a front.

Upstream, a middle-aged woman stands in a pool tossing wet flies and streamers into current. I marvel at her skill. I'm unschooled in fly-fishing: I usually end up wrapping my flies around tree limbs whenever I take a stab at the graceful art.

The woman's hair, mousy brown turning gray at the temples, is tucked under a baseball cap. She stands knee deep in smooth brown water, water distinctly different in hue from that of the trout streams of the North Shore of Lake Superior.

Behind me, the forest demarcates my location. I'm surrounded by stands of oak and maple; hardwoods that aren't found in abundance where I'm from. Here and there, a cedar offers contrast to the grays and browns of the landscape. The leaves on the deciduous trees are still several weeks from breaking out.

"Fish on," the woman cries out.

Her rod bends and her reel whines as the fish, obviously not a sucker, seeks freedom. The angler cautiously follows the fish downstream. The woman's course brings her to an overturned stump in the middle of boiling water. It's clear to me that the steelhead is intent upon seeking refuge in the twisted roots of the cedar.

"I'll get him," I offer, resting my rod against the hollow trunk of a dead oak.

The woman raises her rod and controls the fish. I wade through water. The stream's grip is forceful. I feel cold through the neoprene of my waders as I reach behind me for my landing net.

"Wait a sec while I ease him out from under that branch."

The angler doesn't divert her eyes from her rod as she speaks. Her voice is authoritative. I hang back until she persuades the fish to turn up river.

"Now."

A flash of chrome darts across my boots. I dip the net into the river and catch the fish. The woman slides over to where I'm standing and retrieves the steelhead.

"Thanks."

She gently lifts the fish, a small rainbow trout that has lost its brilliant colors while living in Lake Michigan between spawning runs, from the net. With expert deft, the woman removes the streamer from her prey's mouth and releases the juvenile fish.

Later in the day, as the sun fades over hills and silent oaks, I lean against the railing of a small concrete dam blocking the river. Behind the man-made barrier, the Betsy forms a pond; a momentary delay in the water's rush to Lake Michigan.

"Not many fish in the river," Dad remarks as he joins me. "They're spawning in small numbers. Got real warm in January, way too early. They've been running ever since."

"How'd you do?"

"Hooked a couple, didn't land any. How 'bout you?'

"Suckers. Dozens of suckers. I only saw one steelhead caught all day. I helped a lady land it."

"Any size?"

"Small. She threw it back."

"There's one."

My father points to a pewter missile struggling against the water spilling over the precipice of the artificial falls. A steelhead, compelled by ancient desires, tries to attain the calm relief of the pond just beyond the lip of the dam.

"Let's go see what Bruce wants to do for supper," my dad suggests.

"I'll be along in a minute."

My old man walks towards the cabin in opposition to evening's approach. Though we'll fish for the better part of a week, none of us puts any trout in the cooler. Somehow, it really doesn't seem to matter.

Spring Walk

My wife René and I walk side by side over the pavement of the Taft Road. Jack, our six-month-old son, looks out at the newness of spring from deep within the three-wheeled cart that I'm pushing.

I didn't enjoy the false promise of the past winter. A warm January and February, a lack of snow, the unpredictability of it all was unnerving. Winter in northeastern Minnesota is defined by storms; by below zero temperatures and by mornings that beg for an extra layer of clothing. Not this year.

The sun warms my face as we walk. Having escaped the brutal touch of ordinary winter, I want to deny the sun's impact on my soul. I want to proclaim the falseness of the day. I cannot.

Car after car passes us as we stroll together along the gravel shoulder of the road. René and I speculate as to what the "Townies" are up to.

"Must be checking their cabins," René postulates.

"Probably taking a look at the ice, trying to figure out when it'll go out."

We walk by the house of a neighbor who recently died. Despite the fact that we've lived on adjoining land for over fourteen years, I didn't know the man. In the country, geographic closeness does not always translate into friendship.

"I wonder who's at his house." I ask absently, noting there's a vehicle parked next to his tidy double-wide. "Maybe a son or daughter."

"Maybe."

Jack leans to one side, his body restrained by nylon straps. My wife looks into the cart.

"He's asleep."

"Seems like the smart thing to do."

I contemplate how nice a nap in the sun on our couch would be.

"He's snoring," René remarks, slowing her pace.

"Just like his mom."

"Keep the critique to yourself, Mr. Munger."

176

Crows fly low on a warm breeze. A yellow caution flag attached to Jack's cart flaps annoyingly in my face.

"Poor design," I observe aloud, pushing the fabric away from my eyes.

"Maybe it's designed for taller men."

We turn onto the Fish Lake Dam Road. We leave the blacktop and traverse gravel. An abandoned tavern, its windows covered by plastic, stands near the edge of the road. Walking past the bar calls to mind an evening from the past I spent with Matt, my eldest son, when he was still in elementary school. One cold winter night we walked to the tavern to watch a hockey game on satellite dish. We shared a frozen pizza. Matt had a Coke and I sipped tap beer. At the end of the game, we pulled on our winter coats and walked home through an evening accented by beautiful stars.

The satellite dish has long since been removed. The bar stands empty. I draw no symbolism from the vacancy of the building. It's simply closed.

A heavy residue of winter road sand lines the ditch. Yellow marsh grass and cattails poke through the debris. Despite the dirt in the channel, clear water released by melting snow courses downhill. The temporary stream bubbles and boils as it seeks union with Fish Lake.

René was pregnant last summer. We haven't walked this road in over a year. Unexpectedly, the landscape becomes unfamiliar: The roadway, which was once crowded by white pines and cedars, is now wide open due to clear-cutting; though here and there, sentinel pines remain along the freshly excavated right-of-way.

Jack stretches his tiny arms and legs as we approach the frozen lake. Signs of activity clutter the parking lot of the resort that is our destination. Docks, vehicles, boats, and outboard motors await attention. The sun's brilliant reflection off the lake's ice makes it hard to see. I shade my eyes with a hand. Jack squirms. The strength of the sun forces him to turn his head. I reposition the cart so that the sun doesn't strike his face. Jack opens his eyes.

"I should've put his cap on," René laments.

Before I can respond, a familiar cry pierces the quiet.

177

Peep...Peep.

I strain to locate the source of the noise. The sky is vacant. Only the sun hangs over the bare maples of the far shore.

"Osprey," I observe.

My wife nods.

"It won't be long before the ice is out," I offer.

A ribbon of black water shifts uneasily between landfall and the receding ice. Water gnaws at hardened lake.

"Not long at all," my wife replies.

We leave the resort and head for home. The wheels of the cart bounce over gravel, and, within minutes, Jack is once again asleep.

The Hockey Stick
(In Memory of Jeremy Byrnes)

Matt hasn't worn hockey pads in years. During his amateur hockey career, there were so many games, so many road trips and tournaments, that I don't remember the details of the contests. But I do remember the faces of the little boys he played with. There are objects that I've held onto from Matt's days on ice: team photographs, videotapes of games, snapshots from tournament trips with other parents and their families, and the like. And then there is the hockey stick.

It's eighteen inches long and made of maple. "Cooper" (the name of a Canadian hockey equipment manufacturer) is stenciled in black across on the stick's handle. Someone, a coach, the team mom, or the team manager colored in a blue ring around the stick's handle where the blade meets the shaft and added "Squirt C 1988-1989" in the same ink.

I keep the stick in my office to remind me of more innocent times. The stick represents Matt's last year as a true squirt, the last year of total enjoyment of the fastest game on ice without parental politics. The next year, and each year thereafter until his career ended, Matt faced tryouts and the prospect of "cuts": designations made by a panel of hockey coaches as to which level he'd play at. It's too bad I didn't understand what the future held in store that last year of squirt hockey. I think I would have relished the season even more.

Youth athletics isn't just an opportunity for kids to make friends, learn a sport, and begin realizing that life, like games, involves competition; wins and losses, ups and downs. It's also an opportunity for the parents to learn a few things as well.

That year, a guy I had, and still have, a great deal of respect for, coached our little team. Tim had a hockey background but that wasn't what made him a good coach. He had unflappable patience, a keen interest in the welfare of his little charges, and a steady hand for discipline. His son played on the team; a big-boned, smiling kid, with a wonderful sense of humor and a love of good-natured competition. Tim's son and

179

eleven other players signed the handle of my replica stick. I happen to have their autographs because I was an assistant coach that year.

It was an intense game. I was so wound up watching my kid play; I shouldn't have been on the bench.

"Come on guys," I yelled at the top of my lungs. "Move your feet."

Jeff, the other assistant coach and I worked the doors to our bench and shouted encouragement to the kids. Tim stood quietly to one side surveying the play.

"Brian, get the lead out," Jeff shouted as his son lagged behind the rest of the Hawk forwards down the ice.

Jeff's kid was little, fast, and had a good eye for the net.

"Yeah, Matt. Get up there and help out your team."

Matt turned and gave me look of disdain as he coasted by the bench. He was a forward. We called him the "junkyard dog" because he liked to park himself in front of the opposing net and slam the puck home. It was less work that way. Why waste all your energy carrying the puck up ice when someone else could do it for you?

I don't recall the score of the game. I know we were at home in the Hermantown Arena playing a regular season game. I also seem to recall that it was a close contest requiring extensive vocal intervention to spur on the kids.

"What the heck is wrong with you, ref?" I yelled out when an official missed an easy offside's call against our opponent.

My face was red, my testosterone rushing. I got more and more heated. That's when Coach Tim took me aside.

"Mark. What do you think you're doing?" he asked.

Tim spoke quietly so no one else could hear the conversation.

"The guy blew an off-sides call. They got a goal off that piece of garbage."

"Number one, it wasn't that bad of a call. I've made worse," Tim interjected. "And number two, you're a coach. You're wearing a blue jacket with the words 'Hermantown

Hockey' on it. What kind of example do you think you're setting for these young men?"

A lump formed in my throat. Tim was right. I was acting like one of the hockey parents that I vowed I'd never emulate. I pondered a response. Jeff stayed away from us, unwilling to become the target of a similar lecture.

I study the names on the wooden stick sitting on my desk in the courthouse. Four of the names on the replica went on to play for state tournament teams at Hermantown High School. One kid played in two state tournaments as a goalie. Another never played high school hockey but went to state in track. Justin, one of two kids on the team to battle cancer, became a 1,000 yard rusher his senior year in football.

Five of the boys, including my son, went to college on the strength of their minds, not their bodies. In fact, David, a member of the group, graduated at the top of his high school class. And two of the players from that unit, maybe more, have given something back to the sport by becoming youth hockey coaches, by putting themselves on the line as role models.

The names on the hockey stick bring to mind distant events: some joyous, some tragic. Less than perfect memories reinforce the notion that not every kid who excels in a sport lives up to his or her potential. But there is one signature that stands out whenever I consider the names inscribed on that piece of maple. When I scrutinize the gently crafted letters left behind by that little boy, a boy who passed away at too young an age, Coach Tim's admonition rings as true today as it did twelve years ago:

"Mark, try and remember this isn't real life. These are just little kids playing a game."

The Beaver Pond

Black alders cling to the surface of the stream. To walk downstream in search of brook trout, I press my chest to the water so that I can pass beneath overhanging limbs. Behind me, the tip of my graphite fly rod vibrates with each unsure step. Mosquitoes buzz; ignoring the chemicals I've applied to my face. Sweat forms on my T-shirt inside the impervious membrane of my neoprene waders. It's only 6:30am and already the day's heat seeks to assert its authority.

My eleven-year-old son Christian and I came to the North Shore of Lake Superior seeking trout. We brought sparse provisions, a tent, our sleeping bags, and plenty of dry flies, wet flies, and dew worms. This is the first time Chris has been stream trout fishing. The weather is against us. It's ninety degrees. The sky is cloudless, the day, brutally bright. But I didn't come here with a need to catch fish: I came here with a need to seek solace after a recent death in my family.

We fished a clean, open river not too far from Duluth the first day of our trip. Or I should say, I did. Chris's spin-casting rod was retrieved from the car with a broken tip. Despite my efforts at repairing it with duct tape, the rod remained useless.

"I casted and the tip just fell off," my son lamented as he approached me across the cobbled surface of a gravel bar protruding into the river, the broken rod in hand.

"Can't you get it to stay on?" I implored him as I fished a quiet hole beneath an overhanging cedar.

"It won't work. I tried it a couple of times. The rod just falls apart."

"We'll stop in town and get you a new rod before we head up the Shore."

"What should I do while you're fishing?" the boy asked, careful to keep his voice low, like mine.

"There seem to be fish here. I'll hook 'em and we'll take turns bringing 'em in. How'd that be?"

"OK.'

182

We hooked and landed a few small brook trout, keeping one about six inches in length.

"Take a look at this fish, Chris," I remarked, holding the tiny fish in my hand.

"See the colors? Brook trout and lake trout are the only two trout native to Minnesota," I explained as he studied the beautiful markings of the fish.

We wandered further upstream. The way was easy: There were no branches hanging in the way, no tight places to negotiate. It had been years since I caught a rainbow trout in a stream. When I felt the tug, I assumed the fish was a brookie and handed the rod to Chris.

"Reel slowly and keep him in the current, away from the bank."

The tip of the fly rod danced as the trout sought release. Chris cranked the reel slowly and brought the fish to me. I cupped the silver trout with my bare hands and raised him free of the river's embrace.

"Nice fish, Chris," I exclaimed. "I think it's a brown," I offered. "No, it's a rainbow," I said, correcting myself upon seeing the slight glow of pink across the silver-green sides of the fish.

That was yesterday, when the river was easy to walk and we were within a few miles of civilization. Today we are in the deepest, most secret part of the forest, near the headwaters of another stream. Here, the fishing is not so easy.

Chris stays close to our campsite and fishes a few yards from our tent. We've given up on flies. The warm weather left the trout with poor appetites. They will not rise for dry flies nor nibble at wet flies offered to them. We're using worms. Despite the heat, the water remains cool to the touch. Brook trout need cold water, water oxygenated by constant rapids and kept frigid by overhanging forest. I pause to dip my oilskin fedora in the river. As I place the bush hat on my head, water pours out from under the brim and runs down my face and neck cooling my skin.

I find trout lurking in deep pools near the banks. Most of the fish are six inches long. A few are smaller. I let them all go. I play, land, and keep one nice fish about eight inches long.

Ahead, a thick branch blocks the stream. Because of recent storms, a confusion of sticks left by dissipating water blocks the creek, forming a pool of mysterious quiet. I toss a worm into the middle of the hole and climb over a tree limb. My fly rod bends. A fierce, panicked exchange takes place. I feel the native power of a large brook trout pulling desperately as I try to keep the fish out of the flotsam. Placing one leg on either side of an alder branch, I keep the fish out of the debris and play the trout until it tires. The reds, blues, and yellows of the creature's flank shine as I lift the fish free of black water and into afternoon light. I grasp the trout firmly and remove the hook. It's a beautiful, fat fish, a legendary trout, the sort of trout brook trout fishermen dream of. The fish surges in my hand, a primitive undulating pallet of color fourteen inches in length. I reach behind me to secure the speckled trout in my game pouch. Before I know it, the fish flips out of my hand and returns to the welcoming depths of the stream.

"Crap," I mutter as I watch the white tips of the trout's fins fade from sight. "I'll never catch another one like that."

I plunge on. The sun re-asserts its power. The weight of my waders tires me. I catch and release another half dozen small trout. The course of the creek slows. Beaver have dammed the flowage. With each step the water rises and threatens to breech the top of my waders. I climb a bank and negotiate hillocks of sedge grass. Encountering a beaver lodge, I stop to fish.

Slap.

A solitary beaver warns others of its kind of my approach before vanishing. I toss a worm into the pond. My line tightens. I feel the discrete inhalation of a trout. I begin to retrieve the line and encounter opposition. I set the hook. The fish is on.

"How'd you do, dad?" Chris asks as I stumble my way back into camp, my skin covered with bug bites and scratches from the underbrush, my clothes drenched with perspiration.

"I got a few. I lost a really nice one," I explain through a weak smile, trying to downplay how truly magnificent the dropped brook trout was.

With ceremony and pride, I pull out five trout and add them to the four that Christian caught while fishing ten feet from our tent. I note that my son is not sweating, that his skin displays few bug bites, and that he appears well rested.

"That's a nice one," my son remarks, looking at a fat ten inch brook trout that gave up its life in the calm waters of the beaver pond.

"Yep," I say, carefully refraining from revealing the level of sacrifice I made to catch such a fine fish.

Too Fat Horse

Dylan, my second son was twelve years old when my wife's beloved quarter horse mare, Cisco, died. Cisco was the best horse we ever owned. Anyone could ride her; from the most experienced horseman to the smallest child. When the mare passed away, it fell upon me to find her replacement.

"Here's an interesting horse," I told my wife René one night after supper as I perused the want ads. "A POA, ready to foal, for $1,200.00."

My wife nodded her head.

"You don't even know what a POA is, do you?"

"No, but I'm sure I'm about to find out."

"It stands for 'Pony of America'. Sort of the Dodge Dakota of horses; midsized between a horse and a pony."

"And we need this animal for what reason?"

I looked at René over the edge of the newspaper.

"Dylan needs a horse."

"I'm not so sure Dylan is all that keen on owning a horse," my wife added as she put the last of the dinner dishes away.

Dylan seemed interested, interested enough to drive with me to a farm outside Cloquet to look at the pony. When we arrived at the place, a ramshackle outfit wedged in between stands of greening maples with the last of winter's snow slowly melting off the pasture, I recognized the folks who owned the farm.

"How's it going, Doug?"

"You're the one who called about the horse?" the guy asked, shaking my hand.

He wasn't a good friend. He had dated a friend of a friend. You know, one of those deals.

"Yep. This is my son, Dylan. The horse is for him. He's just beginning to ride."

A mild breeze rearranged my son's blond hair as he studied the farmer through a sideways glance. Dylan rarely looks

186

someone head on, preferring to mosey up to the person before letting his piercing blue eyes lock in on the target.

"Pleased to meet you," the man said, offering my son his hand.

The kid responded with a half-hearted handshake.

"We're working on the handshake thing," I advised.

"My daughter Tiffany is selling the horse. She's had the mare for a couple of years. The stud's that big stallion over there," the farmer said, indicating a massive black creature tethered to a cedar rail fence. "I was just about to mate him with one of my paint mares. Does Dylan want an education in the birds and the bees?"

I'm not sure that my son wanted to see the procreative process of making a foal. But I sure did. I'll spare you the details. Suffice it to say, the stallion was impressive.

After the breeding lesson, Tiffany brought us into the barn where the POA patiently waited. As we walked into the subtle light of the old dairy building, one thought struck me when I saw Starlight, the POA.

That is one fat horse.

There was little question in my mind that the animal was pregnant. Her belly was enormous.

The girl jumped from the top of the stall wall onto the horse's back and rode the animal around the pen. The mare trotted gently, never evincing any bad propensities.

"How long until she foals?"

"Should be a month or so."

"Can she be ridden until then?"

"I wouldn't advise it," the girl stated plainly. "She's gained a lot of weight. I'd take it easy on her."

A deal was struck standing in the dim light of late April. A few days later, Starlight joined my gelding Harry in our pasture. The POA seemed to fit right in.

Not knowing what to expect from a pregnant horse, I called our veterinarian, Dr. Meagher, to look at the horse. The vet came out, drew some blood to check for diseases, and gave the mare the once-over. She didn't do a formal pregnancy test on Star because the animal was obviously with foal.

"That is one fat horse," our friend Nancy McVean commented sometime later.

"She's pregnant," my wife advised.

"How neat for the kids."

"They've seen Labrador puppies and several litters of kittens being born," René added. "But this should be something special."

Another month went by. Starlight continued to gain weight. I managed to get close enough to her motherly parts to determine that nothing seemed to be happening.

"Can you get Dr. Meagher to come out and preg test the horse?" I asked René one day over the telephone while at work. "She's getting bigger but I don't see any signs that she's ready to give birth".

"Sure."

I wasn't there for the pelvic exam. But, as reported to me by reliable sources, it consisted of my wife holding the mare's snout in a twitch to prevent her from kicking the good doctor as the vet stuck her entire right arm, all the way to the shoulder, inside the animal, after which Dr. Meagher declared:

"This horse isn't pregnant. She's just fat."

I'll spare you the protracted machinations that transpired once I found out that the sellers had only owned the horse for a few months before they sold her to us. It turned out the "with foal" part of the advertisement was stretching the truth, so to speak. What's important is not what I did upon discovering the horse's true condition but what our friends Nancy McVean and Kathy Kaneski did afterwards.

Later that summer, Mrs. Kaneski and Mrs. McVean took it upon themselves to conduct an investigation of the pharmacy department of our local Target store.

"Mark, Kathy and I have a present for you," Nancy announced a few days after she and Kathy went shopping.

The announcement came as Kathy, Nancy, and I sat around a picnic table at the McVean place on Island Lake. René was wading in the lake as we sipped ice tea.

"René, you have to see this too," Nancy urged, calling my wife away from the water.

Kathy produced a large white box wrapped with foil and ribbon.

"Here," the women said in unison, "we hope this helps."

Their comment puzzled me.

Helps what?

"Open it," Kathy urged.

I undid the ribbon and tore through the wrapping paper. I was greeted with a large hand-written label, the initials "HPT" prominent across the paper.

"HPT: Horsie Pregnancy Test," Nancy advised.

Inside the box was a contraption of careful design pieced together from various kitchen utensils. It was obvious from the hand written instruction pamphlet and the device's engineering that Mrs. McVean and Mrs. Kaneski had spent the better part of a Saturday creating the implement after carefully inspecting each and every brand of human Early Pregnancy Test kit in the Target pharmacy. The women, including my wife, erupted in laughter. There was no question they were not laughing with me. They were laughing *at* me. I never cracked a smile.

"The next time you think a horse is pregnant," Nancy advised, "just pull out the old HPT."

"You expect me to put this thing..."

"Precisely," Kathy said. "Just make sure the horse pees directly on the Popsicle stick."

Dylan's Shack

Sometimes my ideas are hare-brained. Still, despite my best attempts at self-sabotage, things usually work out. Take, for instance, the day I decided to build Dylan, my second son, a shack. Well, not really build him one. My carpentry skills are too meager for that. Relocate would be a better description.

When we first moved onto the old Drew Place, the hobby farm we bought in 1984 out in Fredenberg Township north of Duluth, there were six structures on seven and a half acres. There was the house: A Sears prefabricated home delivered in crates to the site along the banks of the Cloquet River back in 1921 by draft horse and wagon. There was the original dairy barn; a chicken coop; a pump house; an old garage absent doors, windows, and shingles; and a newer four-car garage. As time passed, I dismantled the old garage and used the salvaged boards for other projects. And before the old barn and chicken coop were burned to the ground as training exercises for our local volunteer fire department, I got the bright notion that the pump house would make a good shack for Dylan.

The building at issue is approximately eight feet by six feet and six feet tall to the rafters. Just big enough for a card table, a couple of chairs, and a set of built-in bunk beds attached to the far wall. When the idea to relocate the structure first popped into my head, the shed's roofing was nearly gone. The siding was painted a hideous shade of blue that didn't match the color of any other building on our property. The floor was hastily mixed asphalt that heaved every spring so that the door, a door I'd retrieved from the local landfill, wouldn't open from March until early June.

Despite the building's shortcomings, René had adopted the shed as her gardening depot. We hung our rakes, shovels, and assorted other implements on hooks in the building. I'd constructed shelves and we'd filled them with gardening hand tools, fertilizer, seeds, and the like. The building was functional if unattractive. But the chicken coop, until we burned it down and built a new pole building, was ample enough to accept the items formerly kept in the pump house. And so, my plans to move the shed were implemented.

"Larry," I said one summer evening, "I need your advice."

I was talking on the phone to my close friend, a former carpenter, now fire fighter.

"How's that?"

"I want to move the old pump house across the creek, put it by the Norway pines along the stream so Dylan has a place to call his own."

"Ya."

"How would one go about picking up something like that and moving it?" I asked coyly, fearful that Larry might sense the barbs of a hook sinking into his mouth.

"Mmm," my pal said, mulling over how deeply he wanted to commit himself to my project. "How big is it?"

I described the shed.

"You could jack it up and move it with a snowmobile trailer."

"A half-day's work?"

"Sounds about right."

There was a pause. Larry knew what was coming next. He'd dealt with his carpentry-impaired pal too many times. I'd worked as a construction laborer with Larry back when I was in college. On the job site, I was never allowed to use tools: Tools are dangerous in my hands. Well, I take that back. The boss of the construction outfit let me use a shovel. But only with supervision.

"Larry, I don't suppose you'd have some free time to lend your old friend a hand?"

It was Larry's turn to pause.

"I've got a few days off next week. What're we gonna pull it with?"

"I've got a hitch on my International," I advised, referring to my utility tractor.

"That'll work."

191

By the time Larry sawed through all of the wall joists sunk deep into the asphalt floor; by the time we'd raised the bulk of the building off the ground, elevating it with four large jacks so that the trailer could be backed under the shed; an entire day had passed.

It was dusk when I put my International 606 in gear and began to pull the shed towards Knudsen Creek. The axle of the trailer bowed. It was clear that the weight on the snowmobile trailer far exceeded the manufacturer's recommendations. Larry, my buddy Eddie (another fireman and a good friend) and I held our collective breath as the wheels on the trailer turned. The axles groaned but the trailer remained intact.

Catastrophe nearly struck when we climbed a small rise and the weight of the shed shifted, causing the hydraulics leveling the trailer hitch to rise precariously. Eddie and Larry intervened. The combined weight of my two pals standing on the trailer's tongue defeated gravity. What can I say? Firemen are well fed.

After unloading the shed at the building site, it remained suspended on timbers for a week while I constructed a new plywood floor. Once the floor was complete, I lowered the structure into place with the jacks and secured the floor to the frame. Dylan and I then painted the exterior walls white. I added a screen door and covered the wall studs with cheap chipboard and built two small bunk beds into the rear wall. When I was finished, despite my meager skills, the place wasn't half bad.

The relocation of the pump house started a new tradition. Beginning in fourth grade, and continuing every year until high school, Dylan invited a select group of his buddies to stay overnight in the shack on the last day of school. My wife René and I supplied soda, hot dogs, chips, and makings for s'mores. We also monitored the festivities from a distance.

Year after year, the boys stayed up late watching the embers of a campfire, playing youthful games of tag, hide-and-seek, and capture the flag long into the night. At times, they took excursions to visit the abandoned cabins at the end of Knudsen Road, all the while listening to tales of murder and mayhem centered on a mythical old man who butchered the children of Fredenberg. Dylan's invented legend still lives on in the form of a

trail sign on one of my cross-country ski trails located on our
property:

Old Man Farley's Trail.

The ultimate highlight of these gatherings was the
ceremonial burning of homework brought by the boys; by Jake,
Ian, Ben, Brandon, Frankie, Cory, and a handful of others who
stayed overnight at the shack after the last day of school. Never
having been invited to witness the boys' celebration, I can only
imagine the theology these festivities involved. I am certain that,
unlike Lenten and Good Friday services, where the pallor of
death and suffering compels solemnity, the boys' celebrations
mirrored Easter's joy: joy caused by watching schoolwork burn.
More than this, I cannot say.

Things, of course, change. Dylan and his pals outgrew the shack.
Girls, not ghost stories, became the primary focus of late night
conversations. Jake's family moved. Their new home came
equipped with a guest cottage. The cottage, which became, by
default, "The Shack", has a loft, electricity, and heat. Girls were
close by. The boys could listen to "tunes".

A final end-of-the-school-year- gathering on our place
occurred at the conclusion of my son's ninth grade year. The
boys had grown too large to fit comfortably in the old pump
house so Dylan borrowed our family tent and pitched it
alongside the Cloquet River. The boys camped near the
disintegrating log cabin Dylan claims was once home to Old
Man Farley, the butcher of Fredenberg.

At least not every dream of youth is forgotten.

Harry's Last Ride

The sun sits diffusely in a June sky broken by innocent clouds. René is looking for me but I'm hiding from her: I'm rigging Harry's saddle and reins. I hear her voice calling me but I ignore her. June days like this one; sunny and bright with a slight wind and no insects are rare in Northeastern Minnesota. I know we're nearing the end of our time in our old farmhouse. I know I'm nearing the end of my relationship with my gelding Harry. I want one last ride on him before he's sold.

"Mark, what do you think you're doing?" René asks when she finds me.

I pretend I don't hear my wife as I mount my horse.

"Mark, are you listening?"

"I'm taking Harry out for one last ride."

"We need to get things packed. I need you to watch Jack."

"The things will still be here when I get back."

With words of protest stinging my ears, I move out. Muscles ripple under the horse's roan skin as the gelding breaks into an easy trot. There's a familiarity to his stride. I leave my wife and don't speculate how she'll deal with me when I return. For now, I'm lost to her and to the rest of humanity.

The animal hesitates, as he always does, at the Taft Road Bridge. His reluctance to trust the bridge with our weight, with our lives, hasn't been cured by repetition.

"Come on boy," I urge, gently digging my tennis shoes into his ribs.

He begins to canter sideways across the bridge deck. His nostrils flare as he examines the water flowing below us. Like everything else on this ride, this is a last; the last time he will likely cross this bridge.

A low, grassy bank defines the north side of the river. Aspen and birch grow thick amongst the saw grass and cattails. Our neighbors have cut a riding trail along the plateau. A breeze tickles the aspen leaves around us. Harry responds to my lead and ducks into the woods. As I ride along the riverbank, I observe our home and outbuildings; our finely manicured lawn; our years of work and dedication to a place; from a distance. Sweat beads on Harry's neck and slides down his skin.

We negotiate our way around deadfalls. The gelding hesitates at a small stream crossing the trail. The rivulet's banks are soft and muddy. I've learned that not all horses will cross suspect ground. Harry will do it for me. Not out of courage but out of trust; trust that I will not ask him to do something that endangers him. He dances a bit as I urge him forward and then, with one mighty leap, he clears the damp spot and moves on.

I loosen my grip on the reins to allow the horse to gallop up a steep slope. His mane, tinged with gold and highlighted by the intermittent rays of the sun, trails his effort and touches my face. At the top of the hill, the horse settles into a walk. His breathing is strong and defiant. The path meanders along the top of the river bluff through balsam, spruce, aspen, and birch. At intervals through the trees I can see our big pasture, the site where our new home will be built. Today, there is nothing on the pasture but grass and the promise of a new beginning.

The trail narrows and then plummets towards another creek. Someone has placed a crude log bridge, perhaps ten feet long and four feet wide, over a culvert at the bottom of the gully. Harry walks across the logs without fear. I feel his muscles tighten as his hooves dig into the dirt of the incline on the far side of the stream. I ease up on the reins, allowing him to bolt up the hill. At the top of the slope, I urge him to stop by applying steady, gentle pressure to the bit.

"Good boy," I whisper to him as I stroke his mane and pat his flank.

I lift my bush hat off my head to untangle the chinstrap. Sitting in the quiet of the forest, I wipe the sweat away from my hairline. The wind picks up and cools my face. Songbirds flit and glide on the breeze, serenading us in cautious jubilation. We ride on. We cross the remains of an old farm field. Harry and I wade through timothy that hasn't been cut in generations. There's no road into this isolated pasture. As we cross the grass, the heads of each plant swaying in the nervous wind, I wonder who first cultivated this plot. The trail narrows down to a single lane. I know, from prior rides that this path ends next to an abandoned hunting cabin sitting a stone's throw from the river.

There have been rumors of a new owner of the hunting cabin: gossip about a developer who wants to build apartments on the site, or, more recently, stories that a rich couple wants to build their dream castle along this stretch of the Cloquet River. The talk disappoints me because at one time, I tried to buy the parcel to keep it wild.

As we approach the cabin, I find the trail blocked by aspen trees felled by an ax. We leave the trail. The horse selects a route through the forest. We rejoin the path next to the once-abandoned structure. Newly peeled aspen logs, obviously cut to serve as roof supports, lean against the walls of the cabin. Though the building appears decayed and suspect, the evidence of recent activity foreshadows an intention to claim and occupy the place. I coax the animal past the shack and down the riverbank.

The big red horse raises and lowers his legs against the weight of the current. As Harry's hooves burst free of the river's hold, water trails from his fetlocks and create tiny rainbows against the sun. I feel our combined weight press into the Cloquet's sandy bottom as we move upriver.

I neck rein Harry into the main channel. We negotiate large stones and boulders. Every so often Harry catches a hoof on an unseen rock and stumbles but never falls. His ears begin to twitch in anticipation of home. Our new pole barn, its yellow metal skin brightened by the afternoon sun, comes into focus. The channel deepens. Only the horse's neck and head remain dry. Black water laps at my thighs and I wonder what it would be like to swim on Harry. I've never done that with a horse and I do not get the chance to do so on this ride. The water level recedes as we approach the old farmhouse. Harry prances impatiently in preparation for a run to the barn but I hold him back.

Horse and rider clamber up the bank. Water slides off leather. My horse of eight years, my friend, pulls against the bit, seeking permission to gallop. Knowing that Harry has given me all that I ever wanted from a mount, I loosen the reins and let the gelding break into a run one last time.

An Old Mantle for a New House

Alvin Douglas wasn't a rich man. Successful, not wealthy, was how he saw himself. How others in St. Paul, Minnesota saw him was problematic. After all, it was the Great Depression and he was a banker. Whether he was a fair-minded man or a tyrant mattered very little in the whirlwind of financial disaster surrounding the farm economy of the Midwest. It was Alvin's job to foreclose on agricultural loans for the Farmer and Merchant's Bank of West St. Paul. Douglas's job was a thankless task even during the best of times.

Oliver Krupp had been a good farmer. Before the drought, before the dry winds from the plains seared his corn and dried up the watering holes used by his cattle on the farm he owned in Rock County in the southeastern corner of Minnesota, Oliver and his family made a living off the land. But the winds, the sun, the lack of rainfall, and a corresponding lack of available money at the local bank forced Oliver out of his ponderous, careful ways. The events of 1932 forced him to take risks with his cattle, with his crops, with his land. Those risks involved going to St. Paul to ask for a loan, a loan that allowed Farmer and Merchant's Bank to acquire a mortgage against the Krupp place.

"I'm sorry, Oliver," Alvin Douglas related as he stood in front of the stark white façade of the Krupp homestead. "There's nothing else I can do. You're sixteen months past due on your loan. I've given you all the rope I can. The board is forcing me to call the note, to foreclose on the mortgage," the banker said in a weary voice.

Krupp stared hard at the banker from beneath the brim of his brown felt hat. The farmer was deliberate and methodical by nature. Those traits served him well when the economy of the 20's was booming but spelled doom in the uncertainty of the Depression when quick action was often the difference between success and failure.

"Here's the thing," Oliver said, his voice parched and dry from the autumn wind. "Next spring my cattle will be fat and

197

ready to butcher on account of the grain my cousin Albert give me. Albert's place went belly up. But before the bank came out, he sold me his grain crop at a bargain. That's what'll carry me through this tough spell."

The banker gazed out across the flatness of the place, seemingly looking for a distant mesa to concentrate his eyes upon. But there were no mesas: He was in southwestern Minnesota, not New Mexico. He wished he were in New Mexico. Alvin Douglas did not want to be here, telling Krupp that the farmer's life, his farm, was going to be taken away by economic forces beyond their control.

"I'd like to accommodate you, Oliver," Douglas offered, "but my hands are tied. I came out to see you as a courtesy before the sheriff serves you with papers. There's nothing I can do to stop the process."

Krupp's huge hands balled into tight fists. The farmer raised his eyes against a forlorn sky. The banker sensed his adversary was near the point of crossing some deeply drawn Christian line. Douglas readied himself for the blows, which he sincerely believed were justified as an attack upon the financiers, the bosses, of whom he was a representative. But the farmer made no move towards the banker.

"How long do we have?" Krupp asked in a defeated tone as he returned his hands to the pockets of his overalls.

"I'm not sure. That's something I leave to the lawyers."

The farmer's eyes drew inward. The deep brown of Krupp's irises became lost behind fatigue. Knowing there was little more to say, little more to comprehend, the farmer turned and climbed the stairs leading to the covered front porch of the farmhouse. Alvin Douglas watched the man's retreat with a sense of pity and shame knowing full well that Krupp would accept neither from any man.

Inside the Krupp home, a fierce fire burned in a brick fireplace. Three children played on the floor within the embrace of the heat. Jonathan, the youngest Krupp child, pushed a tin tractor across a freshly varnished floor. The five-year-old made mechanized noises as the wheels of the toy creaked over smooth wood. Hilda and Oliver Jr., the Krupp's twelve-year-old twins, sat cross-legged around a board game throwing dice. Mrs. Krupp was upstairs, pale and weak from the effects of fighting the flu, moisture dripping noxiously from her limp blond hair as she fought illness. She was asleep, caught in the shallow slumber of recovery, unaware of the pending demise of the farm.

Oliver poured himself a cup of sour coffee and walked quietly into the living room.

"Hello father," the twins said simultaneously before returning their attention to the board game.

"Hello children," Krupp answered dryly, sitting uncomfortably in a store-bought chair, an oak rocking chair crafted in the Mission style.

"Daddy!" the smallest Krupp exclaimed as he leaped onto his father's lap.

The farmer studied the golden tones of the oak mantle surrounding the hazel colored brick of the fireplace. Quarter-sawn columns adorned the piece, revealing the wood's complex grain. The mantle was new: It replaced a simple pine timber above the firebox and was the piece of craftsmanship on the place that Krupp was most proud of. It had taken him two months of careful work to design and build the mantle; two months of painstaking effort that relieved, for a time, the feeling of impending disaster brought about by the decline of the farm.

Oliver Krupp cradled his son in thick arms and studied the fire. He wondered how his family would respond when he told them that they were moving to Minneapolis. His sister Adeline had a house near Lake Harriet on the trolley line. That's where they would live: They'd leave the land, the sacred presence of the country for the uncertain chaos of the city.

I apply thin stain to wood, rubbing the liquid deep into freshly sanded oak with a rag. There's no heat in our new house, a structure built only a few hundred yards downstream from our old Sears farmhouse. Our animals are gone save for our two Labradors. The horses were sold so that we could move to the city while our new home was being built. Wiring, plumbing, and fir studs stand exposed as I work on the antique mantle that will define the great room of our new house. The stain I'm applying accentuates the burl of the quarter-sawn oak. I marvel at the beauty in the wood.

Outside, slick sheets of autumnal rain spatter the ground. The storm's barrage beats a consistent rhythm. The weather's cadence is at odds with a folk song playing over the radio. I pause from my labor to think about the carpenter who built our mantle. I begin to spin a yarn in my head about a man named Oliver Krupp. My sense of history ties the Mission style of the piece I'm working on to the early 1930's. I imagine a farmer, on a distant plot of land, cutting down an old oak, planing the wood, creating the mantle I'm refinishing. Myth? Perhaps. But it's my job as a writer to uncover the truth, or the possibility of a truth, layer by detailed layer so that the reader will understand. And when, as here, the people who know the truth are dead, it's my obligation to create a plausible substitute for the truth.

Oliver Krupp is such a creation. I'll think of his children, the children of the Great Depression, whenever I build a fire in our new house.

Jack's Big Ride

It was one of the few days this winter when riding a snowmobile was possible. Little snow had fallen but it was still winter: We were out of wood for the fireplace and our second son needed to get back in the good graces of his parents.

"Dylan," I called out as the teenager slept in, "we need firewood."

Non-compliant mumbling emanated from the basement of our new house.

"If you want to go to Crosby for your hockey tournament," I yelled, holding the upcoming weekend over his head, "you better get outside and stack some wood."

"Alright."

A few minutes later, I heard the single cylinder of our 1989 Ski-Doo Citation snowmobile cough. The sound of the machine filled the quiet stillness of the late afternoon. I walked to the front window. My eyes followed the progress of the old machine as it carved a path through newly fallen snow. Dylan sat comfortably on the worn vinyl seat of the snowmobile with Jack, his two-year-old brother, between his legs. Behind the snowmobile, an empty red plastic slider attached to the Citation by a white towrope bounced from side to side as the machine roared down the driveway towards our woodpile.

A couple of minutes later I heard the sound of aspen and birch being stacked in the wood rack on the front porch. I opened the door. Jack sat contentedly on the seat of the Citation, hands firmly gripping the handlebars as he pretended to drive. The engine was turned off. A helmet covered most of Jack's face. Ski goggles protected his eyes.

"How's it going?" I asked Dylan as he staggered up the front stairs under the weight of an armload of firewood.

"Fine. How much wood do you want?"

"Fill 'er up. You can leave the rest of the pile out there until we need more."

Dylan, never one to waste words, nodded towards his younger brother.

"Jack likes the snowmobile."

"I can see that."

Satisfied that the work was getting done, I closed the door and settled into my recliner in front of our entertainment center. The latest Crosby, Stills, Nash, and Young album spun in the CD player filling the room with tight harmonies. Outside, the sun sank beneath the rim of the woods. There were only moments of twilight left in the day.

"What's Dylan doing in the trees?" my wife asked a few minutes later as she looked out a window in our great room.

I left my chair and joined René. Down the steep bank of our field's only hill, past a small stand of aspen, a single red light, the taillight of the Citation, glowed weakly from inside a tangle of black alders.

"That idiot," I moaned. "How could he get stuck in the only trees on the pasture?"

"You better go help him. It'll be dark soon."

"No way. If he's stupid enough to drive into the woods he can get out himself."

"He can't do it alone."

"I'm going," I muttered, pulling on my well-worn leather boots and a quilted Hermantown Hockey jacket before walking out the door.

There was scant light as I shuffled through fresh snow towards the idling Ski-Doo. As I approached the snowmobile, it became painfully obvious that the Citation was entangled in brush.

"How in the world did you manage to find the only trees for miles around?"

Dylan stood up from behind the buried vehicle, extended his gloved index finger, and pointed convincingly at his baby brother, a tiny bit of a thing no more than waist high, standing quietly off to one side.

"No way."

A suggestion of a smile broke across Jack's lips. The toddler spoke with the clear and obvious directness of a two-year-old:

202

"Jack goes fast."

Dylan gestured east, towards the pile of firewood remaining to be hauled.

"I bent down to put a piece in the slider. He was right next to me. The next thing I know, the Ski-Doo is flying across the field with Jack holding the throttle wide open. "

My second son smiled with pride at his brother's antics.

"I ran after him but he piled into the trees before I could stop him."

"Did he fall off?"

"Nope. He was still sitting on the machine with the engine running when I got here."

I positioned myself in front of the snowmobile and used all of my leg strength to free the sled. Dylan helped pull the machine into open pasture. A slight moon rose behind us. The teen gathered Jack in his arms and lowered the infant onto the Ski-Doo's seat. My youngest son's eyes twinkled.

"Jack goes fast in the trees."

I watched the Citation plow towards the pale lights of our new house at a deliberately cautious pace, leaving me to ponder how to explain Jack's new found interest in motor sports to his mother.

Driving Too Slow

I'm painting the walls of my wife's art studio. I hear the telephone ring.

"Dad," Christian shouts from the kitchen, "the phone's for you."

"Tell them I'm busy," I yell back.

I'm annoyed that progress is being impeded by interruption after interruption. I took a week off work to get projects done in our new home. I've accomplished little during my time off.

"It's Aunt Susanne," Chris says in an imploring tone. "She needs to talk to you."

My third son appears with the remote phone and hands it to me before I can object.

Outside, it's a dismal day. There's virtually no snow and little prospect of winter. I accept the phone and take note of my downhill skis leaning in one corner of the room. I haven't used them all year. There's been no time and no snow. It's the first winter I can remember that I haven't skied at least once.

"Mark," Susanne relates, "Auntie Ann isn't expected to make it. Wayne and I stopped up there yesterday. If you want to say goodbye, you'll have to do it today."

Auntie Ann is actually my Great Aunt, the last of my maternal grandfather's siblings. She's lived her entire life between the Iron Range towns of Biwabik and Aurora-Hoyt Lakes. She raised two boys to adulthood, took in my Great Uncle Stutz (Steven) who never married, when she was widowed back in the 1950"'s, and has been a loving aunt, mother, sister, and grandmother. Stutz's passing a year or so ago took a horrible toll on her. She's not been the same since.

"Okay. Maybe I can get up there," I say with strained credulity.

I hang up and begin to consider what the old woman dying in the nursing home in Hoyt Lakes has meant to me. Wasn't it Aunt Ann who, when I needed a recipe for roast turkey and stuffing for a stag party almost twenty-five years ago,

204

patiently explained over the telephone what needed to be done with the bird? And when I couldn't get the stuffing right, wasn't she the one who told me to bring the ingredients over to her and she'd stuff the bird for me?

Wasn't it Auntie Ann who always had a sandwich and a beer ready for me when I stopped in unannounced? Wasn't it Auntie Ann who never forgot an important event in my life (confirmation, graduations, marriage, baby showers); who always had time for me even though our blood relationship is fairly distant?

I owe her more than feeling irritated by a phone call.

"I'm going to drive up and see Auntie Ann," I tell Dylan and Chris as I wash my hands in the kitchen sink. "She's not going to make it through the day." I look at the clock. It's 12:15 in the afternoon. "I should be back by five."

I leave the older boys in charge of Jack and climb into my van for the trip up Highway No. 4. Clouds hang heavy over the field surrounding our house. The water of the Cloquet River flows lazily to the west as I pull away from our place. No. 4 is one of my favorite drives. My buddy Jeff has a farm up towards Whiteface; the location of youthful efforts to build a log cabin. We succeeded in a fashion, though the building has long since fallen in upon itself. Driving the narrow two-lane highway north from Island Lake allows me to recall a past where the memories are always artificially pleasant.

At County 16, I take a right, then a left onto 99 and head towards Aurora-Hoyt Lakes. I think about my Great Aunt and the life she has led. Her father, mother, and my grandfather immigrated to this country through Ellis Island at the beginning of the 20th century. There was work for immigrants from Slovenia in the forests and mines of northeastern Minnesota. There was freedom from the prejudices of the Austrian Empire. Auntie Ann was born in this hardscrabble mining country and fell in love, married, and buried her husband and all her siblings here.

A few miles outside of Aurora, the sun breaks through the overcast sky. The Lumina's engine purrs effortlessly as I pass old farmsteads: the remains of the toils of the Finns who tried to farm rocky, stubborn soil. Here and there, a brave soul still raises

205

a steer or two. I see no milk cows. I see no tilled fields. Nature has reclaimed most of what the Finns tried to tame.

I swing into the White Community Hospital parking lot, turn off the engine, and pocket the keys. The building is familiar. Uncle Stutz spent his last days in this place, as did his other sister, my Great Aunt Mary. I visited both of them here. Even in the depths of dementia, during the middle of my campaign to become a judge, Stutz remembered his nephew "Markie"; someone he saw but once or twice a year. That was true until my last visit when his mind would not allow him to recall my name.

I stop at the information desk just inside the door and ask for Ann's room. The attendant directs me down the hallway. I walk the final steps to my Great Aunt realizing that she likely won't recognize me; knowing that she's probably unconscious. It doesn't matter. The visit is as much for me as it is for her.

Arriving at the nurses' station, I note that the place smells fresh and clean, not at all like other nursing homes I've visited.

"I'm here to see Ann Sale," I tell a LPN manning the desk.

I sense something is amiss when the LPN looks over my shoulder and calls for the RN down the hall.

"This gentleman is here to see Ann."

A woman about my age, dressed in a dark blue slacks and blouse, straightens a stethoscope around her neck and advances briskly down the hall towards me.

"And you are…?" she asks politely.

"Ann's nephew from Duluth," I mumble.

"I'm sorry. Your aunt passed away around 12:15. Is there anything I can do?"

"Were her sons here?"

"Yes. They left about a half-hour ago."

"Thanks. I'll stop by and visit them."

I don't ask to see Ann. She isn't here. There's no point in my looking at something that isn't her. I make my way into Hoyt Lakes and stop to visit my cousin Johnny. Over coffee, we tell stories about his mom, marveling at the patience and kindness she shared with us during the ninety years of her life. Silently, I ask her to forgive my slow driving.

A Walk in the Woods

I looked at a wall in our new home and realized that I'd missed quite a few spots when I touched up the paint. The realization shouldn't have been stressful: After all, it was only one wall. At most, it should take half an hour to fully repaint the surface. But it was more than just one wall. There's oak trim that needs to be stained and varnished. I thought I had it all done before the carpenters tacked the trim in place. I was wrong. We were short on the original order. To move in on time, the workers had to put up unstained trim. Small and seemingly inconsequential, the staining loomed larger and larger as I aggregated all of the tasks left for me to complete. Like the windows: The trim around them had been stained and sealed but the windows themselves, constructed of clean white fir, hadn't been stained. Neither had the French doors. Then there are the interior pine doors: I was only able to get one coat of polyurethane on them. I need to buff down the first layer of varnish and apply another coat. On twenty-four doors.

"I'm taking a walk," I said to my wife. "This place is overwhelming me."

"Why don't you do that?" René responded as she chopped carrots at the kitchen counter.

I pulled on my well-worn Sorels and bundled up against an unremarkable January afternoon.

"Here Maggie, here Sam," I yelled as I walked down our long gravel driveway. My voice was solitary and harsh against the quiet of the river valley. Since June, our dogs have lived with our new neighbors, the Kaases's, in our old farmhouse. It's apparent that the dogs would rather live with our neighbors in familiar surroundings than join us at our new home. Every time I let the dogs out, they bolt towards the old place, returning only when offered a meal.

Sam responded first. I watched his yellow torso bound across the thin white blanket of winter defining the distance between past and present. Maggie, fat and lazy from too much food and attention, waddled slowly across the pasture. The yellow dog met me where a whitened hayfield intersects a row of transplanted Norway pines. Maggie appeared a few seconds later with her tongue hanging from effort.

"Good girl," I praised, scratching Maggie's ample belly as she wiggled on her back in the snow. "Good boy," I said to Sam, patting his corn-colored neck.

It was nearly evening when we crossed another field and linked up with my ski trail. The dogs walked in front of me on the narrow path. In the distance, the mournful wail of a Duluth, Winnipeg, and Pacific locomotive sounded as the train crossed a bridge over the Cloquet River nine miles away. If the dogs heard the train's call, they ignored it. I noted that someone had spent considerable time removing deadfall from my trail. Recently trimmed balsam bore evidence of a chainsaw at work. To the south, the distinctive rumble of snowmobiles on Fish Lake disturbed the forest's silence. I stopped and listened to the constant whine of the machines three or four miles distant, understanding that the lake was the only place the machines could safely run due to the disappointing snowfall.

I stopped to watch the black water of the river from a folding chair that someone had abandoned next to a declining cabin. The chair's webbing was fragile from decay. My dogs pranced and snuffled, looking for mice and moles under the snow. In a carefully orchestrated arrival, night covered the river valley. It was time to head back.

My boots shuffled through new snow. I kept my eyes focused on light emanating from our house. Though I didn't see anyone inside, I imagined each member of my family occupied with some pedestrian task. The dogs dashed across the white pasture, their paws kicking up tufts of snow as they broke for home.

"How was your walk?" my wife asked as she opened the front door and stepped on to the front porch to greet me.

"Just what the doctor ordered."

"Wish I could've come with."

"Me too."

The smell of pot roast baking in the oven welcomed me as I climbed the stairs towards René.

The Toilet Bowl

It's pitch black as I drive north on Highway 53 towards Hibbing, Minnesota. Somewhere to the east, below the ridgeline of Lake Superior's hills, the sun searches for open sky. "West Coast Live" echoes from the radio of my Lumina van as tires slap road. Dylan, my second son, the reason I'm up before dawn on a quiet Sunday morning, leans against the passenger door, sound asleep.

Two days earlier. René was invited to the dedication of an alcohol treatment facility in Virginia, another town on Minnesota's Iron Range. She's an employee of Range Mental Health and the building, named in honor of United States District Court Judge Donovan Frank, is run by her employer. She asked if I wanted to attend the ceremony with her.

"You know Judge Frank," René said, recalling that we went to his investiture ceremony at Hamline University.

"Sure," I replied. "We worked together on "Lawyers on the Line" on Channel Eight. He's a great guy. I'd love to go."

Because of our work schedules and a plethora of weekend athletic tournaments involving our sons, the only way we both could attend was for each of us to drive separately to Virginia. Christian, our twelve-year-old had a basketball tournament in Two Harbors the next day. Dylan had a 9:00pm hockey game in Hibbing that night. Someone needed to be recruited to watch Jack, our two-year-old. We're much too astute as parents to try to bring a toddler to a formal dinner. Been there, done that.

"Mom," I said on the telephone a couple of days before the dinner, "can you watch Jack Friday evening? René and I have a chance to go to a shindig on the Range."

"Sure. He can stay the night."

I assured Grandma Barb that Jack didn't need to spend the evening, that René would pick him up after the dinner.

On Friday, I came home from work, picked up Dylan, his gear, and my own clothes and essentials. My plan was to

209

drive to Hibbing, drop Dylan off at the Memorial Building and then make it to the Coates Hotel in downtown Virginia in time for the dinner. René was home, getting dressed. Jack was sleeping. Dylan had his hockey bag, his uniform bag, and his homework packed.

The lights of Hibbing welcomed us as we drove in on Highway No. 169 from Virginia. It had been a few years since I'd been at the Memorial Building. Playing against type, I stopped to ask for directions at a corner gas station. Driving down the residential streets of Hibbing, the arched superstructure of the Memorial Building loomed above the town's streetlights. We arrived right on schedule. I handed my son a ten-dollar bill for dinner and told him I'd be back to watch his game.

"We'll check into the motel when I get back."

"OK," he responded, making his way towards the ice rink under a heavy load.

I met my wife. We sat with some of my judicial colleagues and their wives from the Range. During after-dinner conversation, I noted that it was 8:45pm. Dylan's game was set to begin in fifteen minutes. I said my good-byes and kissed René on the cheek.

"I'll call you in the morning."

"I'll be in Two Harbors."

"I'll call you on your cell phone."

"Don't forget."

"I won't."

Traveling at sixty-five-miles-per-hour wouldn't get me to the game on time but I reasoned that I'd make most of the second and all of the third period if I drove the speed limit.

The parking lot at the Memorial Building was packed with cars. Something was wrong. It was doubtful that a Bantam B hockey tournament, even on the Iron Range, could generate such interest. Walking into the arena, my suspicions were confirmed.

The stands were full: standing room only. Two very fast and very talented high school teams raced up and down slick ice. The distant rafters resonated cheers. I looked into the stands for any sign that Dylan's team was seated together, waiting to get on the ice. I saw no one I recognized.

"Excuse me officer," I asked a policeman working the crowd. "Is there another ice rink in town?"

"About six or seven blocks east, over by the fairgrounds."

"I'm looking for my son. He's a bantam and he's in a tournament."

"That's where he is. The tournament is over there tonight and tomorrow, then over here on Sunday."

"Thanks."

I glanced at the clock on the wall as I raced out of the lobby. It was nearly 10:00pm. There would be little of the game left. But was Dylan there? Maybe he'd hitched a ride to our hotel with someone. I wasn't nervous: He's a big boy, capable of taking care of himself. It was obvious I'd left him at the wrong place. At least he was in the right town.

Walking into the fairground's ice shelter, I saw familiar faces. My eyes scanned the ice. No. 18 lined up a Shattuck player and leveled the kid with a check. I turned to one of the other dads from our team.

"Do you have any idea how Dylan got here?"

"Didn't he come with you?"

"To Hibbing. I left him at the Memorial Building five hours ago. I'm trying to find out how he made it here."

"Beats me."

The Hawks lost. Dylan and his pal Ryan were sharing a room with me at the Motel 6. On the way to the motel, Dylan explained that he'd asked a coach from the Hibbing high school team where the bantams were playing. The gentleman gave Dylan a lift.

It's Sunday morning. My ninth grader is snoring loudly in the front seat of the van. We're on our way back to Hibbing, this time to play a game in the Memorial Building. Normally, I'd be excited about watching my son skate. Not today. Because Dylan's team lost twice during the tournament, he's scheduled to play at

8:00am on Sunday morning in the "Toilet Bowl": the last place game against International Falls.

I-Falls is easily the worst team we've faced all year. It doesn't matter. Our kids play without emotion. There's no incentive for them to do well. It's a shame to play such poor hockey in such a storied arena but that's what happens.

My son and I catch breakfast at McDonald's on the outskirts of Hibbing. During the drive home, I listen to a Vikings game on AM radio, hoping that the Minnesota team gives St. Louis a battle. For one half of football, my hopes are met. During the second half of the contest, the Rams demolish the Vikings. I turn the game off and concentrate on the barren January marsh and forest we pass along Highway No. 7 on the way home.

Our Dad Isn't Sam Cook
(Part One)

(Sam Cook is a nationally known writer from Duluth, Minnesota. Nearly every time Sam sets foot in the north woods, his adventures turn to gold. This set of stories paints a very different picture of a wilderness trip into the Boundary Waters Canoe Area in northern Minnesota.)

I planned our Memorial Day fishing expedition to Perent Lake over the past winter. I used the BWCA's website (everyone, even the wilderness, has a website these days) to make reservations for a trip down Hog Creek into Perent Lake. Matt, my eldest son, would be back from college sometime before Memorial Day. The trip would reunite all of the Munger boys with their parents. Right off, my concept of "family togetherness" met resistance.

"You can't be serious. I'm not taking a baby in diapers into the woods," René said.

My wife's opposition to my plan surprised me. When Christian, our twelve-year-old, was an infant, we made a similar trip into Perent Lake: Of course, we were younger then.

"You can take the older boys. Jack and I'll stay home and fish."

I intended to inventory my fishing equipment, camping equipment and the like well before the month of May rolled around. Other things got in the way. Like Opening Fishing. Like teaching confirmation class. Like laying sod around our new house. A week before the scheduled trip, I was asking myself significant questions.

I wonder if the tent leaks.
Do I have enough fishing rods?
Do the lantern and the cook stove still work?

During 1999, we moved to town while our new home was being built. Our camping and fishing equipment had not been used for a while and I was uncertain as to its condition. But I knew one thing: We had no sleeping bags of merit. I quickly computed the minimum I'd have to spend to purchase four serviceable bags. Not the fancy mummy bags that Sam Cook and other professionals swear by for their winter excursions into the Canadian taiga; just four simple bags that would afford modest protection. I figured at least twenty-five bucks a piece.

Sunday. I'm rummaging through the garage. I find I'm down to two decent fishing rods, not counting the one I bought René last Mother's Day. I know she'll want to toss a line in the Cloquet River over Memorial weekend. I don't dare requisition her rod and reel.

"That's another sixty bucks," I moan. Expensive stuff, equipment like professional fishermen use would cost me hundreds of dollars. I cringe at what my wife's reaction would be if I spent that kind of money on fishing gear destined to be stepped on, thrown into the water, or left behind on some portage.

I find a Duluth Pack. I locate a couple of duffel bags with shoulder straps from my days in the Army. I retrieve my father-in-law's duffel bag dating from WWII. The mice have chewed big holes through the canvas of his old bag. We'll need another pack because we don't have enough bags to carry the equipment and food four people will need for four days and nights in the woods.

A serviceable tent proves to be my biggest challenge. We have two tents. My wife doesn't understand why we have two. She would never understand why we need a third one. I try to envision my sons and I crammed into a two-person tent. Our five-person tent is only suitable for backyard tenting: not real camping. The last time we used our big family tent, my sister-in-law Colleen slept with our two eldest boys on Sawbill Lake in the BWCA. It poured for two days. Their stuff, including their sleeping bags, floated inside the shelter. René and I remained dry in our two-person dome tent.

"Hundred bucks minimum for a decent four-person dome tent," I muse. "This is really starting to add up."

Tuesday afternoon. I purchase two rods and reels at Gander Mountain. I buy myself the cheapest sleeping pad the store sells. I'd like one of the self-inflating models. My budget doesn't allow it. We had four pads but during my inventory, I found we were down to three.

"Dylan, do you know where the fourth sleeping pad went?"

"It was in my fort the last time I saw it. I think the mice chewed it up."

Sure enough, a trip to Dylan's shack confirms my son's memory. Little bits of blue foam litter the interior of the structure. I'm forced to buy a low budget replacement for the destroyed pad.

The local Gander Mountain store has decent sleeping bags on sale. I buy four, keeping my cost below the magic $100.00 ceiling. I also purchase two disposable propane tanks, mantles, and a glass globe for our Coleman lantern, and batteries for three flashlights.

"How much is all of this costing?" my wife asks when I return.

"Not that much."

"I hope you're watching the check book."

"I am."

"It sure looks like you're spending a lot."

"At least I'm not buying a tent."

Wednesday evening, waiting for Dylan to finish driver's education, Chris and I stop at Super One to grocery shop. We race through the aisles filling a grocery cart with boxes of Rice a Roni, Shore Lunch, Kraft Macaroni and Cheese, and other essentials. The bill at the cash register gives me a headache. I remember going to the Boundary Waters with my high school buddies. The whole trip, gas, bait and food included used to run less than twenty bucks a person. My stomach turns over.

At home, I carefully pack all of the items according to my meal plan. Jack scurries around, stealing packages and hiding them. I catch him with the disposable camera I bought before he hides it in a desk drawer.

"Jack, Dad needs that."

"Jack take a picture."

"Not now. Dad needs to pack the camera."

With the food tucked into the Duluth Pack, I organize our fishing gear. In the midst of trying to place line on one of my new reels, the entire reel disintegrates in my hands. I mutter some not so nice words under my breath.

"What's wrong, Dad?"

"Nothing, Chris. I'll have to bring this reel back."

Thursday. Departure day. Both Dylan and Chris are in school. I can't find the maps used on prior trips to Perent Lake. Matt watches Jack while I run errands. On my way back to town, I make a decision.

We need a new tent.

I stop at Wal-Mart and buy the cheapest four-person dome tent in the store. I return the broken reel to Gander, pick out a replacement, and get a five-dollar credit. I feel lucky. I head downtown to buy maps.

"We're phasing out our maps. What we've got is in the cabinet over there."

I'm at the place where I always buy my BWCA maps. The maps I need are missing.

"You could try Gander Mountain."

Why didn't I think of that?

I walk to Minnesota Surplus, a few doors down, muttering the whole way. I'm in search of a cheap alternative to a Duluth Pack. The surplus store has surplus duffel bags for fifteen dollars. At that price, I can buy ten of the rugged sacks for the cost of one Duluth Pack. I buy five. I look up and see a display.

We have McKenzie Maps.

"So you have McKenzie maps?"

"Sure."

"I wonder why the place next door wanted to send me to Gander Mountain."

"They should know better. I send them enough business."

Refreshed by a warm sun, I approach my vehicle only to find a parking ticket waiting for me. I rip the citation from

216

beneath the wiper blade and shove it into my pocket. Then, on the way up the hill, the van's voltage meter goes berserk: All of the needles of the dashboard gauges thrash wildly inside their housings. I sense that my alternator is about to die. I detour to Downtown Service, a couple of blocks away.

My mechanic Woody is a fisherman. He understands my predicament. It's nearly noon. I have to run up to Tofte, more than an hour away on the North Shore of Lake Superior, to pick up our BWCA entry permit and be back to load the kids by 5:00pm.

"If you leave the van here, I can put in a new alternator."

I look around the place. There are ten cars with appointments waiting to be repaired.

Nice guy.

"I need to get Matt before I drive up to Tofte. I can have it back here by 1:30. Is that enough time?"

"That'll work. Just don't turn the car off. You're down to eleven volts. It won't start again."

Back at home I load two canoes on a snowmobile trailer. Without thinking, I turn the van off. It takes twenty minutes to jumpstart the vehicle using Matt's little four-cylinder Mazda. We drop the van at Woody's and race up the North Shore in the Mazda. Jack contentedly munches on McDonald's food as he watches our frenzied pace from the vantage point of his safety seat.

At the Tofte Ranger Station, I get another surprise.

"You can't go into the BWCA until tomorrow. Enter before midnight, and you're in violation," a Ranger explains.

I'm sure my reservation was supposed to begin today. Too tired to complain, I accept the permit and leave.

217

Our Dad Isn't Sam Cook
(Part Two)

Our family's Transport van sits in the Isabella Lake parking lot, the ultimate destination of our four-day canoe trip down Hog Creek. It's 9:00pm as my Chevrolet Lumina van bounces along Forest Service Road No. 354 towards the creek with my three oldest sons, me, our gear, and a snowmobile trailer loaded with two canoes, in tow.

"What the heck is that?" Matt yells as a dark shape bursts onto the roadway in front of us.

"A moose."

"A bull moose," Dylan observes. "He's got a small rack."

The animal lopes straight down the middle of the forest service road. For a couple hundred yards, the animal's hooves slash and pound in fury, seeking to outrun the artificial light of the van's headlights before, without warning, vanishing into forest.

"Cool," Christian murmurs.

"That was cool," Matt agrees.

We negotiate twenty-seven miles of dirt road before we come to Hog Creek. Over that distance, the only other critter we cross paths with is a terrified cottontail that refuses to yield the roadway. In the Hog Creek parking lot, we set up the new tent with ease. Three of us roll out our sleeping bags and take shelter for the night.

"I'm sleeping in the car."

"OK, Dyl. But you're going to be cramped."

I watch my fifteen-year-old son stretch out on the back seat of the van and cover himself with his new sleeping bag. He doesn't respond to my admonition.

"What's for breakfast?" Dylan asks the next morning.

A brilliant sun peaks over the balsam forest and warms my bones.

"There are oranges in the food pack."

"I'm hungry. Don't we have something else?"

"It's all we've got. We'll have lunch when we get to the lake."

The oranges burst with juice and taste good. We launch the canoes, fill them with gear, and head down Hog Creek; a slow trough of muskeg-affected black water that empties into Perent Lake. Chris and I take the lead. Matt and Dylan follow. The rhythm of paddling and negotiating myriad turns takes over. We're quiet as we work.

Once we're out on the big water, we're disappointed to discover that our favorite campsite is taken. A mild breeze greets us as we paddle through a narrow channel. We find another campsite on the mainland. It's not our first choice but a quick survey reveals that the place will do.

"I'm going to take a picture of our first camp."

The older boys pitch the tent while I dig into the Duluth Pack for the disposable camera. It's nowhere to be found. I remove all of the food and supplies on the off chance that the camera has shifted inside the bag.

"Nuts."

"What's wrong, Dad?" Chris asks.

"Jack stole the camera."

"No way," Matt interjects.

"He was really interested in it. I took it away from him once. He must have taken it out again when I was doing something else."

"That kid's going to be a juvenile delinquent when he hits puberty," Chris opines.

"Oh, oh."

"Now what?" Dylan inquires.

"I forgot to pack the rain tarp. It was in another duffel. I forgot to put it in here."

Ignoring my mistake, I inventory the food to locate perishables that need to be kept cool. I make another disappointing discovery. Four packages of lunchmeat, along with a brick of cheese, are missing. Then I remember. I pulled several items out of the freezer and packed them but I never bothered to double-check the refrigerator.

René and Jack will have plenty of ham and cheese to eat while we're gone.

Things get worse. I discover that one of the new collapsible fishing rods I bought is missing its last guide. I find an old rod tip in the campfire pit and jerry-rig the new rod.

"You should bring that back to Gander, Dad," Matt observes.

"For a quarter I can put a new tip on it."

"Yeah, but it's brand new. Why not just get another one?"

I ponder my eldest son's suggestion. Chris and I decide to go fishing. Matt and Dylan join us. The older boys insist on still fishing in the lee of a gigantic boulder. They catch nothing. Chris and I drift spinners and dew worms across rocky reefs under a clear blue sky. A breeze sets up a perfect "walleye chop" and propels our canoe across the water at just the right speed. Chris and I catch fish. We keep two nice walleye for the frying pan. The other canoe is skunked.

The night air is cool. I burrow deep inside my new sleeping bag and dream of wilderness. There is no sound but the whistling of the wind, the lapping of the waves, and the solitary call of a loon gliding gently off the rocks in front of our camp.

"Crap," Matt remarks late the next afternoon as we fish.

"What's wrong?"

"I lost your fishing rod."

"You what?"

"I just lost your rod."

"It's brand new. You're gonna have to pay me back. Forty bucks, mister."

This exchange takes place as Chris and I work the shores of an inconsequential island. On each pass through the narrow channel we pick up walleye. Up until Matt lost his rod and reel, he and Dylan were catching fish as well. But Matt made the mistake of trolling the shoreline without securing the rod.

"I lost my spinner," Dylan adds.

My patience wears thin.

220

"Matt, you know better. You should've tucked the rod under the seat so it wouldn't be pulled out if you got a snag. You two might as well head in and get supper ready."

"Matt, you're a bonehead."

"Shut up, Chris," Dylan retorts.

I watch the other canoe fight waves as it heads back to camp.

Chris and I catch and release another ten walleye before the day is done. When we're ready to turn for home, we stop in the vicinity of the great rod disappearance. I toss a monster Daredevil from shore towards the spot where Matt lost the new rod. After a half-hour of trying to snag the submerged rod and reel, I give up.

"Let's try one more pass for fish."

"Sure Dad."

We lower our spinners into black water. The sky turns overcast. The woods are tinder dry. There's a great need for the sky to open up and douse the forest. I study the trees and the clouds as Chris reels his line in.

"I think you caught Matt's line," I observe as Chris tries to untangle two lines.

"I thought it was yours."

"Nope. Hold on while I try to pull the rod in."

I fumble with the line trying to determine which end the lost rod is attached to. The bail on the reel is obviously open: I pull handfuls of twisted monofilament line into the bottom of the canoe until there is no more line to retrieve. I gently pull on the line, trying to coax the rod free of the rocks below.

Snap.

The line breaks. The adventure is over.

"I prayed that we'd find the rod. I guess God answered my prayer," Chris explains quietly.

"That he did, son, that he did."

Back on shore, I fillet six fine looking Perent Lake walleye on a rocky slab of the Canadian Shield. Matt takes the fish and batters them as I paddle across the straits to chop up and deposit the leavings for the birds. Gulls circle above me, drawn by the freshly cleaned fish. As I pull myself away from the rocks, the birds land with boldness and claim the carrion.

"This stuff is spicy," Dylan says between mouthfuls of fish.

"You're a wuss."

"He's right Matt. I need more Kool-Aid. This Cajun style batter is hot!"

"What a bunch of pansies."

We sit on jack pine logs in front of a reluctant campfire and watch evening pass. Pink light glows from somewhere beyond the western horizon. For a moment, the lost rod is forgotten. For a moment, the only sound to be heard is the contented munching of four hungry fishermen.

Our Dad Isn't Sam Cook
(Conclusion)

We hope that the sun breaks through the high gray clouds so that we can see the lost rod and reel in the black water. Matt lost my new fishing rod close to shore. Without direct sunlight, our chance of seeing anything on the bottom of Perent Lake, even in the shallows, is non-existent.

Our canoes drift lazily over the uneven lakebed. I'm positive the rod is wedged between boulders.

"I'll walk in and see if I can feel it."

Dylan, a high school freshman, volunteers to strip to his boxers and wade into the icy water.

"You're nuts," is our universal response.

Matt eases the green plastic Old Town canoe into shore. Dylan carefully removes his clothes and stacks them in a neat pile on top of the Duluth Pack. Both canoes are loaded for the trip down the Perent River. We're leaving the great fishing and easy life of Perent Lake for adventure. At least that's how I've been selling our departure to the boys.

I know that there are twelve portages, thirteen if you count the final one to the parking lot at the lake, ahead of us. None of them are long. But the respite between them is short, making it necessary to pace yourself.

Dylan's skin immediately bristles with goose bumps as he enters the water. He has no luck finding the lost rod.

I study a map. I've led us up a small creek several miles off course. I realize my mistake only after I note that the water is flowing *against* us: We should be headed downstream, not upstream.

"Can't you read a map?" Dylan scolds.

"Give me that thing," Matt demands.

"Chris, just paddle. Let's get away from those yahoos," I urge.

223

My partner pulls hard. Our fully loaded Coleman canoe plows through tannin-clouded water as I try to escape my critics.

"Wait up. I wanna see the map."

I ignore Matt and push on.

"Oh great, he's looking at the map again," Dylan chides.

Studying the map, I determine my error: I was relying on a map of the Isabella Lake area. We're too far east for that map to be of any help. It's useless to stop and explain my discovery to my two eldest sons. They'll simply heap further denigration on their old man.

We arrive at the first portage, the longest we'll encounter, and empty the canoes. In short order, the packs are safely across the isthmus.

"I think we can make it."

"I'm game."

Matt and I study the rapids. The water is low. There is not much force behind the river. We decide to run the tempest in empty canoes. We do so without incident.

At the far end of the first portage, I dig into the food pack and pull out makings for peanut butter and jelly pita sandwiches. Using pita bread is a stroke of rare genius: Pita bread maintains its shape and stands up to the rigors of the trail. A bright sun bathes us in white light as we eat. I pull several wood ticks off my shins and feel the warmth of spring enter my body.

At the second portage, Matt struggles to carry the Discovery by himself.

"It's not about strength," I say. "It's about balance. Both you and Dylan are stronger than me."

"It feels like crap."

"Put a life jacket under the portage bar."

"That doesn't help."

I double portage the canoes over the first few portages to help out. The boys carry the packs. We run another set of rapids. This time, both canoes get stuck on rocks. I stand waist deep in devious water holding our canoe while Chris sits patiently in the front seat.

"Let Chris go down by himself," Matt urges.

I look at the vicious tongue of water. I hold the canoe against the current. Out in the open water of the next pond, Dylan is swimming with the Discovery. The big green canoe is full of water, making it difficult for my son to tow the craft to shore.

"No way, Dad," Chris whines.

I detect fear in my twelve-year-olds' voice.

"Get out on a rock. I'll guide the canoe down."

Chris complies and stands timidly on solid ground. I send the canoe crashing through the gorge. Matt tries to guide the vessel away from the rocks with a rope but slips and bangs his knee on a boulder.

"Shit."

We run another set of rapids. No one is injured; the gear and canoes make it through without incident. By the seventh portage, Matt and Dylan have discovered that, with the two of them working together, they can easily portage a canoe.

We pass through a succession of ponds. A small flock of Goldeneyes takes wing. A pair of mergansers hangs with the other ducks for protection. Muskrats dive from warm perches into the cool water at our approach. Chris and I try unsuccessfully to sneak up on three mud turtles basking on a bleached log. The air is clean.

At the eighth portage, the trail climbs an onerous ridge before plummeting to the river. I follow Matt and Dylan on the trail as they struggle with their canoe.

"Look at the size of these white pines."

"Ya, right. That's just what I was thinking too, Dad."

"Come on Dylan, you've got to appreciate these trees."

The portage trail splits two magnificent white pines. Both trees tower in excess of a hundred feet above the forest floor. I watch my sons plod onward without so much as a glance upward.

At the end of the day, we stop and discuss whether we should try to make Isabella Lake.

"I'm not going any further."

Dylan wants to camp at the first available site.

"We might as well make it to the lake, Dyl."

"Matt, shut up. I'm not going any further. This is the stupidest trip I've ever been on. Why couldn't we just stay on Perent Lake and fish?"

I admit to myself that the boy has a point. By portaging twelve times in one day, we've covered distance but have not really accomplished anything, unless you count the subtle lessons the boys have learned regarding teamwork. I don't tell them that one last portage awaits us before we achieve our destination.

"We'll stop at the first campsite."

Our camp at the end of the Perent River is perfect. We situate our tent on a stone outcropping above the river. A cool breeze keeps black flies and mosquitoes away. Chris and I fish from separate canoes. In less than an hour, we catch and release a dozen small perch and northern.

Memorial Day, the last day. A stiff west wind greets us as we rise. I urge the boys to move fast. The sky looks like rain. When the clouds clear, the boys are left even more skeptical of my outdoor skills. We make the short portage into Isabella Lake without complaint. By now my sons are old hands at portaging. It's a long paddle against the wind across the lake to the trailhead.

"What'd ya think of the trip?"

"I'm never going canoeing again," Dylan responds.

"Really? That hurts my feelings."

"No offense Dad, but your trip didn't make any sense. We should've stayed on Perent and caught fish rather than portaging so many friggin' times."

I mull over Dylan's observation as I walk to the car. The trail leading to the parking lot passes through an arid, desert-like grove of jack pine. I'm astounded that the place doesn't burst into flames. The woods are tinder dry, ready for disaster.

In the parking lot, I inspect the left rear tire of our Transport van. The tire is dangerously low. It's thirty miles one-way to Hog Creek and the other van. I scrutinize the wheel.

"Well, it's not flat yet," Matt advises.

I motion for Matt to get in the Pontiac. We leave the other boys sitting on top of our gear as we drive back to get the other van.

226

I'm bone tired and thirsty when I pull back into the Isabella lot driving the Lumina with the trailer in tow. Matt is just ahead of me driving the Transport. Just before reaching the Isabella lot, the suspect tire on the Transport gives up the ghost. I'm too exhausted to complain. I pull out the tools and the jack, lower the spare from beneath the rear chassis, and change the tire. I'd taken a bath in the frigid waters of the river the night before. The grime of the road and the exertion of changing the flat leave me less than clean.

We stop at a little tavern in Isabella. I have twenty-six dollars to my name. Matt is broke. Thankfully, both vans have full gas tanks.

"We can only spend four bucks apiece," I tell Matt and Dylan. Chris is outside and doesn't hear my instructions.

Once he's seated, Chris tries to order a six-dollar item. I quietly admonish him. He pouts. The boys order sodas. I order a cold tap beer. It tastes good. It tastes like another. I can't chance it. I don't want to end up doing dishes. My stomach is in knots in anticipation of the bill. The total comes in under budget. I have enough money left after the tip to give the boys a buck apiece to buy a cold soda for the road.

"Dylan, would you change your mind if I made some concessions?" I ask as we stand on the dusty gravel of the tavern's parking lot getting ready for the return trip to Duluth.

Blue eyes stare at me as Dylan tries to fathom what I'm up to.

"Like what?"

"Like letting you boys plan the next trip."

"That might work."

I hope it does.

Black Water

When my eldest son Matt recently returned from a Boundary Waters trip with three of his buddies, I experienced trout envy. The brook trout Matt displayed on our kitchen counter were huge. They ran nearly a full pound each. I stared at their fat, swollen bodies and wondered how they had fought, how Matt's eyes must have lit up when he pulled the first fish clear of the clean waters of the little border lake he was fishing.

In desperation, I took a package of my stream trout out of our freezer in an attempt to mollify my jealousy. When I placed the brilliantly colored trout next to Matt's giant fish, the result was predictable. My heart, rather than being uplifted, sank into a fisherman's depression.

I thought about Matt's brookies all summer. An opportunity arose for me to try out brook trout fishing on Minnesota's Iron Range when my wife René drove to Biwabik, for work. With René safely entrenched behind a desk, I headed north. I'd read about an Iron Range stream that was labeled, at least in the book I consulted, as a premier brook trout stream. There were also rumors of huge brown trout (reported to be reproducing naturally) in the cold waters of the river.

The thing about trout envy is that, once it hits you, you can't shake it short of going fishing. No amount of golf, walking, weight lifting, or biking can substitute for taking your shot at native trout in wild water. Lake fishing is a poor second cousin. When you're in a stream, wading through rapids in search of that next great pool, it's you against God and the fish: No fish locators, no gasoline engines, no trickery.

The sky was heavy. There was no question that the North Country needed a deluge. Dust kicked up as my Lumina took tenuous corners on the logging road. It was cool and pleasant as I stopped just beyond a plank bridge crossing a stream. A pickup passed by as I pulled my jeans and golf shirt off in favor of shorts and a T-shirt. I brought extra clothing in anticipation of stopping at Howard Street Books, a local bookstore in Hibbing, when I was done. I had a new novel to promote, one invoking memories and scenes from the Iron Range. I didn't want to show up at the store, asking for a book signing date, smelling like fish. The driver of the truck waved as a cloud of fine dust settled over my van. I pulled on my waders and picked up my fly rod.

The bottom of the stream was partially sand, partially loon crap. Black alders hung over the banks. Norway and Jack pines loomed above the marsh grass on either side of the water. There were few birds: It was as if the birds anticipated a storm that would not break.

A few moments into fishing, I felt a tug but I knew it wasn't a trout. I pulled a four-inch shiner from the river. The minnow dropped off the barbless hook, taking my night crawler with it. Minnow-1, fisherman-0.

Wading became more difficult. It was obvious that beaver had been at work and that humans had used extraordinary efforts to destroy their handiwork. Here and there the remains of lodges and dams interrupted the natural flow of water. Silt had settled deep in these artificial pools, making walking nearly impossible. At intervals, I caught more minnows but no trout.

I came upon a gorgeous pool. Switching to dry flies, I awkwardly presented several types. My efforts yielded more minnows. The wind picked up. Though I sensed that it was about to storm, the weather remained noncommittal. It was the middle of the day; a poor time to try to pick up native brook trout or to raise always-skittish German Browns. I'd hoped my diligence and effort would result in a few strikes. It seemed my faith in books was misplaced.

Wandering downstream, I encountered a large jack pine blocking the river. On the left, a high bank soared. On the right, the landscape boasted lowland marsh filled with thistle. There seemed to be no path open to me but straight down the channel.

The stream's foundation suddenly gave way. My boots sank in bottomless loon crap. I reached for a nearby log. I lunged forward and snagged the palm of my left hand on a branch. Despite the gash in my hand, I held on to the limb. My boots floated free of the bottom. Exhausted, I pulled myself onto the log

Blood oozed from the wound in bright whispers. There was no pain; only a constant flow of red. I ripped a piece of cotton free of my T-shirt and wrapped it around my bleeding hand. I sat heavily on the rough surface of the dead pine, my rod and reel balanced precariously on another log. I tried to shift my weight to gain stability. Pulling my left leg free of the mucky bottom, I strained my hamstring.

The impromptu bandage was soaked with blood. I dipped my hand into the river. After a few minutes, I removed the wet cloth and examined the wound. It wasn't deep. I'd merely peeled back a layer of skin, exposing white fat. The bleeding had stopped.

It took some doing to negotiate the steep bank out of the river valley. I climbed heavily to the crest of the ridge. My drive back to Hibbing was reflective: I convinced myself to give up the notion of catching fish, of satisfying trout envy. Sometimes it's safer to admit that you've been bested.

Swimming with Loons

Round Lake sits peacefully against a backdrop of hardwoods and pines. It was a complicated journey from Fargo, North Dakota. Our eldest son, Matt, is changing colleges. After two years at Michigan Tech (located in Upper Peninsula Michigan) he's had enough snow. He's had enough five-to-one boy-to-girl ratio. He's had enough serenity and contemplation.

It was nearly impossible to convince our two eldest sons that the six of us should cram into our minivan and drive to Fargo to visit North Dakota State University and our friends the Floms. Spencer, our pro forma adopted son and Christian's best friend, came along for the ride. Seven seats. Seven people. A four and a half hour drive. Use your imagination.

We pulled into Moorhead just after 11:00pm. I stopped at a service station, looked in a phonebook, and found Jan and Joel's address. I verified our location on a map so that I wouldn't wander aimlessly through cornfields in search of their house.

Traveling down the highway, I spotted the side road I was supposed take. I pulled onto gravel under a barrage of criticism.

"They don't live on a dirt road," René enjoined.

"You've gone too far. We're in the sticks," Matt lamented.

"I'm thirsty," Christian whined.

"When we gonna be there?" Dylan intoned.

I mumble under my breath, pull a U-turn and head back north.

"Jan, this is René. We're on No. 75. How do we get to your place?" my wife asked over my cell phone.

There was a pause in the dialogue.

"Jan says you missed the road that would have taken us right to their place. She can see our van from her living room window."

I muttered. The dirt road I'd been admonished to pass by was the correct road.

"She says to take the next right, follow it around the bend by the river."

I started to say something. Objections from my kids and wife silenced me in mid-sentence. René continued to chat with Jan. I heard Jan's voice over the cell phone:

"Turn here!"

A woman appeared out of nowhere, and stood defiantly in the light of the van's headlamps. The Lumina stopped inches from our friend. Jan was standing in her pajamas in the middle of the road pointing at her house.

"Jan, you're nuts," was René's only response.

The Flom children are growing up. A.J., their eldest, is a senior at Moorhead High School. Sarah, the middle child, is entering ninth grade. Both are athletes. Peter, the youngest, is a musician. Joel and Jan were law school classmates of mine at William Mitchell College of Law in St. Paul. They wed shortly after we all graduated; a year or so after René and I were married. Then they moved to Moorhead where Joel became a partner in his own firm. Jan hung up her briefcase and became a mom, watercolor artist, and sculptor.

Matt, René, Jack, and I toured NDSU the next day. We weathered moments of minor conflict but handled our differences well despite the ninety-eight-degree heat.

We've made a visit the Flom's nearly every year since our friends bought a place on Round Lake. Their cabin is an hour drive from Fargo-Moorhead; located in the rolling hills and black earth of Becker County between Detroit Lakes and Park Rapids. Joel and A.J. went ahead of the group to open the place up. I was responsible for getting all my boys and Spencer to the lake in the Lumina. René and Jan followed in Jan's Blazer with groceries.

I glanced at the van's fuel gauge when we left Moorhead. Over a quarter of a tank, plenty of gas to make it to Detroit Lakes. Jack slumbered behind me in his car seat, I turned onto US No. 10. About fifteen miles from Detroit Lakes, the van started to act up. It chugged and wheezed. I glanced at the fuel gauge. It still reads a quarter of a tank. I pulled over to the side of the road. Vacation traffic flew by as I contemplated my next move.

"Must be vapor lock. I'll just let it sit for a minute or two."

"Try it without the AC," Matt offered. "Maybe that'll help."

We opened the windows, allowing hot, dry air to engulf us. The vehicle traveled a few miles before it started to labor again.

"I'm gonna turn off here and let it sit."

We exited the highway and parked next to a gasoline pump at a convenience store. I examined the fuel level again. Nothing had changed. I turned the key. The car started. We moved a few hundred yards down the highway before the engine quit again. Matt called René on the cell phone. Jan's Blazer pulled in behind us. I transferred the four younger kids to Jan's car. Matt and I decided to wait for a wrecker.

Sitting in the rising heat, I studied the gas gauge. It hadn't moved. I looked at the trip odometer. Three hundred and seventy-eight miles. I did the math in my head. The van gets a little over twenty miles to the gallon. It has an eighteen-gallon tank.

"Matt, we're out of gas."

"No way."

"Look at the odometer."

"Didn't you pay attention to the gas gauge?"

"See for yourself. It's still above a quarter. It's busted."

When the women came back, I sent them for a gas can. Twenty minutes later the Lumina's tank was full and we were back on the road.

A soft, hot wind greets René and I as we stroll past the Flom's log cabin to look at the lake. The cottage is stained a dark brown. A stone fireplace chase interrupts the horizontal harmony of old logs. Clear water laps expectantly against riprap along the shore. I lower my hand to take the lake's temperature. I look back at the cabin. Somehow the nostalgia of the place acts as a subtle

233

barrier against the assorted complexities and demands of the 21st century.

Early the next morning, I wade into Round Lake. The sun has not yet risen, though tendrils of orange climb the eastern sky. The lake shimmers like a vast emerald. René walks onto the dock with a mug of coffee in her hand. Steam rises from the cup in the morning air.

"Look, a loon."

Without my glasses, I have difficulty seeing. Squinting, I confirm René's discovery. I dive and move silently towards the bird. When I surface, the loon is further away.

"Swimming with the loon?"

"Loons, plural," I reply. "After yesterday, I feel like one."

Traveling Blues

I was, as always, in a hurry to make the event. I figured if I got out of court by 3:30pm, I'd have an outside chance of making it to a cross-country meet in Maple, Wisconsin. My twelve-year-old son Christian was running in the race as a seventh grader. I made sure of the time and location of the event by cross-examining Chris earlier in the morning:

"What time is the meet?"

"4:00."

"Where?"

"Northwestern. The golf course."

"You mean Norwood?"

"That's the one."

"You're sure?"

"If that's the one in Maple."

My afternoon calendar allowed me to leave the courthouse by 3:30. I raced across town and picked up Jack at daycare well before 3:45. I had fifteen minutes to make Maple. The odds of doing that without a speeding ticket were against me.

The colors had not yet peaked as my van roared along U.S. Highway No. 2 east of Superior, Wisconsin. Hints of autumn touched the highest reaches of the maples. The aspen and birch were as yet untainted. Jack watched the panorama of rolling farm fields, wild trout streams, and adolescent forest pass by from his safety seat.

Approaching Poplar, Wisconsin, I noted a golf course sign on my left. I veered onto a county road. It was 4:05. I figured I'd get to the course just in time to pretend that I'd seen the race and congratulate Chris on a fine run.

What the kid doesn't know won't hurt him.

There was only one car in the golf course parking lot. The dearth of big yellow school buses convinced me that my kid was somewhere else. An old man ambled gingerly across one of the fairways pulling his golf cart and clubs behind him. He was the only soul around. I didn't stay to watch his game.

The van accelerated towards Maple where Northwestern High School is located. I was certain that the only golf courses around were in Poplar, where I'd already been disappointed, and to the south, on the road to Solon Springs. I wanted to make sure the teams weren't assembled and running somewhere close by.

The Northwestern Tigers football team was practicing when I drove past the school. I saw no cross-country runners in the area. Jack continued to study the countryside. We headed south.

Norwood Golf Course was deserted. It was 4:30 and I'd missed Chris run, wherever his meet was actually being held. We stopped at a filling station along Highway 53 to refuel. Jack came into the store with me and picked out a candy bar and a sucker.

I headed back to the Hermantown Middle School to await the arrival of the cross-country team. Given it would be nearly 6:00pm by the time I got to the school, I calculated that we'd only have to wait an hour or so for the team bus.

"I play on the swings."

"OK, Jack."

I lifted my youngest son out of the van. He ran towards the playground next to the middle school. There was a boy's varsity soccer game going on. I watched the game to its conclusion. It was 7:00pm. Still, there was no bus. I called home, using the telephone in the school lobby, to find out whether anyone had heard from Christian.

"Chris called about a half-hour ago. He won't be in until nine," Dylan advised.

"Nine? Why would it take until nine to drive back from Maple?"

"Maple? Dad, I hate to tell you this but Chris is in Grand Rapids!"

"What?"

"His meet is in Grand Rapids. At the golf course."

I hung up the phone. Muttering under my breath, I grasped Jack's hand and walked quickly through the deserted hallway of the middle school. It was a quiet ride home.

It was difficult maintaining my composure when I picked up Chris later that evening.

"How was the meet?"

"Fine."

"When did you realize that you'd sent your father to the wrong state, a hundred and fifty miles away from where you were running?"

The boy remained silent.

"Was it when you got on the bus to leave Hermantown?"

No answer.

"Was it when the bus drove northwest across the State of Minnesota instead of southeast across the State of Wisconsin?"

Christian remained mute.

"Was it when you arrived in the wrong city, in the wrong state?"

More silence.

Then, in a timid voice, Christian finally advanced this admission:

"It was when I crossed the finish line and realized that you weren't there."

Occurrence at Hunter Lake

This past winter I got the bright idea (no pun intended) to go cross-country skiing during the eclipse of the full moon. At first blush, the concept seems straightforward. But think about it. Yes, the moon would be full. Up until the eclipse. But once the eclipse comes to fruition… Do you see the problem?

I skied hard and fast as the sun slowly covered the yellow globe of the full moon. Darkness enveloped the trail. Night took on a dangerous aspect. I started to wonder why I hadn't brought my two Labradors, Maggie and Sam, with me. I started to think about the timber wolves and the occasional cougar lurking in the forest surrounding our home, both of which are active at night and not at all bothered by winter. My heart raced. I picked up the pace. I made my way back to the house safely despite the eclipse.

I tell you this so you can understand that not all of my ideas for adventure along the banks of the Cloquet River are well thought out.

"Do you and Ron want to go canoeing tonight?"

I listen as my wife René calls our friend Nancy to find out if she and her husband want to canoe from our house down to Hunter Lake (an ox-bow in the Cloquet River) a one and a half-hour paddle from our place.

"They're going to try and make it. Randy and his girlfriend want to come with," René explains as she hangs up the phone. Randy is the McVean's middle son. He's a resident medical student living in LaCrosse, Wisconsin. "Randy's got a new canoe. Ronda's coming down tonight so she'll want to go too," my wife adds, noting that her good friend and blueberry picking partner from Ely will be staying the night with us.

I scurry around, locate four canoe paddles, stock a cooler with beer, pop, and ice and ready two of our canoes for the journey. Nancy stops over with her mom around dinnertime. She wants to firm up our plans and show her mom our new house.

"I'd like to pull the canoes out at Wahlstens," I suggest, knowing that Nancy is a good friend of the Wahlstens. For some reason, I leave my reference to our take-out site oblique. Though there are no words exchanged, I believe that Nancy understands that it's her job to call the Wahlstens and warn them that we'll be landing on their shoreline sometime after midnight.

A haze descends: The moon rises in the east as a dim bulb. There's enough light to see but not enough light to make the evening memorable. At 9:30pm, the McVeans arrive.

"We need lifejackets," Nancy laments. "We forgot ours at the lake."

I wander out to our garage and locate four adult life preservers.

"Nance, you really don't need these. The water's only thigh deep and the current isn't moving much," I say as I hand the vests to her.

"I'll feel better if we take them."

"Suit yourself."

The moon's limited power isn't much help as we descend the steep bank to the river. I've made it a priority sometime during the summer to put in stairs. I haven't hit that part of my chore list yet. I help Randy carry his canoe, a Kevlar beauty, down the boulder-strewn slope to the water. His girlfriend Jen slips and bangs her knee.

"She's already got a concussion from water skiing," the doctor-in-training observes. "Are you alright?"

A slight nod from Jen. The first canoe enters the water. Randy and Jen sit in the Kevlar craft suspended in the current, waiting for the rest of us. I help Ron and Nancy into my Old Town Discovery. They promptly paddle backwards into overhanging brush. A few critical comments and their canoe drifts free of the alders. Ronda and René hand me the cooler and paddles. The women step gingerly into our 15' Coleman canoe, its red plastic skin worn thin by encounters with boulders and rock ledges. René claims the front seat. Ronda sits on a cushion on the floor in the middle. I push the canoe away from shore, sit heavily in the stern, and begin to paddle.

There are only two places along this stretch of the Cloquet where canoes are in danger of hitting rocks. Both our canoe and the one carrying Ron and Nancy manage to find those places. Randy tosses a derogatory comment or two our way. My response is honest and forthright:

"Hey, take a look at the weight in this canoe. I've got beer, two middle-aged women, and an out of shape dad in the stern. You've got two twenty-somethings in a lightweight Kevlar. Is it any wonder we're hitting bottom and you're not?"

I ignore the angry looks that René and Ronda flash my way.

"How can the moon be on our left and then straight ahead of us?" Nancy asks sometime later.

"Simple, Nancy, the river is changing directions and we're following it," I explain.

"It doesn't make any sense."

"René, I notice that you're very conservative with your strokes," Ron needles.

My wife and her pal from Ely engage in extended conversations as the shoreline slips by.

"I paddle only when I need to."

The pale light of the moon never intensifies. There's scant current to assist our progress. Just above Hunter Lake, John Mellancamp echoes over the water. We drift by a brightly illumined cottage fully expecting to see throngs of partying people but there's no movement in or around the building.

Randy and Jen paddle into Hunter Lake. Their Kevlar canoe is a slash of bright yellow against a black and white world. There are no bugs. Here and there, the faint glow of artificial light signals an occupied home or cottage along the shoreline. The far side of the lake remains shrouded in darkness. We turn back towards the river and our take-out point. I switch on my flashlight. Inadvertently, the halogen beam reflects off the windows of the Wahlsten home.

"Watch your light," Ron cautions. "You'll wake them up."

A beam of light appears suddenly from behind trees. Someone approaches the shoreline. The lamp illuminates Ron and Nancy as the bow of their canoe meets riverbank.

"Hi Bruce. It's Nancy."

"You scared the heck out of me," Bruce Wahlsten replies as he stands in his bathrobe in the dark. "I was in bed."

Bruce is surprised. Nancy thought *I'd* called the Wahlstens. I thought *she* did. No one had bothered to tell our neighbors that seven adults would be stumbling around their yard at half-past midnight.

Bruce helps land the canoes.

"Good thing you recognized us," Ron says with a smile as he shakes Bruce's hand.

"Good for you, you mean," Bruce says, exposing the grip of a nasty looking automatic tucked into the waistband of his pajamas. "Mom's got a bead on you from the house with the back-up gun."

As we portage the canoes to waiting vehicles, I ponder whether Bruce is serious about the back-up gun. I can't ask him: He's already back inside his house.

A Big Snow

"**You're** crazy. No one's going to show up for a book club on a day like today. You're going to end up eating breakfast by yourself."

My wife had a point. Snow fell at a steady pace. Our quarter-mile long driveway looked to be socked in. I was supposed to meet a book club at the Buena Vista restaurant, read selections from my debut novel, *The Legacy*, and discuss the book and the writing process with the ten or so female members of the book club. Looking at the snow that had already fallen, it seemed unlikely there'd be much of a turnout.

I'm male. Big snow means a challenge. My wife had just bought a Toyota Rav4 SUV a few weeks before the snowstorm. I hadn't driven the car. The book club excursion was the perfect excuse for me to try out the vehicle's four-wheel drive.

"I'm sure at least some of the members will show up."

"Women are not going to go out in this weather for a book club. Why don't you call the person in charge and re-schedule it?"

I was already out the door when my wife's comment floated across the warm air of our kitchen.

Of course, she was right. I made it to the restaurant in plenty of time. I ate wild rice pancakes, sausages, and fried eggs by myself and drank piping hot coffee in the silence of the near-empty establishment. Wind-driven snow pelted the thick windows of the place. There were only three or four other brave souls eating, holding private conversations in distant corners of the room. No one from the book club showed up.

"They canceled the meeting," I admitted to René after returning home.

"What'd I tell you? I made a nice breakfast and you missed it."

"The wild rice pancakes I had while I was waiting were really good. We'll have to go there for breakfast sometime."

"I knew it. You ended up reading your paper and having breakfast by yourself, didn't you?"

"Yep."

"Did you find Jack's money?" I asked later in the afternoon as we were getting dressed to cross-country ski.

That past Wednesday evening, in the back seat of the Toyota, Jack, our three-and-a-half-year-old son, had decided to ingest currency. The only admission he'd make to René was that he'd "swallowed a penny".

A trip to the urgent care center confirmed Jack was a serious saver: A large, bright circle on Jack's X-ray showed that the kid had actually swallowed a quarter. The coin had cleared Jack's stomach and was on its way through. René, being the mom, was assigned the job, by me as the dad, of making sure the money was retrieved upon exit.

"No. I haven't seen it. He keeps getting on the toilet without telling me. I'm not sure if it's been passed yet."

Knowing better than to criticize my wife's fecal inspection abilities, I zipped up my nylon pullover and headed out the door.

White cloaked the field in front of our house as I waxed our skis. Fragments of frozen water, more sleet than true snow, fell from the sky. Twelve inches of new snow covered the ground. There was no wind.

Our skis cut slow, steady paths through shin-high drifts blanketing the trail. At one point we stopped and rested, listening to the distinctive rumble of a Duluth, Winnipeg, and Pacific locomotive crossing the trestle downriver from our house. Halfway through our ski, René and I stood quietly beneath an arbor formed by stately Norway pines crowning the highest point on our land. We didn't talk beneath the canopy: We simply breathed fresh air and relished the quiet.

Shadows lengthened across the white land. A northwestern zephyr formed a hedgerow of snow across our driveway. My wife broke through the drift and skied towards the house. I made for the garage. I clicked out of my skis, took off my ski boots, and I slid into Sorels and insulated overalls. Dressed against the gale, I fired up my International tractor and began the slow process of removing snow.

Sailing

My son Christian and his buddy Spencer stand in refreshing water. They're waiting for me to rig the jib and mainsail of a Hobie Cat. With thick fingers and the limited dexterity of age, it takes me awhile to finish the job.

We came to Round Lake in rural Becker County to spend a couple of days with old friends from law school. It's a ritual that we've kept up as a family for the better part of a decade: The Floms drive east from their home in Moorhead; the Mungers drive west from Duluth. We meet at their 1930's vintage log cabin near Detroit Lakes. There's never a lack of food, kidding around, or friendship at their place.

The boys sit on the catamaran's pontoons. The sails gather wind. It takes several false starts before we're able to tack and work our way out of the protected bay in front of the cabin.

Round Lake is part of the Ottertail River. Being part of a flowage, the water is clear and clean. Osprey and bald eagles soar above us seeking the benefit of the same wind we rely upon to move the boat. The Hobie Cat gathers speed. I learn how to use the jib and weave a path out into the main lake. The catamaran glides.

"Mission Impossible," Chris shouts as he hangs below me, moving hand-over-hand along ropes suspended beneath the flexible tarpaulin that forms the boat's deck.

"Indiana Jones," Spencer responds.

A gust bends fragile reeds in the lake's shallows.

"Hold on, boys."

The pontoon carrying Chris dives beneath the waves. The float carrying Spencer breaks free of the water. I lean heavily away from the submerged float. The rope in my hands sings in the wind. I hold the rudder in place by pinning the rudder's handle against the canvas deck with a leg.

We dance across the lake. The colorful sails fill with brisk country air. Though it's Saturday, there are no other boats on the water.

We beach the boat several hours later. The boys pull the Hobie Cat onto land for the night. I notice Jack looking out the cabin's big picture window.

Later that evening, my older sons, Matt and Dylan, join the adults in a game of contract rummy. The action is lively: the banter, unforgiving. The other children, Peter (the youngest Flom), Christian, and Spencer play video games. A.J. (the Floms' eldest) naps on a leather sofa. It's amazing that he's able to sleep with the racket we make playing cards.

The next morning, Joel and I drive to Moorhead to pick up Sarah, Joel and Jan's daughter, and one of Sarah's friends. When we arrive back at the cabin, Jack is waiting for me.

"Go in the boat, Dad?"

"Sure, Jack, but you need a lifejacket."

"Go fast in the boat, Dad?"

I study the lake. Ripples barely disturb the water's calm. What breeze there is seems unpredictable. I look at my son's face. There's little I can do but agree to try. I enlist Chris and Spencer to help raise the sails. With the boat is in the water, it becomes apparent that the older boys have got to go: Their weight is impeding progress.

"Ouch," Chris cries as I smack his bare fingers with my elbow.

My gesture forces Chris to drop into the lake.

"Hey, watch it," Spencer exclaims as I shove him off the canvas deck.

The boat surges forward.

"All I had to do was lose the dead weight."

"I'll get you for this."

Chris's words are an idle challenge: The catamaran has moved into deep water.

"Lay down, Jack."

My youngest son, his arms and legs brown from the summer sun, reclines on the tarp. His orange life vest dwarfs his body.

"That's it. You don't want to get hit by the boom," I say, pointing at the horizontal pipe connecting the mainsail to the mast.

246

We clear the bay. I use the jib to make the boat come about. The wind remains slight. Jack doesn't seem to mind. Once or twice, we catch temporary gusts. In these fleeting moments, water moves rapidly beneath the catamaran and Jack smiles.

"Dad go faster."

"I'll try."

I turn the boat around. Approaching shore, I see René, Jan, and Joel lounging in lawn chairs, sipping gin and tonics in the shade of tall spruce trees. The smell of grilled bratwurst permeates the still air. I lower the mainsail. As the pontoons of the Hobie Cat scratch sand, I study the earnest smile of my youngest child and realize there's no better way to spend a weekend.

A Fine Day

My father is getting on in years but time hasn't seemed to slow him down much. Oh, he's had the odd heart malady and the occasional back twinge. These minor challenges are appearing more regularly; evidence, despite his hardened demeanor, that age is creeping up on the old man. Still, as I watch him walk the far edge of the stubble, his red label Ruger twenty gauge held at port, his black Labrador retriever working the rippling stalks of dead corn, it's hard to believe Grandpa Harry just turned seventy-five.

We're here, beneath a clear blue sky, on a gorgeous late October day, to celebrate our respective birthdays. North, across the flat table of land that we're hunting, a large pothole sits immobilized by early ice. There's a high ridge to the south, its spine covered in maple, aspen, and birch, dead leaves chattering in the heavy breeze. Like everything around us, the leaves seem reluctant to let go. Summer has been long and dry. Autumn has been more of the same with folks golfing into October on the area courses.

That we're hunting a game farm, a private plot of land in northeastern Minnesota, intent upon shooting domesticated pheasants released earlier today doesn't reduce the serenity of the landscape or the impact of the occasion. The birds are skittish. They fly with quick abandon and native skill when flushed, providing at least the appearance of a wild hunt.

The dog stops dead in her tracks and goes on point. Sleek black fur reflects the morning sun. The Labrador's nose snuffles a dollop of broken corn.

"Watch her Mark."

"I'm on her."

The kid who's our guide for the day raises a twelve gauge automatic to his shoulder. I bring my over-under to the ready and take a step.

Caaack.

Caaack.

A beautiful rooster pheasant flushes from cover. Beating its wings to reach altitude, the bird sets a course towards the pothole.

Boom.

My first shot is low.

Boom.

My second shot is behind the fleeing rooster.

"I'm a little rusty," I admit as the three of us watch the pheasant sail across the frozen pond.

"That one's fox food," the guide muses.

As we continue our walk, I notice a pair of red tailed hawks soaring high above the open field.

"Hawks," I say, pointing up into the sky.

We stop to watch the raptors soar. The guide explains that the birds are here to collect the pheasants that we miss, pheasants that foolishly set their sights on escaping into the forest with the misguided belief they can outwit danger. Most of the escaped birds will perish within a day; their ability to evade predators dulled by generations of domestication.

Another pheasant flushes. I take my time, following the low course of the hen.

Boom.

"Nice shot," my old man says as the dull gray bird folds and drops to the ground.

"Thanks."

Cleo retrieves the hen pheasant with style. The Labrador holds the bird firmly in her mouth as she trots through swaying grass and corn.

"Here girl."

The dog stops at my side and deposits the dead bird on frozen ground.

"Good girl," I praise, stroking the ebony fur of the dog's neck.

Cleo's long pink tongue slides in and out of her mouth. Droplets of spit fly as she pants. The morning is just beginning. There's much work left to be done. There's little patience in the dog for sitting around when she knows there are birds to be hunted. She moves towards a virgin section of corn, indicating that break time is over.

Several pheasants take wing only to meet steel shot before I miss another bird, reminding me that I am, at the core, a mediocre marksman. My dad hits every bird he aims at. The age thing, I decide, is vastly overstated. We work the marsh surrounding the pond. I draw the job of stomping through the rushes and cattails with the dog. I learn that the ice doesn't support my weight. My boots break through. My feet get wet. There's nothing to do but trudge on.

Caaack.

A brilliantly hued rooster explodes from a tangle of alders, acting more like a ruffed grouse than a pheasant as it takes wing.

Boom.

The bird glides on.

Boom.

The rooster achieves the far side of the pond with impunity.

"Damn," I curse, opening the breech of my shotgun. Two spent shells drop into my gloved hand.

"You get him?" Dad asks from behind a veil of brush.

"Nope. He's hawk food," I reply, sliding two new shells into the gun's chamber.

A few steps later, I miss a hen that was keeping company with the rooster. The bird seems to stagger momentarily at the report of my second shot but I remain unconvinced that any pellets hit home. My dad and the guide take Cleo to work the edge of a logging road that marks the limit of the swamp. The hen I missed landed somewhere near the road. After a concerted effort, the bird flushes. My dad's desperate shot falls short. Another pheasant escapes.

"Missed her," my old man admits with regret.

I study my dad. He stands next to his dog on top of a slight rise, his orange hunting hat and vest stark and vibrant in the autumn sun. In middle age, he would have been angry at missing a bird. Now, deep into maturity, there's a calm acceptance about him that seems foreign in a man who has always lived life at seventy-eight rpm. It doesn't bother him that a bird has flown free: It's just not that important.

I take Cleo down an old logging road near where one of the escaping roosters landed. The ridge marking the southern boundary of the old farm rises off my left shoulder; a steep pitch covered with hardwoods. I work a thicket of wild raspberries with the dog. Nothing. I work a patch of young aspen. Nothing. The Labrador is spent. Her tail has ceased wagging. She's ready for a well-earned nap in the back seat of my dad's Tahoe.

As I round a bend in the trail, a fat male pheasant saunters into the open. The bird hesitates in the middle of the path. Cleo is so tired that she doesn't see the rooster break from cover. I stop. The dog continues to work the edge of the path. The bird twitches and then explodes into the yellow sky. Cleo watches the bird's erratic flight. I wait until the rooster is well above the dog.

Boom.

The bird flits away from the first shot and turns to take advantage of a strong gale blowing in from the east.

Boom.

The last pheasant of the day falls to earth.

René's Fence

"**The** deer are at it again," my wife lamented. René was standing ankle deep in the sandy loam of the vegetable garden surveying broken corn stalks and nibbled bean shoots. "We need a fence."

I'd approached the garden to talk to her about transplanting four apple trees we'd placed along the edge of the pasture surrounding our new house. My belief that the trees would be safe from deer was misguided. Within weeks of being set in the firm dry ground, the new trees had been reduced to stalks. It was obvious that any fruit trees we wanted to plant would require greater security.

"I'm gonna move the apple trees alongside your garden," I responded. "When I build a fence, they'll be protected from the deer."

"You sure the trees are worth saving?"

"I think they'll be all right if we can keep the critters at bay."

At our old house, our vegetable garden, flower gardens, and fruit trees never experienced deer. Whether because of the electric fence surrounding our horse pasture or because of the close proximity of our two Labradors retrievers, the deer stayed away. It was a shock to learn how insistent white tail deer can be once we moved onto the new place. It didn't help that our dogs chose to remain behind at our old Sears house once we moved. But that, as they say, is another story.

I'm not much of a carpenter. I can, however, with some guidance, build a respectable fence. A few days after our conversation, René deposited t-posts and wire livestock fencing on the ground next to the freshly tilled soil of the vegetable garden. I think she envisioned that the fence would erect itself.

A July sun hung over the hayfield. Wet air enveloped me as I began the process of clawing at the parched soil with a post-hole digger. I intended to use reclaimed cedar posts for the corner supports of the fence: T-posts alone wouldn't keep the wire mesh snug. I glanced at the deer-ravaged vegetable garden and wondered whether the effort was worth it.

"The fence is looking good," René interjected at various intervals during the project. "But don't you think that post over there is a little out of line?"

Her veiled criticism flew across my sunburned brow like a cannon shot across the bow of Old Ironsides.

"You want it straighter? How about picking up the sledge hammer and lending a hand?"

"You're doing such a nice job," my wife demurred, ignoring my jab. "I'd hate to have one or two posts detract from the finished product."

René's compliment didn't mollify me.

"I thought you'd be further along by now," she added with just the right hint of sarcasm, as she turned towards the house.

I'd started the project early Sunday morning, missing church, violating the commandment about working on the Sabbath. I sinfully labored straight through the noon hour, pausing only in the late afternoon to cool my scarlet skin in the slow current of the Cloquet River. I took to the water again to avoid further conversation with René. She expected the fence would be completed in a day. But after eight hours of steady labor, the project was far from fruition. Rather than engage in doomed dialogue, I chose to cool off.

We're facing a major drought, at least in terms of flowage out of Island Lake, the large man-made reservoir formed by the Cloquet River a mile and a half upstream from our place. Despite the deluge of rain we were blessed with during late spring and early summer, the river in front of our home is at an all time low. Wading in the cold water, I longed for depth. I made do with a headlong plunge into waist-deep water.

Dog-tired, I slept soundly Sunday night, rising on Monday morning to the rigidity and stubborn pain of a middle-aged body. Despite creaking joints, I pieced together the final

253

section of my wife's fence after working a full day at the courthouse

"Where do you want the gate?" I asked René.

"By the compost pile."

I tore into the sod with the post-hole digger. A half-hour later, admiring my proficiency, ready to run the last of the fencing, I realized we'd made a mistake.

"I think the gate should be over by the garden shed," I offered, pointing in the direction of a gleaming white building on the north side of the garden patch. "It makes more sense over there."

I stared hard at the cedar posts I'd just erected with the realization that my most recent effort had been a waste of time.

"I think you're right," René agreed.

"The gate'll have to wait until tomorrow. I need to pick up some treated lumber and hinges."

A brief flash of disappointment clouded my wife's features.

"Will it be done tomorrow?"

"Yes," I responded carefully.

I'd been forced to redo many of the t-posts as the path of the fence drifted off line. I didn't want to stand around justifying the time I'd expended. I just wanted the thing done.

"Like my gate?" I said, beaming proudly as my wife approached the finished enclosure on Tuesday evening. I'd spent the better part of another three hours manufacturing the gate.

René opened the stainless steel latch and pulled the door towards her.

"It needs to be higher off the ground."

Blood surged into my face.

"Fine."

Another hour passed. The deer flies and horse flies that had plagued me over three days diminished, replaced by nearly invisible mosquitoes. Between angry swats at insects, I managed to re-hang the gate, trimming the jam so that the door swung freely and fit snugly against its frame.

"That's better," René said after a final appraisal of the project. "You know, the deer have stayed away since you began

254

building the fence," she added in an attempt at polite conversation.

I didn't respond. My legs carried me to our back porch where an old pair of cutoff jeans hung wet and heavy over the railing. Under the cover of a beach towel, I undressed and slid the shorts on before lumbering with age towards the waiting river. Immersed in the flow, I watched dusk overtake the heat of the day. Details of the shoreline disappeared. The intricacies of the forest vanished. Individual trees merged and formed a singular black silhouette against a velvet blue evening sky.

"I wonder where the deer are?" I asked quietly as I looked across the parched grass and admired my handiwork.

Another Deer Story

Those of you who know me know that I'm not much of a hunter and even less of a deer hunter. The last time I seriously stalked whitetail I did so on the spur of the moment with a borrowed shotgun loaded with slugs. I ended up haggling with another hunter over a dead six-point buck. That incident pretty much soured me on deer hunting.

This year, with an over-abundance of deer around our country home, I decided to buy a hunting license. My plan was to hunt our land. In anticipation of the opener in November, I took to the woods while the leaves were still in color to build deer stands from salvaged lumber and aspen logs. Things were set for a good hunt.

The Opener. I climbed into one of my new stands before sunrise. I was already comfortable when Gunnar Johnson (that's a real Minnesota name now isn't it?) and another guy I'd given permission to hunt my land, ambled by. I whistled. The sleepy hunters kept right on walking.

After Gunnar passed by, the forest became quiet. There was significant sun. It was warm: not at all reminiscent of the deer hunting weather of my youth. What I remember from nearly every hunt with my father and younger brother at our old shack up by Comstock Lake was shivering; from the moment I sat down in my stand to the moment I walked back to the shack at the end of the day. It didn't matter whether I roamed the woods, sat in a stand, or found an overlook on a ridge above a swamp: I was always chilled to the bone. Not this year.

Sometime after eight in the morning I heard the snap of a branch. I'd already been fooled by innumerable red squirrels darting across leaves decaying on the ground. The noise disturbed the gentle slumber I'd fallen into. I forced my eyes open, sat heavily in my stand, and wondered whether another rodent was toying with me. Then I saw her. Her movements were hesitant. The doe stopped and stared at me. More sounds of hooves dragging through leaves: another deer followed the doe. I didn't have a doe permit but I was hoping that the trailing deer was a buck. The doe studied my location. I waited for its companion to show itself.

The second animal hesitated, its neck and head concealed by a conifer. A slight wind rose and pushed my scent towards the deer. Before I could react, the flags of the two animals went up and they were gone.

Despite the warmth of the sun, my toes ached from the cold. I decided to take a walk. Unloading my twelve gauge over-under, I climbed out of the stand and set out towards the Taft Road. My plan was to follow the road for a few hundred yards, turn into the woods, and follow the small creek that feeds the Cloquet River on the eastern-most border of our land.

I climbed a small rise next to the road, loaded my shotgun, and entered forest. As I reached the shadow of the trees, two deer bolted. The animals leaped over fallen aspen, their brown and white bodies graceful against the sunshine, before vanishing into swamp. Even if I had a doe permit, I wouldn't have taken a shot. I couldn't. I was frozen by the sudden grace of the animals.

I hunted hard. After lunch, Christian joined me. He sat with me in another stand. After an unproductive hour or so, I left my son up in the stand and took a short walk in an attempt to drive deer. I pushed a doe but saw no bucks. As the sun set, my son and I met up and walked home.

Strolling down our driveway, the sky turning faint orange as it disappeared in the west, does and fawns materialized on the pasture surrounding our house. My son and I looked at each other and smiled.

The next evening. Nightfall cloaked the river valley as I drove my wife's Toyota down the entrance road to our house. An enormous buck manifested in the middle of the gravel lane.

"Holy crap."

"He's gotta go eight points," René whispered.

"Ten," Chris corrected from the back seat.

The buck was ancient and obviously smarter than the dozens of deer hunters combing the woods. Vapor from the

257

animal's nose framed the buck's magnificent rack before he turned and fled. As the Toyota rounded a corner and climbed towards our garage, two shadows blocked our path.

"I can't believe it."

"Not again," Chris moaned.

Another trophy buck and his female companion stood defiantly in our driveway.

I guess there's not much more to say about that, now is there?

A Little White Lie

"**What** happened to your finger?" I asked my son Dylan, who was, at the time, thirteen years old.

"I jammed it playing shinny hockey in Nick's basement."

I stared hard at the index finger of my boy's left hand. The second knuckle was swollen.

"You sure you don't want to have it looked at?"

"Nah, it's OK."

Fast forward to a funeral a week later. Pipe organ music echoes off the thick stone walls of St. Paul's Episcopal Church in Duluth. Mourners gather to pay their final respects to the wife of one of my former law partners. It's a contemplative moment. The weight of mortality hangs heavy.

"Hi Tracy," I say to Nick's mom. She's sitting behind me, waiting for the funeral mass to begin. "Dylan's finger is still pretty swollen from that hockey game in your basement."

"Oh."

We discuss how it is that each of us knew the deceased. The music flares. The service begins. I reflect on the thick wood beams and high ceiling of the cathedral. Ever the perfectionist, I note that, despite expensive repairs to the building's roof, water stains remain visible against the white plaster of the sanctuary.

I'm cognizant that Dylan is visiting the doctor today, and is in fact, likely at the physician's office that very moment. Dr. Knutsen will examine my son and x-ray the knuckle of the left index finger to ensure no bones have been broken, no ligaments torn as an aftermath of the floor hockey incident. René has taken off work to be there with our son. Things will go smoothly.

Tracy taps me on my shoulder. I face her. Her eyes are clear and somewhat hesitant. She speaks in a quiet voice.

"Mark, about Dylan's finger…"

"Yes?"

"Well, I don't really want to tattle on him but, that's not how he got hurt."

"What?"

There's a short gap in our dialogue. Sacred music fills the background.

"He and Jake were shooting at each other with BB guns. I think there's a BB stuck in Dylan's finger."

A vision of my wife sitting in Dr. Knutsen's office, having related my son's version of events to the physician, becoming upset as the terrible truth is suddenly and certainly revealed to her by x-ray, manifests in my mind.

"Are you sure?"

"Positive," the woman whispers. "I feel awful having to tell you this."

"Don't. I appreciate it."

There's no way that I can diplomatically leave the funeral. Instead, I mumble a prayer on my wife's behalf that the service will end soon enough for me to reach her by telephone. My selfish plea is injected into the stream of petitions whispered by the congregation on behalf of the departed.

"This is Mark Munger," I say urgently, talking to a nurse on the telephone after the funeral. "I need to speak with my wife before Dr. Knutsen sees Dylan."

"You're too late, Mr. Munger. The x-rays have been taken and the doctor is already in the examination room with your wife and son."

As René later related the incident, the physician walked into the room, our son's finger swollen and throbbing in pain, placed the developed film on the view box, and left mother and child alone to consider the image.

"What do you suppose that is?" René remarked, pointing to a shadow on the film, clueless as to what was actually wrong with Dylan's finger.

"Maybe it's one of those marker thingies they use."

"Maybe."

Dr. Knutsen wandered back into the room. He held his face tight with his right hand to suppress a smile. His other hand held a laser pointer. With the click of a switch, a red dot appeared on the surface of the x-ray. The pointer came to rest on the artifact on the film.

"What do you suppose this might be?"

René became uneasy. She shifted in her chair. Her eyes scrutinized Dylan's face. Something was up. She wasn't certain what was going on. But something was up.

The boy remained silent.

"I don't think it came from playing floor hockey, do you?"

More silence.

"Dylan?"

"I guess not."

"What do you think it might be?"

"It could be a BB...I guess."

Of course, I wasn't there for this part of the story. I was standing in the social hall of St. Paul's Episcopal Church trying to envision what was occurring in the doctor's office. What I imagined wasn't far from the truth.

Turtles

I have the opinion, based upon personal experience, that turtles are archaic, that they simply don't understand automobiles.

Every year we've lived in the country, ancient snapping turtles, their thick green shells covered with prehistoric nodules, their beaks wicked and curved, seek out loose sand and gravel on our property in which to deposit their eggs.

When we lived in the old Sears house, I encountered huge female snappers digging up our vegetable garden to secure clutches of eggs. In fact, there's an old photograph of me standing proudly on the newly mown grass of our front lawn. I'm holding a snapper by its tail and it's clear from the picture that the heavy weight of the animal is straining my arm as the turtle hangs in the thick summer air. I caught that turtle as she planted eggs in the moist soil of our potato mounds. The photograph was taken just before I released the animal back into the Cloquet River.

Sometimes I skinny-dip in the river. I often speculate that the same mother turtle (or one of her descendents) lurks in the black water beneath the overhanging bank, waiting to lash out at something resembling a… Well, you get the picture. As a male, it isn't a happy thought.

Though such an assault has never materialized, once, a few years ago on nearby Island Lake, a snapper bit my niece Kelly's big toe as she dangled it over the side of an inflatable Fun Island one hot Fourth of July. I view that attack as verification that my manly nightmare is likely a vision shared by a dim-witted turtle or two.

Our new house has a quarter-mile-long gravel driveway that passes over the throaty gurgle of a creek. Every summer, we find female snapping turtles hunkered down in the gravel laying their eggs smack dab in the middle of the road.

Driving home from work last week, I came upon not one, not two, but three snappers depositing their offspring-to-be in the warm gravel of the road.

"Jack, look at the momma turtles," I exclaimed, stopping my van just short of the preoccupied reptiles.

My son sat upright in his car seat. I rolled down the window so he could see the reptiles.

"Turtles!"

"They're laying eggs."

The drawback to having turtles use our access road as a nursery was reinforced the next day. Returning from work Wednesday evening, I found one of the snappers lodged in her hole. I exited the van. My son Dylan followed. I pushed an alder branch in front of the animal. The turtle blinked but did not snap.

"Something drove over it," Dylan remarked. "There's a crack in its shell."

My son pointed to a thin line crossing the turtle's protective covering. There was no question a vehicle had driven over the animal.

"Must have been the garbage man," I replied, grasping the tail of the injured animal.

The turtle did not move. It was obvious that a vehicle had crushed the reptile's spine. The animal was alive but paralyzed. Clear water swirled below the edge of the roadway as I hoisted the snapper and launched her towards the creek.

Splash.

The turtle landed heavily in the shallows. The snapper's head rose above broiling water. Her body spun aimlessly in the current: It was apparent she couldn't resist the force of the stream.

"Something will come along and eat her," I reflected as I returned to my vehicle.

A day or two later, Jack and I were driving the narrow causeway between the Eagle's Nest and Blue Max Resorts where the Beaver River fans out to form Fish Lake. A bright sun sat above the shimmering shoreline. On the hot blacktop of the road, a painted turtle, significantly smaller and less ominous than its snapping cousins, considered traffic. I stopped the car.

"Stay in your seat."

The turtle made no attempt to evade me as I approached it. When my hands closed around its smooth shell, the animal retracted its head, tail, and legs.

"See what Daddy found?" I asked Jack back at the van.

"Turtle."

"A mud turtle. It's not a snapper but it can still bite."

Later that evening, Chris and Jack released the painter in the pond of our rock garden. The artificial limits of René's garden pool could not hold the animal. Within a matter of minutes, the turtle was digging up our front lawn. She filled the hole she created with a dozen or so leathery white eggs, ensuring another generation of turtles on the Munger place.

Confronting the Green Eyed Monster

I was reading the *Duluth News Tribune*. My reading habit is unchanging. I start with the sports. Then I read comics (my eyes grow fuzzy trying to find the hidden picture in that one strip). I move on to the arts section. And I conclude my reading of the newspaper with the news section. I stick to this order regardless of what may have happened in the world because I'm a man comforted by consistency.

Now, I have to admit, the arts section is a new interest, one spurred on by my writing avocation. But my interest in the arts isn't altruistic: I'm profoundly competitive. I read the arts blurbs to discover what other writers and poets are up to in the Northland: what new pieces they've written, what awards they've been blessed with. I have a fierce inner need to be vindicated; a desire to feel that my efforts at writing and self-publishing have importance.

This Sunday, I read a piece in the *News Tribune* about a Proctor woman who, after moving to the Twin Cities, wrote her first novel in her late thirties. Since I also began writing later in life, my initial reaction to the article was:

How neat: Another writer who started late is getting her due.

Her name is Sarah Stonich. The book is *These Granite Islands*. Like my debut novel, *The Legacy*, Ms. Stonich's book is set on the Iron Range of Minnesota. Unlike my book, a large New York publishing house picked up her debut effort. Savage Press of Superior, Wisconsin, a small, one-man effort captained by Mike Savage, published my book. The difference between being published by Little Brown and Savage Press cannot be overstated.

Along with the national marketing power of a large publishing house, authors lucky enough to find a mainstream publisher also sign lucrative contracts paying generous cash advances. And, like any major player in the game, Little Brown will send Ms. Stonich across the country to promote her novel. She'll do reading and signing events at flagship bookstores in

New York, Chicago, and on the West Coast at the publisher's behest, I, on the other hand, continue to schedule my own events with minimal assistance from my publisher. It's not that Mike doesn't try: he does. But being a small publishing house means his efforts are concentrated on publishing first, marketing second.

When I discovered the measure of Ms. Stonich's success, I was unprepared for the extent that envy would well up inside me. Confronting jealousy can be a helpful thing, spurring one to seek greater rhetorical mountains to climb. However, I was wholly unprepared for the rush of envy that overcame me as I read the *News Tribune*.

"This really irritates me," I confessed to my wife, the professional therapist in our home.

"What's that?"

"Oh, this woman from St. Paul. She writes some book about an old woman on the Iron Range and all of a sudden, she's an overnight sensation."

Of course, the underlying and unspoken sentiment was:

Why couldn't that be me? Why, after nearly seven months of constant personal marketing efforts on behalf of my little novel, why hasn't it won awards? Why hasn't The Legacy *received national acclaim?*

"Patience, Mark. It'll come."

"Yeah. You know how patient I am."

In truth, I'm one of the least patient people I know. It's a trait that I struggle with at my "real" job, where, as a District Court Judge, I'm constantly called upon to exercise restraint. I'm nowhere done learning that facet of my job. I'm nowhere near being able to say, "I am a patient man."

I tossed the arts section of the *Tribune* aside. My wife's admonitions didn't curb the tacky, ugly feeling of resentment stuck in my craw. I know better than to invoke God to deal with my sin. He or She has bigger fish to fry, so to speak, than to listen to me whining about my hobby.

I found my way into the three-season porch of our house. The room serves as my sanctuary. It's where I go to write, and sometimes, to read what others have written. Sitting heavily on a cushioned chair, mired in a cesspool of self-pity, I placed my feet on a stool and perused the latest issue of *Writer's Ask,* a newsletter for neophyte authors published by *Glimmer Train* magazine.

Glimmer Train is one of the most beloved literary journals in the nation. I've entered short story after short story in the publication's writing contests. I've received rejection after rejection from the editors of the magazine: little notes of condolence that I file away with hundreds of other similar messages I've received from a variety of other publications. Despite the fact that *Glimmer Train* hasn't liked any of my stuff, I covet the writing in the magazine. I consider it to be a guide, a "how to" manual of short story writing, which is the reason I subscribe to *Writer's Ask.*

As I scanned various interviews in the newsletter, a curious thing occurred. Even though I'd followed my earlier inclination and refrained from asking the Almighty for intervention and guidance, a power beyond humanity interceded on my behalf. There, set out plainly on the printed page were words of sage advice from a world-renowned author:

Don't write for publication: Write for yourself. Don't worry about what other writers are achieving; worry about your project and whether or not you are being true to yourself. Don't disregard envy but don't dwell upon it. Use small doses of jealousy as motivation.

The passage contained an answer. Maybe not the answer I was looking for, but clearly a thoughtful, well-reasoned response to dealing with the "green eyed monster" that was lurking beneath my writing table. In reality, it was the same answer, stated in slightly different terms, as my wife's:

Be patient. Good things will come if you do the work. Keep your spirits up and remain true to yourself.

Sunday evening, I tried to get back to work on my second novel. My soul held too much residual envy for me to write. After creating several poorly constructed paragraphs (efforts that ended up in the wastebasket) I turned off my notebook computer and went outside to help my third son, Chris, put together a new trampoline. By nightfall, the three youngest Munger boys were leaping exuberantly through cool evening air. Watching their antics, I felt the weight of my jealousy dissipate incrementally with each gleeful bounce.

When I got to work today, I turned on my computer, went online and visited Northern Lights Books, a local independent bookseller. I didn't need to peruse the store's selection of new offerings. I knew which book I wanted. Without hesitation, I bought *These Granite Islands*.

The Short Life of Doc the Bunny

"**I'm** buying Jack a bunny for Easter," my wife René advised over her cell phone as she drove towards Dan's Feed Bin in Superior, Wisconsin.

"I'm not so sure about the wisdom of that."

"What's that? It's hard to hear you over the static."

I'd already taken a risk by broaching the topic of early rodent death. I decided to keep my predictions to myself.

"It's not important."

"What?"

I hung up my phone and concentrated on driving. I was on my way to pick up Jack from daycare. The rabbit would have to remain incognito for three days, until Easter Sunday, when it could be revealed to our five-year-old son.

Easter. Things went well. The brown and white bunny hopped around the great room of our house depositing droppings in nearly every corner of the space. Jack chased him and cuddled him and learned about rabbit claws, ending up with scratches across both wrists that resulted in significant welts. I placed a cage in Jack's room. Before leaving for church, I spread clean wood shavings in the bottom of the cage, freshened the rabbit's water, and added pellets to the food dish.

"What's the bunny's name?" I asked Jack as we drove to worship.

"Doc," he replied without hesitation.

There was no sense asking how the kid came up with the name. He just had. I left it at that.

Christian attempted to litter train Doc after going online and reading up on the process. Apparently Doc was computer illiterate. He never really accepted the notion of pooping in a box. Instead, he chose any convenient corner of the room he was in to do his business. After a few of weeks of finding bunny pellets in the farthest reaches of the house, I put an end to the experiment. The litter box was relegated to the storage shed and Doc was confined to quarters.

Jack continued to love and cuddle Doc but wisely adopted the strategy of doing so only when wearing long sleeves. The scratches faded. The bunny grew.

"René," I asked, "is Doc a dwarf rabbit?"

"No, he's a full sized rabbit."

"Well, there may be a problem. The cage you bought is for dwarf rabbits. Doc's still growing. He'll out-grow his cage."

"Do you always have to be so critical?"

After more than twenty years of marriage, I knew better than to respond. I walked out the back door, intent on providing Doc with outdoor grazing space. Shoots of new grass were appearing in the back yard. I'd promised my sister Annie that she could use our outdoor playpen, essentially a plastic corral that folds up for transport, for her little girl, Madeline. But the playpen also seemed to be an ideal fence for the new bunny. I found the contraption buried in tall weeds next to our storage shed and set it up.

Each morning before driving Jack to daycare, I placed the rabbit in the enclosure. Jack would climb into the playpen, hold the growing bunny, stroke its smooth soft fur, and say a daily goodbye. I cautioned Christian and Dylan to make sure our two Labradors remained in their kennels while the rabbit browsed. I'd seen enough Easter bunnies reduced to puffs of fur by family dogs over the years to know that dogs don't understand the niceties involved in declaring a rodent to be a family pet.

Tuesday afternoon. I drove my Honda Passport up the gravel drive towards the house after work. Jack munched M&Ms in the back seat. The sun was high. The day was warm. I'd left the rabbit secure in its enclosure free to nibble clover to its heart's content. I parked the car in the garage and watched Jack exit the Honda and amble out the service door. A blood-curdling cry arose. I jumped out of my seat and raced on to the back lawn where I discovered that the bunny corral had been upended.

I rushed to Jack's side. Doc (or what had once been Doc) rested between my son's tiny feet. Two blank eyes stared up at us from the rabbit's severed head. In the distance, Daisy, our mutt retriever, cowered in deep grass.

I carried Jack into the house, sat him down on the sofa, and bounded down the carpeted stairs leading to the lower level of our house.

"Who's the idiot who let Daisy out of her kennel?"

A lock clicked.

"Matt," Chris sheepishly revealed from behind the security of his locked door.

I stormed down the narrow hallway leading to my eldest son's bedroom.

"Matt," I yelled, throwing open the door to his room, "did you let Daisy out of her kennel?"

My eldest son works nights. My accusation rousted him from sleep.

"What?"

"Did you let the dog out of her kennel?"

"Ya, so?"

"Well, she just tore the head off your brother's bunny," I seethed. "You walked right by the rabbit when you came home. How could you not put two and two together?"

"What?"

In danger of losing it, I withdrew.

"Jack," I said in as consoling a voice as I could muster, "Doc is dead. Daisy didn't know any better. She's a dog. Dogs are supposed to chase rabbits. You stay here while I go outside, OK?"

Jack nodded. Tears streamed down his face.

I locked Daisy in her kennel, picked up the rabbit's head, walked to the edge of the trees, and gave the remains a heave. There was no sense in holding a funeral. It would only serve to upset Jack all over again.

Matt felt so bad about the whole ordeal that he and Chris drove Jack to the pet store that evening in search of a replacement. I suggested something smaller, a Guiana pig or a hamster: Something that could remain inside, out of the reach of marauding dogs. Jack selected a white hamster with beady red eyes. He named her Shirley. The first time Jack picked Shirley up Shirley bit his pinky. Then she learned how to escape from her cage by standing on her plastic igloo and squeezing through the bars.

One evening, Matthew knocked on the door to our bedroom. He'd been out with friends. The hamster had been AWOL for two days, her disappearance causing Jack mountains of little boy angst.

"Come in," René responded.

Matt entered our bedroom. The bottom edge of his t-shirt was rolled up.

"I found the hamster," Matt said, holding the fabric of his shirt tightly to his stomach.

"Where?"

"She was running around in my room."

"Put her away," I mumbled, my head pressed against the softness of my pillow, "and go to bed."

"Goodnight."

I listened as our eldest boy opened Shirley's cage. Immediately, the rodent found its metal wheel and began to run in place.

Squeak. Squeak. Squeak.

Likely getting in shape for another escape attempt, I thought as I faded off to sleep.

Last Chance

The sky is gray. The wind blows. Rain slides down the trunks of the three birch trees supporting the deer stand I occupy. It's not my stand but one built by a friend. Ron Envall is a substantial guy. The platform reflects Ron's need to have a sturdy place from which to scan the woods. The stand is constructed of treated 2"x 6" timbers, plywood, and twenty-penny spikes. The thing is built to hold Ron. It's excessively sturdy for a man of my size.

Everyone around me has been shooting deer. Does. Spike bucks. Mammoth swamp bucks with gargantuan racks. I've seen two deer. The flash of a tail and a snort of warning. The flank of a doe retreating through a thicket. No chance for a shot. No need to discharge my over-under twelve gauge loaded with slugs. Christian has had similar luck. He's heard a few animals crashing through the forest but has seen no deer.

Snow fell this past week: Snow dampens the sound of deer on the move and makes the animals less wary. Snow also provides contrast in the forest, making the deer easier to see. But the snow has largely melted. What remains has been hardened by the early winter sun and polished smooth by recent rain. The deer are nervous. The noise of their hooves chattering over ice-covered trails makes them wary and the woods are crawling with humans. Deer hunters march endlessly through the forest in search of animals to shoot. The noise of the advancing florescent army forces the deer deep into the swamps. Given the circumstances, I'll be lucky to see any deer on this dismal day.

It's the last day of deer season. I've managed to get into the woods for a total of six hours of hunting. Book selling events in Canada and here at home have eaten up prime hunting time. I missed opening day. Chris related that I really didn't miss much other than below zero cold. He fired no shots. He hit no deer. No venison was taken off our acreage.

I hunted the second day of the season. It warmed up enough to make the few hours I spent in Ron's stand enjoyable.

There's something spiritual about sitting ten feet above the floor of the forest, a weapon in your hands, your ears and eyes attuned to the sounds and sights of the woods, a slowly rising sun warming your face. But, as I've already confessed, I saw only glimpses of deer; phantoms that couldn't be shot during that earlier watch.

Today, the wind is brisk but does not chill. The drizzle is so light that it doesn't penetrate my clothing. I remove my fluorescent orange hat and gloves and sit silently amongst gently swaying trees. I rest my shotgun across the corner supports of the stand and scan slight openings in the deep forest for signs of movement. I see nothing. Nothing but sedge grass, balsam, aspen, birch, and three large red pines, remnants of the forest that once covered this piece of land.

By the age of the pines, I speculate that the trees sprouted in the aftermath of the Great Cloquet Fire of 1918, a conflagration that consumed hundreds of thousands of acres of forest, destroyed entire cities and towns, and killed upwards of five hundred people. The red pines in front of me likely sprouted from soil blackened by that fire. The pines are impressive against the surrounding second-growth birch and aspen but are mere twigs in comparison to the white pine and red pine forest that once covered this part of Minnesota.

I hear rustling on the woodland floor. My ears perk up. I move my right hand towards the stock of the shotgun, alert and ready should a deer appear. A red squirrel skitters. My heart returns to its normal pace.

Not long after the rodent disappears, I hear what sounds like a pair of bison crashing through the underbrush. There is no question that the noise is the result of a doe being chased by a buck in rut. The sound grows louder. The deer are moving closer. I slide my hands under my gun and lift the weapon to the ready. My index finger moves into position outside the trigger guard. The disturbance stops. I can tell from the direction of the noise that the deer are off to my right, concealed from view by a row of balsam. I try to control my breathing. The skin of my bare hands chills. I wait. And wait.

I never hear the deer again. Like ghosts in the mist, they vanish. I never see them; never have a chance of a shot. Dusk arrives. The rain intensifies. My glasses fog but I do not get wet. Distant gunfire booms across the Cloquet River. I do not hear any shots fired on my side of the river.

Finally, it's too dark to hunt. I empty the breech of my shotgun and climb down Ron's well-built ladder until my hunting boots, the leather aged from use and lack of care, rest firmly on wet ground. I walk home. I have failed as a hunter. Still, I am satisfied.

A Bitter Harvest

After days of unrelenting cold and gray, the sun has finally decided to shine. It's Sunday afternoon. Dylan is working at the Minno-ette. Christian is hiding somewhere on the lower level of our house with his buddy Spencer playing video games. Matt is sitting in front of the television watching another putrid performance by the Minnesota Vikings. Jack, our youngest, is in his bedroom playing with action figures, his imagination aglow with possibilities.

The wind is raw despite the low globe of the sun hanging to the west. Dead cornstalks chatter in the breeze as I trudge through the wet loam of our vegetable garden. Squash, painted bright orange by a heavy frost and shaped like emaciated footballs, sit on moist ground. I hack vines with a hatchet, releasing the squash before placing them into a waiting trailer attached to an old Yamaha four-wheeler. I haven't been in the garden for over a month. I despair at the weeds that've overtaken what was once a neat and orderly plot. Migrating raspberry canes choke out the blueberry bushes that René planted last spring. Similar intruders overshadow the new black raspberry canes that I planted with visions of sweet homemade jam.

Huge acorn squash, their girth equal to a man's waist, the globes weighing in excess of thirty pounds, their skins still hard and green, prove to be a challenge as I hack them free of their vines and drop them over the fence onto our lawn. I stare at the squash. It seems impossible that these vegetables would fit in a conventional oven: They're simply too big.

I fell corn stalks with a ground ax, leveling the residue of the best sweet corn crop we've ever grown. I pull offending raspberry canes free of wet dirt. The plant roots are stubborn and unyielding and I wrench a shoulder in the process but there's no one around to listen so there's no point in complaining.

Jack dances across our lawn in a brand new winter jacket, dress slacks, and new light-up tennis shoes. He's clearly intent on joining me in the garden but his apparel is wholly inappropriate for the task.

276

"Jack, you need to put on your old jacket and boots."

The boy stops in his tracks. Sampson, our fourteen-year-old yellow Labrador and Daisy, a black Labrador mix, lope behind the child, distracted by their own play.

"I don't wanna."

I'm short on patience. The circumstances of last Friday weigh heavily on my mind as I consider my son.

"Just do it or you'll have to stay inside."

Jack crosses his arms over his chest. The hood of his new jacket obscures his face. I can't see Jack's eyes but I know that they're filled with refusal. After an interlude, the child wheels and darts towards the garage. The dogs run after him. I return to piling dead vegetation in a wheelbarrow. It takes a good half hour to transfer the debris to our compost pile. By the time my task is completed, Jack is playing with the dogs. He's changed his jacket, pants, and shoes causing me to consider how much he is like his older brother Dylan. Both will complain to high heaven about doing what they're asked to do only to ultimately comply.

My eyes search the high silver sky for signs of rain or snow. The clouds contain no moisture. If the sky had been like this on Friday, it wouldn't have happened. Tragedy would have been averted. But that wasn't the case. The skies over Eveleth, a small town located on Minnesota's Iron Range, were low and dense with ice. The difference between what's above me now as I work in my vegetable garden and what confronted the Senator's plane is patently obvious.

Though we weren't close friends, I knew Paul Wellstone and his wife, Sheila, peripherally.

The first memory I have of Paul was as an organizer in the Jesse Jackson for President Campaign. René and I took Matt to see the Reverend Jackson speak at the University of Minnesota-Duluth. The UMD gym, the same venue where I saw President John F. Kennedy speak when I was a child, was packed. We were lucky to have tickets. I don't remember what the reverend said that day. But I certainly remember Paul Wellstone.

When Wellstone picked up the microphone and challenged all of us in the room to work to defeat the

Republicans it was as if someone had disturbed a herd of Angus with a cattle prod. There are no words to describe the vitality, the energy, the emotional connection that Paul conveyed on that occasion. It was, and remains for me, through all my years in politics, a singular moment.

Over the years, our paths crossed. René and I hosted fundraisers for Paul. On several occasions I reminded Senator Wellstone to remain true to his populist roots; to remain, in the face of a tide of conservatism and selfishness assaulting the nation, a Liberal. He assured me that he'd never back down, that he'd never yield philosophical ground. And he never did.

Whether you agreed with his politics or not, no one could argue that Senator Paul Wellstone wasn't a man of principle. This is best illustrated by his first and last major votes in the United States Senate. When newly sworn in, Paul was called upon to show his support for the United States' invasion of Iraq under the first President Bush. Paul Wellstone opposed that war. He refused to accept that peace was not an option in dealing with Iraq. He voted on his convictions. More recently, in what would turn out to be the last major vote of his career, Senator Wellstone once again refused to yield to the advice of pollsters. In an act of courage, against conventional wisdom in a tight re-election campaign, Paul Wellstone refused to support the second war with Iraq. His constituents loved it. His standing in the polls climbed. Integrity, it seems, does matter.

When my first novel was being printed in the summer of 2000 and I needed folks of prominence to endorse the book, I thought of Senator Wellstone. As I said, we weren't close friends but the moment I asked his staff if he'd take a look at my novel, there wasn't any hesitation. He read it and critiqued it himself. He was the same way with everyone. Whether you were a new judge with a recognizable last name or a retired teacher from Buhl who needed help with Medicare, the Senator rolled up his sleeves and did what needed doing.

The tiller churns. My boots are caked with soil. No geese fly despite the hunter's sky. I am careful to till around slumbering carrots, the plants still green despite the advent of hard frost. I avoid tilling up our asparagus, a mistake I've made in the past.

After an hour of following the slowing churning tires of the Troy Bilt, our garden is finally at rest. I return the tiller to the shed and head towards the banks of the Cloquet River in search of inner calm. I sit at the top of stairs that descend to flowing black water.

I went to church this morning. I prayed for the Wellstone family and for the others who were on the Senator's plane. It's unclear to me whether my prayer achieved what I'd intended. As I watch the river roll past my family's home, I ask God to speak to me. I ask the Great Judge to explain to me why eight innocent people had to perish. I want the Creator to reveal to me why this United States Senator, one of a handful of politicians possessing the remarkable moral clarity to oppose a war waged solely for personal gain and familial reputation, had to die. But on this Sunday afternoon in Fredenberg Township, Minnesota, I hear nothing but the passing of a slow wind through dead leaves.

Smooth

Winter once again challenges the order of life for folks living in the country. It's February and I'm lacing up my old Bauer hockey skates for the first skate of the year. The reason I'm so late in taking to the ice? Last week it was nearly fifty degrees. The Fredenberg ice skating rink, the work of many hours of donated labor by our local volunteer fire department under the careful scrutiny of a part-time rink attendant, deliquesced.

Normally, when the ice thaws this late in the season, there are no second chances. But a cold snap stalled over northeastern Minnesota during the week, allowing the skating rink to be re-flooded in quick fashion.

It's near zero. Jack and I sit in the warming shack. An electric wall heater spits dry warmth into the room. A bare light bulb glows. I bend over to tighten my son's skates.

"This should be fun," I say to Jack as I pull the laces taut.

"Yep," the child responds curtly, his face buried in the fabric of his hat, his ears and cheeks covered by flaps of fleece-lined nylon.

"That should do'er," I say, pulling gloves over my hands.

It's an odd year for me. I've had a kid playing organized hockey for sixteen years. No more. Some years back, Matt was cut from the Hermantown High School team as a sophomore and, for the most part, hasn't held a hockey stick or laced up his skates in seven winters. Dylan felt the unkind blade of a coach's cut this past November. After returning from a tournament in Warroad, Dylan was advised by the head coach that his services were no longer needed. Consequently, I haven't watched a hockey game this season. Not one minute. Not one shift. Not one period.

Christian never played the game. His skating shows it. He's a lot like his old man in this respect. I didn't learn to ice skate until late in life; as an adjunct to taking Matt to his practices.

280

Jack is five. Given our family's history with the sport, I don't see Jack taking up organized hockey. It's not worth the effort. But skating for pleasure, with winter tickling your exposed flesh; now that's something worth passing on to a kid. And so, earlier this evening, I asked my youngest son to go to the rink with me.

We walk outside. Laughter greets us as we waddle along the black rubber path linking the warming house with the rink.

"Come on Jack," I urge, sliding a child's chair towards my son across the ice. "Grab on. Use the chair for balance."

Jack moves forward with unsteady steps. Vapor trails from his mouth. Fathers and their children (there are no mothers at the rink on this frigid night) skate lazy circles at the far end of the rink.

"I'll give you a ride," I offer, skating up to Jack, spraying him with ice as I stop.

The boy takes a seat in the chair. I crouch low and push off with the inside edges of my battered skates. We sail over the ice, stars visible and clear in the black sky stalled above the rink. We pivot around a net, narrowly missing a little girl and her father. Air rushes past us. We gain speed. A bare remembrance of the moon climbs the eastern sky above the darkened land. We circle the rink. I stop. Jack resumes pushing the chair.

One by one, the other folks depart. Soon, it's only Jack and me and the ice. Cars and trucks come and go at the Minno-ette across the road from the warming shack.

"Time to go," I say as I complete an awkward crossover turn.

"One more ride."

I search Jack's eyes. I witness in them the hopes of my youngest son and I recall the disappointments of his older brothers. I nod. Jack settles into the chair and I begin to skate.

Beanie Babies

It's an annual tradition. Every year, I bring my sons and wife to the local Ducks Unlimited (DU) fundraising banquet. This year, I shelled out two hundred bucks for my wife René, Dylan, Jack, and myself to attend. That's just the cost of dinner and our DU memberships. Once we're at the event, we spend more money on raffles and other contests in an attempt to win prizes.

Though we haven't won consistently at these events, when we do win, we usually win big. About ten years ago, I won an over-under twelve-gauge shotgun. When Chris was ten years old, he won a beautiful oak gun cabinet handcrafted by a local cabinetmaker. Three years ago, Dylan won a semi-automatic ten-gauge goose gun. All told, I figure we're still ahead of the game.

DU spends millions of dollars each year in the United States (more in Canada) attempting to preserve prairie marshlands and ponds so that waterfowl and wildlife have a place to propagate. Some cynics would say that the only reason DU does what it does is to ensure plenty of ducks and geese for hunting. I don't buy that. The men and women that I've met at these dinners over the years are not just here to support hunting: They're here to preserve clean water, air, and wildlife habitats for all species that live in the marshes and alongside the great waters of North America.

Without the efforts of DU, herons, swans, egrets, and countless other non-game species of birds, not to mention otters, beaver, musk rats, and a myriad of other mammals, would likely disappear from many of the places they're still found.

"Dad, I wanna win somethin'," Jack observed as he followed me from auction table to auction table at the DU dinner.

I was scouting out the silent auction items, placing my name on bid sheets in front of things I liked.

"OK. There's a Green Wing table across the room for guys your size."

We walked across the carpeted floor in the Proctor Blackwood's Restaurant and stood in front of the kids' table.

"How much to enter the Green Wing drawing?" I asked an older gentleman decked out in western style clothing complete with bolo tie and Stetson.

"Ten bucks a ticket," he replied. "Say, little fella," he continued, looking down at Jack, "you havin' a good time?"

The man tousled Jack's brown hair. The child smiled and nodded.

"I'll take one."

The cowboy tore off a ticket and handed it to Jack.

"Put the big end in the drum and keep the little end."

Jack did as he was told. I took the small end of the ticket and tucked it away in my shirt pocket with the other raffle tickets I'd purchased.

Dylan was antsy. There was only one other couple at our table, an elderly psychologist and his wife. It was a Saturday night and my son had places to go and girls to see.

"Dad," Dylan said, wiping the last bit of food away from his mouth, "I'm gonna hit the road. I'll be home by twelve."

"I'll watch your tickets for you," I replied, unwilling to force him to stay any longer. He'd done well to stick it out two hours.

"See ya, Jack," the teenager said as he ambled towards the door. "Win somethin'."

The slow parade of silent auction items began. The raffles that I'd entered proceeded to conclusion. Despite spending nearly two hundred dollars on tickets, we didn't win anything. Finally, we were down to the last event: The Green Wing raffle.

I leaned over to speak with Jack. My instructions were whispered.

"Jack, if he pulls your name," I said, pointing to the cowboy at the front of the room, "take the shotgun."

There were seven or eight items to choose from on the Green Wing table. There were nice limited edition prints of dogs and ducks. There was a fishing outfit, complete with rod, reel, and tackle box. And there was a gleaming brand new twenty-gauge semi-automatic junior shotgun resting in the middle of the prizes. The gun was a real gem, worth nearly three hundred dollars.

I glanced around the room. There were only four or five other kids present. Jack had a legitimate shot at winning the gun. My message, though said softly, was said with firmness so that my five-year-old understood the gravity of his decision.

"Take the gun."

Jack's face tilted towards mine. His mouth parted. I strained to hear his acceptance of my direction.

"I want the Beanie Babies."

My eyes darted. The volunteer's hand dipped into a jar filled with tickets. On the Green Wing table behind the cowboy I spotted five small stuffed animals.

"Jack, I'll buy you ten Beanie Babies. Just take the shotgun."

"And the winner is…Jack Munger."

As we walked through the crowded room, other patrons murmured things like: "Oh, what a cute little boy" and "Isn't he precious?"

I continued petitioning.

"Jack, when we get to the table, take the shotgun."

We stopped in front of the one hundred and fifty or so folks in the room. I handed the cowboy Jack's ticket.

"What will it be, pardner?" the man said in a *faux* western voice.

I bent over to counsel my son.

"Take the friggin' shotgun."

Jack stared at the table but his eyes never focused on the shotgun.

"But I only want just one of the Beanie Babies."

I looked back at René. She smiled and shrugged her shoulders. I was on my own.

"OK," I relented. "He wants the Beanie Babies," I said, gathering the five small stuffed animals into my arms.

Jack's face broke into a broad beam as I handed the animals to him. His feet fairly flew back to our table. The psychologist and his wife chuckled as I sat down, the sting of defeat etched on my face. Another name was drawn. The second kid was whisked to the front of the banquet hall by his father.

"He'll take the shotgun."

Back at home, Christian was appalled to learn of Jack's decision. Chris ripped the stuffed creatures out of Jack's embrace and raced into my writing study. After five minutes of computer research Chris re-entered the great room of our house and tossed the Beanie Babies on the floor.

"Eleven dollars and twenty-five cents. You passed up a shotgun for eleven dollars and twenty-five cents."

"Relax, Chris," I admonished. "I'm OK with it. Jack told me something that made it easier to accept when we were walking back to the table after he turned down the gun."

"What's that?"

"Well, he looked right at me and said: 'Cheer up Dad. You can always buy me a shotgun.'"

Escape

"**I'm** taking the day off," I announce to René, my wife of twenty-three years.

"For what?"

"For my mental health," I assert. "I haven't been trout fishing all summer. The season ends soon. I'd like to put in at least one good day on the water."

My spouse looks at me with understanding. She knows that I'm trying to cram a few centuries of living into one life. It's a defect in my character that she accepts.

"You can't keep adding and adding. You're not going to be able to keep this up," she warns, her words a repetition of countless prior admonitions.

"That's exactly why I need to go fishing."

The following morning, I drop my youngest son off at his preschool and head up the North Shore of Lake Superior. I have a list of streams in my head that I want to explore. One in particular stands out. I plan on saving that river for last.

I've admitted it before. I am an inept fly fisherman. I grew up plying the waters of Miller Creek in the Piedmont Heights area of Duluth for native brookies and planted browns using worms for bait. Occasionally, I'd hop on my old Schwinn 5-speed Collegiate, the handlebars and seat modified to affect a touring bike, and pedal to the banks of the Midway River or Keene's Creek in Hermantown. I was a poor fisherman as a teen. I rarely caught trout. I don't want to decrease my chances of success by trying to tempt fish with flies: I'm a worm fisherman and proud of it.

It's a cool, over-cast late summer morning. Despite near perfect conditions for trout fishing, the first two streams I try produce no strikes. I pull into a small grocery store in Finland, Minnesota for a packaged sandwich and a bottle of juice.

"Any luck?" the female cashier, a woman looking to be in her late fifties, asks.

"Nothing. But a bad day on the river is better than a good day at the office," I reply, repeating a timeworn cliché.

"That's for sure." She takes my money. "Good luck."

"Thanks."

My shins ache. The waders I'm wearing rub my shins, where my stockings droop. I pull the socks up to cover the abrasions, the left ankle more affected than the right, in hopes of preventing further damage.

I drive over a logging trail through the bleakness of a northeastern Minnesota cutover. The loggers have left a meager buffer of timber (mostly aspen and birch, augmented with an occasional pine or spruce) along the streambed. I find a spot where the river, really no more than a creek, passes beneath the gravel road in a culvert. I park my car and pull on my waders.

My socks don't insulate my skin from the neoprene. I grimace as I pick up my rod (a cheap collapsible spin cast outfit) and ease down the bank on wounded ankles. Overhead, a big flock of Canada geese swings south. It's too early for the birds to be migrating but not too early for them to be obnoxious.

As I enter the river, I remain concerned. The summer has been unnaturally warm and virtually rainless. These fragile North Shore streams cannot survive without cool, filling rains. I dip my fingers into the lifeblood of the river. It's cold: cold enough to sustain trout. I'm glad. This is my favorite trout stream. I would hate to see it destroyed (the way other local streams have been) by beaver dams that raise the temperature of the water and negatively impact the survivability of speckled trout.

I struggle through cedars shading the creek and toss my hook and worm into places that look trouty. I marvel at the determination of the Minnesota DNR. Every hundred feet or so, I find evidence that some worker from the state has sliced through logs dropped across the water by intrepid beaver, chain sawing potential logjams out of the way, allowing the river to flow.

It's late afternoon before I land my first fish, a small native trout flashing blue, red, and yellow dollops of color under the muted sky. I shove the fish in the pouch of my fishing vest and continue to fish. I encounter a quiet pool. Beaver have managed to string not one, not two, but three dams across the river, slowing the gushing water to a meander. As a fisherman, I recognize that, in the long term, the dams are not beneficial. But in the short term, I know that larger fish lurk here.

The banks of the river are undulating mounds of swamp grass, interrupted by shallow pools of standing water and deep access canals cut by beaver. I take a step and watch my leg disappear to the limits of my waders while my other foot remains affixed to solid ground. Never much good at doing the splits, I extract myself from the deep hole just as water begins to enter my waders.

A red tail hawk glides over valley. A bluff, its crown covered with spindly pines and leafy deciduous trees, rises behind me. A clear-cut looms beyond the timber. I toss my hook and worm into the slow current and wait.

My line disappears from the river's surface. I set the hook. I'm into a nice fish; far more powerful than the one I've already taken. The brookie seeks refuge in a tangle of roots along the far bank of the pond. I horse the fish and ease it towards my waiting hand. The fish breaks the plane of the water. It's a nice ten-inch speck. Luminous and vibrant, the fish dances across the water against the cool air. I grasp the fish firmly with one hand, remove the hook from its jaw, and deposit the trout in the game pouch of my vest.

"That's why I'm here," I mutter to myself. "There must be more where that one came from."

Indeed. Several minutes later I latch into a beauty. The strength opposing me is significant. I let the fish race up and down the pond. The brookie finally tires and I pull it from the grip of the river.

"Wow," I muse, studying the powerful flanks of the trout, a specimen over twelve inches in length. A gorgeous catch for any stream. A trophy from the small waters that I'm working.

A few more casts. I snag a log. I pull hard hoping to dislodge the hook. I hear a snap. My cheap collapsible rod breaks.

"Crap."

There's nothing left to do. I've caught all the fish I'm supposed to on this day. If one measured the success of the day in dollars, I'm deep in the red. The gas. The lunch. The license. The bait. The ruined rod. All expended for less than a pound of fresh fish. The exchange isn't exactly even.

But that's not how brook trout fishermen, even those that use worms, value things.

The Opener

Thirty-five years. That's how long my father and four of his high school cronies have been spending the Minnesota Fishing Opener at Bob Scott's place on Whiteface Lake north of Duluth. Over that time, there've been many lean years at Whiteface in terms of fish being caught. But fishing isn't why we spend nearly every Mother's Day away from our wives and mothers: Catching fish has very little to do with the Opener.

Before the males in my family ventured up to Scott's cabin for the Opener, my dad brought us to the Seagull River at the end of the Gunflint Trail for the Opener. Seagull is a legendary walleye factory. It's where I hooked the only truly remarkable fish I've ever caught. The story went something like this.

We motored up the Seagull River under cover of night so we could be at our fishing spot by midnight. At the Narrows, we met up with hundreds of other like-minded folks searching for trophy fish. We anchored our boat amidst a raft of other boats and started fishing. But my big fish wasn't caught at night in the Narrows: I hooked it while trolling another stretch of the river in broad daylight. I was tired from spending the night on the water and inattentive to what I was doing. I held my fishing rod (an old fiberglass cast-off with an open-faced reel) loosely in my hands.

Somewhere along the path we cut through a myriad of other boats, my line went taut.

"Dad, I think I'm snagged."

"That's about par for the course."

Dad was forever untangling my line, baiting my mom's jig with a new minnow, or trying to keep my brother David's hook out of someone's eye. My father is not a patient man. Putting him in a small boat with three amateur fishermen was a real test of his mettle.

My father backed the boat up. I tried to reel in the monofilament line but whatever I'd hooked wasn't budging. Then, without warning, my line began to ascend.

"It's coming up."

"Probably a log."

I won't belabor the tale. After five minutes of playing the fish, I pulled a ten pound, three ounce walleye out of the Seagull River. Though the fish provided little fight and even less excitement, it remains, to this day, the largest fish I've caught. And that walleye was only one of a half dozen fish that we netted during that Opener that exceeded six pounds.

On the Seagull, we were angling over walleye spawning grounds, catching huge females and preventing them from perpetuating their species. This fact wasn't lost upon the Minnesota DNR. Eventually, the state closed the Seagull River to fishing during the Opener. By the time the Seagull was closed, the Munger boys had already started spending the Opener at the Scott cabin.

Let me tell you this: Compared to the Seagull River, Whiteface, a slender reservoir lake created by a small dam on the Whiteface River, is the Dead Sea. Oh, every year, the five fathers (we've recently labeled them "The Iron Five" because they're now all over seventy years old) who originated this tradition, brag about years when we caught oodles of walleye and huge northern pike during the Opener. Well, to my memory, if anyone ever caught a limit of fish on Whiteface, it must have been while I was asleep. I can't remember taking more than a handful of nice walleyed pike, fish over three pounds, from the Lake in our thirty-five years of trying.

Our wives, girl friends, and mothers know this to be true. They'd tell you that, despite the fact they've been deserted on most Mother's Days, they've yet to see more than a meager packet or two of walleye fillets come home. This year wasn't any different.

The sky never really cleared. There was near constant drizzle and wind. Fishing was terrible. In my Northland fishing boat, powered by a fifty horse Force outboard, I took, at various times, my father, his pal Red, and my two teenaged sons, Dylan and Chris, across the Lake in search of walleye. We never caught a single walleye. Red netted three perch. Dylan caught a northern suitable for a tropical fish tank. My dad, Chris, and I were essentially skunked, unless you count the two slimy snake Northern Pike that Chris reeled in using other people's rods.

It really doesn't matter. The Opener is about eating vast quantities of food, re-telling old stories, and having a libation or two; though sometimes the two becomes three or more, creating memories that, unfortunately cannot be shared in a family story collection.

This year, there were twenty-six of us at Bob and Pat Scott's place. For a quarter of a century, Pat Scott has permitted a bunch of carousing fisherman (no daughters, wives, or girlfriends allowed) to invade her lake cottage during the Opener. It's even more astonishing that, for the past ten years, what was once the Scott cabin, is now the Scott home. Can you imagine your mother, wife, sister, or daughter putting up with several dozen smelly beer-swilling fishermen in their home for two nights and two days?

We were out on the lake. The wind had calmed but low rain clouds and shifting rain remained. Dark shrouded the landscape. I turned the ignition key to start the Force. Instead of the satisfying roar of the motor, all I heard was the whining of the starter.

"What the....?"

"You remember when that happened last summer, Dad," Christian advised. "You took off the cover and fixed it."

"I did no such thing," I said, certain that I'd never encountered this particular problem.

I'd already discovered that my trolling motor, a two horse Johnson, was inoperable. I had the thing repaired last summer after Dylan, my muscle-bound son, pulled the recoil rope right out of the unit. His antics broke not only the rope and handle but the recoil spring itself. When I tried to start the motor on Saturday there was no handle and no rope to pull. The shop had replaced the spring but not the handle and rope.

"That happened once last year to Matt and me," Dylan announced.

"You fixed it before, Dad," Chris insisted.

"I'm telling you that I've never had this motor act like this."

"I think your dad would remember if he'd done this before," Grandpa Harry interjected.

"What did Matt do to fix the problem?" I asked as I removed cowling.

"I dunno," Dylan responded.

I muttered something unprintable and fiddled with the armature of the starter. The cog on the starter moved. After further tinkering, I was able to get the starter to connect. The outboard roared to life.

Back at the Scott place on Sunday afternoon, I dig my swimming suit and towel out of my overnight bag. The lake water was measured by John (Bob and Pat Scott's eldest son) to be forty degrees. I strip off my clothes, pull on my trunks, and enter the Scott family sauna. Inside, Bob, John, and Joe Scott (John's son and Bob's grandson) sit in heat. I find a place on the cedar bench.

As steam rises from the rocks of the sauna stove, the four of us (one Munger and three generations of Scotts) talk about life, love, politics, and sports. We do not discuss fishing.

Satellite Blues

I'll be the first to admit that I am not a techie. My son Matthew is. So is my brother-in-law Alan. When the two of them get together and talk, it might as well be in Russian as far as I'm concerned.

Sure, I'm typing this story on a computer. It's the same dinosaur Texas Instruments notebook that I used when I was in private practice as a lawyer. But just because I know how to type on a 486 50MHz piece of history (you thought I was gonna say something else, didn't you?) doesn't mean I know squat about how the thing runs. To me, it's a bit of black magic that my fingers touch the keys and words appear on the screen.

Anyway, Matt came home. He's been away touring the public colleges of the Midwest. He started out as an engineering student at Michigan Tech. Then he migrated to Fargo for a year at NDSU. Now I think he's finally found his niche: He's at the University of Wisconsin-Superior taking courses in business technology systems. A fancy way of saying he's learning how to integrate computers into the business world.

"Dad, we need faster Internet," was one of the first phrases our oldest kid uttered when he came back home.

"Why?"

"I'm gonna be downloading all kinds of assignments from my professors and I'll need to be able to do it quickly."

"We don't have access to fiber optics or cable out here," I advised.

We live on the banks of the Cloquet River twenty miles from town. Where we live, we're lucky we have telephone service. Given this reality, I thought the issue of high speed Internet was dead. Unfortunately, I didn't figure on two techies putting their heads together.

"Alan, what do you know about satellite Internet?" Matt asked when my brother-in-law was at our house for Christmas.

Alan works in the Twin Cities in the technology field. I've never really understood what he does. When he's around Matt, there's precious little conversation about such details.

"Funny you should ask," Alan responded. "I bought a new dish for work. I was going to use it at one of remote sites in Ohio but I haven't tried it yet. I'd be willing to haul it up here and let you try it to see if it works. If it does, you can just buy it from the company. If it doesn't, I'll take it down."

"Dad?"

I feigned deafness. My deception didn't last.

A Saturday morning in early February. I'm waiting for Alan, his wife Colleen, and their two kids to arrive. I'm slated to assist my brother-in-law with the installation of the satellite dish.

"Where are you going to put that thing?" René asks as she wanders into the kitchen. "I don't want some ugly satellite dish standing out like a sore thumb in the front yard," she adds.

"Alan needs to aim it to the southwest. The front yard is the best place to put it. It's gonna be on a wooden pallet. It's only temporary."

René's look is stern.

"It's not going to be standing in my front yard," is all she says between sips of strong coffee.

Later that morning, my wife's instruction clear in my mind, Alan and I lug a pallet towards the back of the house as we discuss a location for the temporary installation.

"Can we put it off the three season room in the back?" I ask. "It'll have a clear shot over the pasture to the southwest."

"That'll work."

Despite the fact that he's a techie, I genuinely like Al, though I've never called him that. I've never asked him if he'd respond to Al rather than Alan. Probably not. Alan suits him.

"Twenty-three," I call out over one of Alan's walkie-talkies.

The dish is positioned precariously on the pallet, pointed between two gigantic white pines off to the southwest. I gave Alan a woodsman's approximation of southwest. My brother-in-law insisted on checking the orientation with a GPS. Turns out my instincts were within a degree of true southwest: A triumph for man over machine.

Alan is outside with another radio wiggling the dish up and down and from side to side in an attempt to increase the percentage of connection to the computer from twenty-three percent to something over thirty-five percent, the minimum required to get a useable signal. Despite the fact that it's February and windy, it's not cold. This is not a job you'd want to be doing in below zero weather. Not that I'm shivering. I'm sitting behind a keyboard in Matt's bedroom. My sole job is to relay numbers from the computer screen to Alan via the walkie-talkie.

I don't want you to think that there wasn't debate as to whether Matt's personal computer or our home computer, located in Christian's room, should be hooked up to the satellite dish. There was considerable discussion of that topic amongst our three oldest boys. But in the end, given that Matt was the one who "needed" a faster Internet connection, the cable is being routed to his room.

Alan and I work throughout the morning trying to increase the satellite signal. By 1:30pm, when it's time for lunch, we've actually gone backwards.

"I don't know why we can't get a better connection," my brother-in-law laments between bites of pizza.

"Maybe it's just not gonna work."

"We're missing something. It'll work."

Matt comes home from his job and I escape further involvement in the project. Before abdicating my role, I leave my eldest son with a parting shot:

"It's never gonna work."

For the remainder of the day, I am smugly satisfied. Instead of increasing the percentage of connection between the computer and satellite, the number plummets further. Finally, even Alan admits defeat. My wife diverts his attention from the Internet project to wiring under-the-counter lights in our kitchen. *That* project turns out to be an overwhelming success.

"Sorry it didn't work," Alan mutters as he steps away from our front porch. It's near nightfall and the Schostags are headed back to the Twin Cities.

"Not your fault," I say, trying to conceal my "I told you so" glee.

Later in the evening, René and I go out to dinner with friends. Matt enlists Christian to monitor the computer screen. My eldest son mounts the dish to the wooden posts supporting our three-season room and manipulates the unit in search of a better signal. My wife and I arrive home around midnight. We hear voices in the basement.

"I've tried that," Matt advises to someone over the telephone. He's a true techie. He's wearing a headset, his cell phone strapped to his waist, as he walks around the room. "That too," he continues.

"How's it going?" I ask as I enter his bedroom.

I note that that graph on the computer monitor shows a twenty-three percent connection to the satellite, exactly the same number that Alan and I obtained when we first turned the thing on at ten o'clock that morning.

"I'm on the phone with Hughes," my eldest son admonishes, naming the manufacturer of the ill-fated dish.

"Dad, I wanna go to bed," Christian laments through an open window. My third son peers into Matt's bedroom from outside. His face betrays that he's cold, tired, and fed-up with his brother.

"You're not any further along, are you?"

Matt ignores me.

"Ten more minutes and then let Christian go to bed," I warn.

Matt continues talking on the phone.

Fifteen minutes pass. I crawl into bed. René is in the bathroom brushing her teeth. I hear a blood-curdling cry from the bowels of the basement. I leave the comfort of our king-sized platform and pad down the stairs.

"What's up?"

"I can't believe it," Matt says.

"Can't believe what?"

"Alan."

"What about Alan?"

"I asked him about the little labels covering the ends of the dish receiver. He said they wouldn't make any difference. The guy at Hughes asked if I'd taken them off. I asked why. He said the dish won't work with the labels on."

"You're kidding me!"

My son beams. His eyes are heavy with fatigue but his face clearly betrays an "I told you so" look.

"Check it out. I took the covers off and the thing jumped to sixty-eight percent. I'm logged on to MSN right now."

The graph on the computer screen proves the obvious and it's my turn to eat crow.

Ron's Turtle

My neighbor Ron McVean has only part of his left arm. The details of how and why he lost the limb aren't important to this story. The fact that Ron, in a very limited sense, is physically challenged, is relevant to this tale.

A couple of summers ago, René and I were visiting Ron and Nancy's motor home on Island Lake. The details of why we were there aren't significant. I remember it was a Saturday during the summer and that lots of other folks were milling around the place, enjoying the hospitality of the McVeans.

I was trying to play horseshoes. I say trying because I consider myself to be lawn game challenged. With the exception of volleyball, where I can use determination to compensate for my lack of athleticism, I'm pretty much a failure at standard picnic games.

Thud.

More often than not, my horseshoes would land in the grass great distances from their intended target. Sometimes the shoes would turn sideways in the air and land on the run, rolling hell-bent-for-leather towards innocent bystanders. Only once out of every hundred or so throws did I hit the stake. Only once out of every thousand tosses did my horseshoe catch the post.

Ron was absent from the game. He usually supervises my ineptitude by offering gentle pointers such as:

"You throw like a girl, Munger."

Or:

"Didn't you ever play this game growing up?"

But Ron wasn't by my side as I launched ponderous metal objects into the summer sky.

"What 'cha doin'?" I asked when I caught up with Ron later that afternoon.

My friend was on his dock immersed in a task. A pair of mallards floated contentedly on the black water of Island Lake as a breeze worked up a walleye chop.

"I'm trying to fillet this darn turtle."

The stump of Ron's left arm secured the rough shell of a snapping turtle.

"Why?"

"I want turtle soup. This critter was eating the fish on my stringer and wouldn't let go when I picked him up so I whacked off his head with a hatchet."

My friend raised the heavy reptile with his good hand and beamed proudly.

"She's a big one."

"Should be good eating."

"Ever tried it?"

"Nope, but I hear it's good."

To set the record straight, despite the fact that Ron has only part of his left arm, I've learned over the years that there are very few things Ronald McVean cannot do when he puts his mind to it. He's bested me at one-on-one basketball. He's slammed a volleyball down my throat on any number of occasions. He's good with tools; better with computers; and recently wired the entirety of his new house. But that day, watching Ron struggle with the snapper under the stump of his left arm, it seemed to me that my friend could use some help. Still, offering aid to a person with an obvious physical impairment isn't something one does cavalierly. I weighed the fact that Ron is a proud and hard-working man, someone who has not let a little detour on life's road impact his love of life, his God, and his family, against the fact that he wasn't making much progress cutting up the critter.

"Want some help?"

Ron didn't hesitate.

"You bet. I can't hold the thing and cut at the same time."

Though I'd never dissected a turtle (my high school biology experiences having been limited to cats, frogs, and a fetal pig) it didn't look all that tough for someone with two functioning hands to cut the meat away from the shell of a dead reptile.

The sun came out. The day grew long. Ron wandered off to entertain guests. I sawed away at the unforgiving sinew of the turtle's musculature. Deer flies and horse flies appeared, teased into activity by the heat. My progress was continually interrupted as I swatted insects trying to burrow into my scalp. I cut my thumb trying to slice and swat at the same time. Blood flowed from the wound.

"I need a band aid."

One of my kids located a bandage in Ron and Nancy's motor home. I covered the cut and continued working.

Dinner hour came. Ron reappeared with a plastic baggie for the turtle meat: lean, red muscle that looked a little like beef.

"Is that all the farther you are?"

"Shut up," I said, half annoyed, half amused that my dissection of a dead animal had consumed the better part of a beautiful summer day.

"You don't have to get testy."

"This is a lot harder than it looks."

"Looks like we'll have enough for soup."

After two and half-hours of diligent effort, the shell was finally clean of flesh.

"Cool," Ron said, hanging the shell of the turtle on a nearby birch limb. "The birds can peck off the rest."

My thumb stopped bleeding. I removed the bandage and washed my hands in the lake. Ron's wife walked onto the dock.

"Ronald, what are you going to do with that?" Nancy asked, pointing to the bag of turtle pieces in my friend's right hand.

"Put it in the freezer. Some winter night we'll invite Mark and René over for turtle soup."

"That stuff will sit in our freezer forever. You're never going to make turtle soup."

"That's it," I exclaimed, rinsing my hands in the cool lake water of Island Lake. "Where do you want the guts?"

"Put 'em over there," Ron responded, pointing to weeds along the shoreline. "The gulls can eat 'em."

"They'll stink to high heaven," Nancy objected.

"Put 'em over there," Ron commanded.

I did as I was told.

Years intervened. The McVeans built a beautiful home on their lake lot. In the process of moving, Nancy discovered the turtle meat congealed in a lump at the bottom of the family deep

301

freeze. Ron was away at work when his wife removed the hard-won gains of my reptilian autopsy and tossed the mess into the garbage.

Floating

There is water everywhere. It's rained like cats and dogs for weeks. The past month has seen only brief interruptions in the precipitation. The days without moisture have, with rare exception, been unnaturally cold.

Pewter clouds roll overhead as I set the bow of my Grumman square stern canoe in the Cloquet River. I'm determined to fish the river. It's Memorial Day weekend. I should be up north, in the Boundary Waters Canoe Area with my three oldest boys, enjoying a pristine wilderness experience. But I am not.

Matt, my eldest, was the first to break the news to me.

"Hi Dad. About this weekend…" he related over the telephone.

"Huh huh."

"I have to work."

"Matt. I've had the permit for months. You've known about the trip since January."

"I know Dad. They want me to work. They're short-handed. I can't turn them down. I can't pass up the time and a half. I need the money."

A wave of upset rose inside of me. I tried to maintain a calm demeanor. I couldn't very well fault the kid for trying to put some money the bank. After all, he was paying his own way through college.

"Fine."

"Fine" is an interesting word. Paradoxically, the phrase generally denotes situations where things are anything but "fine".

"Don't be upset, Dad."

"I'm not."

"Yes you are. I can tell."

Of course, he was right. I let my anger cool.

"How about trying some brown trout fishing if I can find some time later this summer?" I asked, thinking of a well-known river not too far from where my eldest son was living at the time.

"Sure."

I let it go at that. The same night I had virtually the same conversation with Dylan, my second son.

"Dad, I can't go this weekend."

Lucky for Dylan, Matt had already softened my resolve.

"Gotta work?"

"Yep."

"OK."

That left Chris and me. I knew that René and Jack weren't interested in fighting the forecast that called for prolonged rain and cold. Under ordinary conditions, my wife would be more than willing to tromp around the BWCA but she wasn't about to volunteer to do it in the pouring rain.

"Dad, Curtis wants me to go camping with him."

One of Christian's classmates asked if Chris could go with his family to Wisconsin for Memorial Day Weekend. The request came as I was contemplating whether or not the two of us should venture up to Brule Lake in the BWCA. My son's intense brown eyes reflected a clear desire to go with Curtis.

"Fine."

Funny how that word seemed to roll off my tongue and linger in the air.

I pull the recoil on the little Johnson two horse to make sure that the motor will start. The outboard coughs. A cloud of blue exhaust spits into the cool air. The fuel ignites and the canoe surges through the water. I shut the outboard down. I'll need the engine for the return trip. For the trip down river, the natural flow of the river is sufficient.

At intervals during my float, I toss lures into locations that normally produce game fish. I manage to hook and land a three-pound sucker. Nothing else bites. Several pairs of wood ducks, the males resplendent in their plumage, rise from the river and scurry out of my path. I munch on Ritz crackers and sip bottled root beer while I fish. Stray raindrops tumble from the sky and strike my raincoat as the canoe floats along. There isn't enough precipitation to make me run for cover: just enough to make me wet and uncomfortable.

I drift through a series of modest rapids and come to rest in a flat pool. I cast and cast and cast but nothing strikes the floating jig head and dew worm I offer. I scan the shoreline for signs of nature. No deer appear. No rabbits scurry beneath the bramble. No beaver plow through the water.

My stomach rumbles. It's past dinnertime. Chris is somewhere in Wisconsin, splashing in the pungent water of a chlorinated swimming pool. Matt is hoisting and carrying boxes at work. Dylan is keeping a close watch on plumbing supplies.

I start the motor and begin the short journey home. In a matter of seconds, the sky opens up.

Indian Lake

The Lumina bounced along the blacktop highway north of Pequaywan Lake. Matt sat in the front passenger seat. Christian occupied the seat behind me as I drove.

"This seems like an awfully long ways," Chris noted. "You sure we can do this trip in four days?"

"The map says..."

"Oh no, not the map thing again," Matt lamented.

"You got somethin' against reading a map before you go on a canoe trip?" I asked.

"It's not *that* you read the map, Dad, it's *how* you read the map that concerns me," Matt observed.

I remained quiet, unwilling to enter into a debate at eight o'clock in the morning heading into the weekend. The forest, a mixture of evergreens, aspen, and birch, slipped by. Finally, the sign I'd been looking for loomed ahead.

"Here we are," I said as I made a left turn onto a gravel road.

We were to begin our paddle on the upper Cloquet River at Indian Lake, a dime-sized pocket of water located near Brimson, Minnesota. Matt was along to drive the van home once Chris and I launched our canoe. Home was our target. Because our house sits on the banks of the Cloquet River a mile and a half below the Island Lake dam, it was my vision (hopefully not a nightmare) to canoe from Indian Lake, forty to fifty miles north of our property, down the Cloquet, through Alden Lake, back into the Cloquet, and then, with one final rush of enthusiasm, cross Island Lake. At the western end of Island Lake, we'd portage around the dam, drop the canoe back into the river, and finish the trip home.

A cold Lake Superior wind greeted us as we exited the van. Matt and I flipped the canoe off the vehicle and left it next to the lake for Chris to load. I took a deep breath of country air and admired the scenery as Chris piled duffel bags and fishing equipment into the bottom of the battered Coleman canoe.

"Good luck," Matt said as he stood next to the driver's door of the van watching the Coleman float free of the sandy bottom of Indian Lake.

"It'll be nice if the wind keeps coming from the east," I replied.

Matt entered the Lumina and slammed the door. The van's tires spun in the gravel. My attention shifted. I searched the lake's shoreline for the outlet to the river.

"The channel's over there," Chris said, pointing to a funnel of water flowing south as we began our paddle across the water.

"You're wrong." I said with confidence.

My guess turned out to be a dead end. Chris was right. Thankfully, he didn't chastise my navigational skills after we'd paddled aimlessly around the small lake before edging the Coleman into the slow current of the river. The river exited the lake right where Chris had pointed.

The Cloquet River begins its descent from Indian Lake as a series of winding turns through sandy banks. White pine, spruce, jack pine, and an assortment of broad leaf trees shelter the watercourse.

"What are those?" Chris asked as we slid by a sandy bluff.

"Turtles."

"There must be fifty of 'em."

"They're wood turtles. They're rare. You only find 'em on the upper reaches of the Cloquet."

We pulled up to shore to investigate. The reptiles were lounging in the intermittent sun, preparing nests. Chris crawled out of the canoe, hoisted a specimen, and gently placed the turtle back on the loose sand.

"That was neat," Chris said as we pushed away from the bank.

After several hours of paddling we arrived at the first portage. In higher water, the rapids ahead of us could be run.

But with the river level the way it was, there's no way a kayak, much less a fully loaded canoe, could make it through.

Chris and I donned our caps and began unloading the Coleman. A stranger appeared. The man was old and doubled over but his eyes sparkled as he spoke.

"Headed downriver?"

"To our house below the Island Lake dam."

"Water was higher last week."

"You ever catch any fish around here?"

"Walleyes, northern, crappies, and the occasional brown," the old man said, squinting at me as he took in my face.

"Really. I thought there were supposed to be brookies up this way."

"Browns. The water's perfect for fishing right now. It was too high for the Opener."

I asked some more questions, mostly about the landscape beyond the first rapids and the locations of campsites further downstream. The old man confirmed that there was a formal campsite complete with fire ring and primitive latrine just below the rapids we were skirting.

Chris and I passed the first campsite. It was too early in the day to stop. We pushed on. The landscape reminded me of the river in front of our house. Black water sliced between low banks strangled with pines, birch, balsam, and aspen. Towards dusk, we scared up a muskrat. Evidence of beaver was everywhere in the piles of slashings, felled trees, and impressive habitations along the river.

"See that little pool?" I asked Chris as we rounded a sharp corner. "According to the map, there should be a campsite here."

Chris muttered something about "Dad and his maps" but didn't voice any serious opposition to checking out the shoreline. We found a campsite complete with fire ring, cooking grate, latrine, and a supply of cut firewood exactly where the map said it should be.

After setting up the tent, starting a campfire, and eating dinner cooked in a pouch, my son pulled out a traveling chess set, placed the board on a balsam stump, and began arranging chessmen on their appropriate squares.

"Wanna play?"

"Sure," I replied. "I'll kick your butt."

A propane lantern hissed from its perch on a flat rock as we sat on folding camp chairs and plotted our moves. The day departed and velvet settled over the campsite as I achieved checkmate.

Morning broke. Mist rose from the cold water and merged with warming air. I awoke from the sort of desperate slumber gained when one sleeps on rocky ground. Age is not kind to canoeists: One's ability to sleep on a thin pad of foam does not become easier with maturity.

Chris was still asleep as I filled steel pots with river water, started the single burner propane stove, and cooked breakfast. Instant oatmeal, hot cocoa, tang, and hot coffee were soon ready.

"Get up."

Chris didn't stir.

"Time for breakfast."

A slight moan emerged from the tent in reply. I sat on a stump and ate hot cereal. A beaver cruised upstream, passing a spot where I'd encountered a set of timber wolf tracks. The tracks went right through our camp behind those of a small deer. I wondered about the drama that likely unfolded between hunter and prey somewhere downstream.

Slap.

The beaver detected our presence and gave warning. Chris climbed out of his sleeping bag, donned his clothes, and joined me. In short order, we finished breakfast, cleaned the dishes, and packed the canoe for the second day of our trip.

We entered a slow, meandering portion of the upper Cloquet River that can best be described as maple savanna. Tall grass and spindly trees defined the inconsequential banks of the river. Gone were the high bluffs and conifers that marked the beginning of our journey. White pines and red pines were visible on the horizon but did not crowd the water. A white tail deer, the amber color of its fur set ablaze by the morning sun, browsed marsh grass along the bank in front of us before sauntering off.

Our progress halted. Beaver had successfully bridged the Cloquet River by dropping a massive burr oak from one bank to the other.

"Looks like a good place to have lunch," I said. "We'll have to portage around the beaver dam anyway."

"OK."

The muddy banks surrounding the dam were steep. It took an effort to drag the fully loaded canoe up the incline and on to flat ground. Evidence of beaver infestation was everywhere.

"Look at all the beaver crap," I said, my feet mired in ooze.

"Gross."

After finding a patch of ground clear of beaver leavings, we ate lunch before portaging around the dam. We resumed paddling. I tossed a spinner and a night crawler along the shore. No fish bit. Chris slept as we floated. A stiff wind out of Manitoba prevented warmth.

"Another portage," I said as the Coleman rounded a lazy bend. "Must be getting close to Alden Lake," I surmised. I didn't bother confirming our location on the map. We had ample daylight left and we weren't in a hurry.

The sound of a four-wheeler rumbling in the woods greeted us as the bow of our canoe struck land. A Polaris ATV, the driver, heavy set and circumspect, pulled into view.

"Where you headed?"

"To our house on the lower Cloquet," I replied, climbing over a Duluth Pack and a stack of duffle bags in the middle of the Coleman. "We started at Indian Lake."

"Water's going down. Was higher last week."

We inspected the portage. The guy sat on his vehicle, his ample belly covered by a "Minnesota Vikings" pullover, as he reflected on the churning whitewater.

"Doesn't look so bad," I said to Chris as we viewed the rapids from a rocky point. "Wanna try?"

My son studied the water.

"What about that?" Chris said, pointing to a plume of water spouting between two gigantic boulders.

"I think we can slide between the rocks. It'll be tight, but if we crank it to the left as soon as we come over the lip, I think it's doable."

Gray cloaked the afternoon. The sun had vanished. A chill infiltrated my bones.

"Well?"

"Sure."

"You gonna try 'er?" the stranger asked as he pulled alongside our canoe on his ATV. "My son does it all the time in higher water. Last week would have been perfect."

"I think we'll give it a whirl," I replied, climbing back into the Coleman.

"Good luck," the man offered without conviction.

We paddled across the river and sat quietly in the last bit of calm water above the rapids. I studied the rocky ledge, looking for an entry point that wouldn't leave us hung up. The last thing I wanted to do was get stuck sideways on a rock.

"Ready?"

"Yep."

"Just keep your paddle in the canoe until I ask for help," I reminded my son. "Let me steer. If you put out your paddle before I tell you to, we'll likely end up wet."

Chris didn't respond.

The entirety of the Cloquet River was gathered between the two boulders. There was no water to the right of the ledge: only more boulders. To the left, the water thinned out until it was only a few inches deep.

"Here we go."

Gravity grabbed us. Spires of water rose around the canoe. A boulder loomed. I dug deep with my paddle and tried to pivot away from the rock. The canoe didn't respond.

In a panic, Chris stuck out at the rock with his paddle. The shift in my son's weight caused the canoe's left gunwale to dip. River poured into the bottom of the Coleman.

"Don't reach!" I shouted. "Keep your paddle inside the canoe until I tell you otherwise!"

There was an instant, as water surged over the plastic edge of the canoe, when I thought we were going to roll. But

311

Christian shifted his weight back to center and I dug hard against the current. The canoe slid through the narrows.

"Alright!" I shouted, raising my paddle in triumph as the Coleman shot into the flats below the flume.

"That was something."

"Paddle!" I shouted, angling the canoe across the shallows.

The bottom of the canoe bounced and slid across rocks as we continued downstream.

"Look," Chris said, pointing towards the left shoreline.

The big man sat expressionless on the ATV watching our progress. It was obvious that he'd selected his vantage point in hopes of witnessing disaster. I was happy to disappoint him. He waved half-heartedly as we passed by.

"Oh, oh."

"What?"

"There's more."

Another set of rapids, a complication not apparent from our former vantage point on the trail, loomed ahead of us but we passed over the second barrier without incident.

Afternoon grew into evening. I heard the sounds of an outboard motor up ahead.

"We must be getting close to Alden Lake."

"You said that two hours ago."

"Ya, but this time, I really mean it."

We passed the intersection of the Little Cloquet River and the Cloquet. The channel widened. The watercourse took on the attributes of a lake. Rounding a bend, a pontoon boat came into view. It was the first boat or canoe we'd seen in two days. Two men worked on an old outboard motor in the middle of the channel trying to get the engine to idle. Blue exhaust drifted against the pewter sky. We paddled past the boat. One of the guys, his sweatshirt covered in motor oil, raised his hand in a slight wave. I nodded. We pushed on.

OK, so I got us lost on Alden Lake. I know what you're thinking. Alden Lake, a modest bulge in the upper Cloquet River, is too small to get lost on. Well, that might be true if you're simply looking to stay on the lake. But if you're searching for the lake's outlet, it isn't that hard to get turned around.

"Dad, why are we paddling back where we came from?"

"I messed up."

"But you're the guy with the map."

I didn't respond. I simply paddled.

Eventually, we found our way into the river and camped on a small island just below the outlet from Alden Lake. During the night, a thunderstorm rolled in from the west. Though the bad weather only lasted half an hour or so, the force of the wind was remarkable. Our dome tent, sitting as it was on a small island in the middle of the river, was unprotected from the gale. As a hard rain fell, the wind increased until it sounded like a freight train lumbering across a crossing. The thin fabric of our shelter billowed and lifted off the ground, restrained only by tent pegs thrust into shallow soil and the weight of two worried campers.

"I hope it holds," I whispered as the tent rocked and pitched. There was no response from my son.

Dawn came quietly to the river. The clouds were gone when I left my sleeping bag the next morning to light the stove. A pair of wood ducks flew down the river valley. The sun had not yet climbed into the eastern sky but the day was already beginning to warm. The tent had held. We had stayed dry. All in all the experience had been, to use a common adjective used by today's teens, "awesome."

Below our island campsite, we ran numerous riffles and small rapids without incident. The landscape became familiar. The flat savanna that we'd negotiated gave way to terrain nearly identical to that surrounding our home. Pines and balsams became prevalent. The river channel began to feature boulders, rocks, and ledges as its pitch increased.

Late in that morning, we encountered significant rapids and beached the canoe to scout our approach.

"Looks doable," I said. "We'll have to pull like hell to make it from the top section across to that chute," I noted,

313

pointing to a tight passage near the middle of the rapids. "But I think we can make 'er."

"Let's try it," Chris agreed. "I don't want to portage."

It was the fastest water we'd run. The bottom of the Coleman never touched a rock as we blew through the first flurry, pulled hard across the current, found a line, and scooted down a second set of riffles before the river spit us past an island in the middle of the channel.

"That was a hell of a paddle," a guy observed from the comfort of his canvas camping chair on the island. A group of five men, the first canoeists we'd seen on the trip, nodded approvingly as we drifted by their campsite. "You made it look easy," the guy added as he sipped something hot from a tin cup, the steam from the cup wandering against fragile morning light.

I nodded. The current pulled us away. The Coleman slid easily through other riffles and rapids. Our speed began to increase as we neared Island Lake: a large reservoir lake holding water for Minnesota Power's hydroelectric system. Chris and I had canoed this stretch of the upper Cloquet when my uncle Willard, a state representative involved with environmental preservation, led a group of legislators and conservationists down the river.

Three bald eagles left their perches and soared westward, apparently intending to race us to the lake.

"I don't think we can portage that mess," I advised as we scrutinized a set of rapids just above Island Lake. "There's no channel."

"Time to portage," Chris reluctantly agreed.

The trail was rutted and muddy from rain. We made several trips across the slippery path with our gear and the canoe.

Bathed in late morning sunlight, we ate peanut butter and jelly on pita bread, drank Kool-Aid, and munched beef jerky. Water coursing over rock provided a noisy backdrop as we filled our bellies with food and our souls with beauty. Across the water, two nylon dome tents rustled in the breeze.

"The wind will be in our faces when we hit the lake."

Chris nodded as his teeth fought tough beef.

314

The Coleman slid over the final boulders demarcating the border of river and lake without incident. Fishing boats bobbed in the water. We were no longer alone: We were back in the 21st century, surrounded by outboard motors, jet skis, and year-round lake homes.

The wind was strong. Despite the steady breeze and white-capped waves, Chris was a trooper. He never whined or complained as we plodded across the open water of the lake.

"Let's have dinner at Porky's," I said as we passed beneath the Island Lake Bridge, my arms tired, my legs cramped from two hours of paddling.

"I'll go for that."

We beached the canoe and made our way up to the highway. A short walk on blacktop brought us to Porky's Drive-in, a throw-back to the 1950s: a vintage roadside restaurant where you order your food at an outside counter and eat at tables under an open sky.

"I was thinking," I offered between bites of well-done cheeseburger and onion rings, "that maybe we should surprise Mom and come home a day early. If we keep paddling, we can probably be across the lake before evening. It's only a mile and a half down river to the house from there."

"OK," Chris agreed, his mouth full of burger.

The wind hadn't lessened. With little discussion we paddled across another five miles of open water as whitecaps rolled under the plastic spine of the canoe. I was thankful that we'd taken the Coleman: It's the only one of our canoes with a keel. In surging waves, even an inch of raised plastic running down the hull of a canoe can be significant. A keel keeps the craft on line between dips of the paddle making course corrections less frequent.

"I think that's the bay we turn into to get to the dam."

"I'm not sure," Chris said, his mistrust of my navigational skills obvious. "I think it's further down."

Again, the kid was right and I was wrong: We had another mile to paddle. As we approached land, the shoreline on either side of the dam was bustling with people.

It was clear from water stains on the concrete portion of the dam that Island Lake was five to six feet below its normal water level. I'd suspected that this was the case. As we'd passed through the lake, we'd seen pontoon boats resting on extended beaches and docks that didn't come close to reaching water. The rain the past evening had not made a dent in the drought. It would take a storm of Noah-like proportions to bring the lake's level back to normal.

I portaged the canoe across the dam and down a steep rocky slope before resting it on a gravel beach. As Chris and I lugged gear down the same path, brown skinned Native American children flitted through newly leafed aspen trees playing tag while their parents fished from shore. Other anglers stood waist-deep in the river wearing chest waders and tossed spinners and jigs towards the lake's outlet. The water exiting the dam foamed, accentuating the illusion that the lower River was a giant vat of root beer. We loaded the canoe and slipped into the current.

Water frothed. The Coleman bounced off boulders as we slid easily through rapids. Mallards and teal escorted us as we paddled home. The concrete bridge over the Taft Road loomed ahead. We passed through the bridge's shadow and floated by our old farmhouse, the place that originally drew our family to the Cloquet River. As we drifted towards our new home, the voices of my wife and Jack echoed across the water. A yellow sun dipped in the west just above hills marking a familiar bend in the river.

"René," I shouted, "we're here."

My wife appeared at the top of the riverbank.

"You're home early."

"We thought we'd surprise you," Chris added.

An unfamiliar bark broke the quiet interlude. The furry head of a yellow Labrador puppy appeared next to my wife at the top of the slope.

Yip.

Jack materialized from behind his mother. The puppy cocked its head and took a defensive stand as if to protect my wife and my youngest son.

"Meet your new dog."

316

Transitions

The trial lasted six days. Even though being the judge on a complex civil case isn't as taxing for the judge as it is for the lawyers, there's a certain amount of stress that makes its presence known by the end of a long case even for the judge. I was ready for respite. I was ready for the North Shore of Lake Superior.

"Remember, I'm taking Friday off," I reminded my wife René on Wednesday as we cleaned up after dinner. "I think I'll head up the Shore to do some trout fishing, maybe bring a shotgun with, take Copper for a walk in the woods."

"I have an appointment Friday morning. I guess I'll have to get someone to watch Jack."

I was happy my wife didn't try to talk me into foregoing the trip. She seemed to know that I needed a day off.

6:00am came early. I forced my eyes open, stumbled through the darkness of our bedroom, and ran a hot shower. The Lumina was already loaded with my waders, a fly rod, my fishing vest, rain gear, Grandpa Jack's side-by-side .410, and a box of thirty-year-old Number 7 shells. Dressed in blue jeans, a heavy fleece shell, and wool socks, I rambled to the basement level.

"Dylan, time to get up," I hollered through my second son's closed door. "It's six-thirty."

There was no answer.

"Dyl!"

"Wake Chris up," was the response, "he needs to take his shower first."

I stepped to the next door.

"Christian!" I yelled, "time to get up."

There was a low moan in reply. I left the basement, walked into the cool dark of the garage and loaded a travel kennel into the back of the van for our five-month-old yellow lab pup.

"Here, Copper," I yelled. "Here boy!"

The pup pranced into the garage. An open door revealed the ascending light of a new day. It was going to be sunny and clear, a great day to hunt partridge: not so great a day

317

to catch brook trout. Copper leaped into the kennel without hesitation. I shut the cage's wire door and closed the van's hatch. Sampson, our old yellow lab, a dog decrepit with arthritis, hard of hearing, and gun shy, looked up from his place on a rug next to the garage service door. He didn't move: His limbs were frozen with age.

I watched the sun climb over Lake Superior as I drove the back roads from Fredenberg to Two Harbors with a loose grip on the steering wheel and a travel mug of hot coffee in my right hand. Vapor rose from the slumbering land. The sun's mounting light reflected off wispy spider webs linking grasses in the roadside ditches. I pulled into the Two Harbors McDonald's drive-through and ordered an orange juice and an Egg McMuffin to go.

"Can he have a treat?" the clerk asked as she handed me a bag containing my breakfast.

"Sure."

The woman passed me two dog biscuits and I slipped them through a slit in Copper's kennel.

"Thanks."

We arrived at a stream. The dog remained in his cage while I fished. I had no intention of letting a young Labrador disrupt the solitude of a morning spent on brook trout water.

My first cast of the day landed behind a small boulder. Water curled around stone, white and fast on its plunge towards the Big Lake. I felt a strike and set the hook. I reeled my line in. A brilliantly hued trout danced above the flowing stream. The fish arched and wheeled against the tension of the fishing line.

Splash.

The fish went free. Morning fog rolled off the river. Here and there, hints of autumn touched the maples, birch, and aspen lining the water. Trout season was due to end on Monday. When I purchased my trout stamp and fishing license in May, I vowed that I'd get in plenty of fishing. It's my first time out brook trout fishing this year.

A sleek doe, her nose wet, her eyes large and wary, stepped gingerly into the stream. She entered the water twenty

318

feet from where I stood. I watched the animal, its fur shiny in the fresh light, its caution evident. A yearling fawn nearly the size of its mother stepped into the river behind the doe. I stood transfixed. The animals stopped halfway across the river to drink.

"Hey," I shouted after allowing the deer an extended visit.

The animals were upwind. They didn't detect my scent.

"Hello deer," I called out, waving my free arm like a maniac as I continued to fish.

The doe's nostrils flared. Then, without so much as a splash, they were gone.

By noon I had four fat trout in the game pouch of my fishing vest. The sun was high. The brookies had disappeared beneath overhanging cedar roots and jumbled boulders to escape the warming day. By noon, I was hungry and convinced that the fish had stopped biting.

Lunch for the fisherman was a ham salad sandwich, a bottle of juice, a Hershey chocolate bar, and a bag of potato chips purchased from the Cooperative store in the little hamlet of Finland, Minnesota. Lunch for the retriever was an ample supply of dog kibble.

"Come on Cop," I called to the pup as I began to walk down an old logging road in search of ruffed grouse after finishing my sandwich on the tailgate of the van.

The dog lifted his head from the remnants of his meal before padding down the trail after me.

We walked the better part of two hours without seeing any game birds. Copper was perfect. He worked the edges of the trail with gusto. He never strayed more than a dozen paces ahead of me. He sniffed dead leaves and grass. He followed the scent of flickers and blue jays into the brush but always returned when called. After a bit, I raised Grandpa Jack's old .410, flicked the safety off, and pulled the trigger. I wasn't aiming at a bird: I fired the old gun to see the pup's reaction to the noise. Sampson is so gun shy that he's totally useless in the field.

Boom.

At the sound of the gun's discharge, the young dog simply stopped and turned as if to ask:

So did you hit the bird or what?

"Good boy," I praised as I urged the pup into his kennel at the end of the day. The dog's tail beat a steady pattern against the plastic walls of his cage. He let out a howl, the sort of lonesome call you'd associate with coon dogs. I emptied my shotgun and pulled my fishing gear out of the van.

I worked the river in hopes of finding big trout. The section of the stream I was on had yielded four or five nice trout the year before when I'd stumbled onto a beaver pond chock full of fish. But the water level was low and the streambed was littered with silt. I tried hard to catch another brook trout but it was not to be.

Frozen Ground

There has been an absence of winter. Though the ground froze solid early this year, there is no snow cover.

Saturday. For the past several years, my two middle sons, Dylan and Christian, have been assigned the task of organizing our family's recycling. It's a job they're required to accomplish every month. Not that they easily comply with my requests to "take the recycling in". They don't. They're teenagers. It takes a lot of yelling and cajoling, accompanied by threats, to compel their cooperation.

It's ten o'clock in the morning. Both boys are fast asleep. I decide to accomplish two very dismal tasks on my own. One of them is to bring paper, plastic, glass, tin, and aluminum to the recycling center.

I dress for winter. The sun is shining. It's warm for December. Two or three days earlier, the mercury reached forty-five degrees. I'm hopeful the warm spell will make my second task of the day manageable.

I begin my chores by dumping three barrels of recyclables onto bare ground. Much of the refuse is contained in white trash bags. My first task is to open the bags and sort through the mess; plain glass in one pile; brown glass in another; tin cans to the side; aluminum into a cardboard box; plastic into a large black trash bag; junk mail, newspapers, and magazines in plastic bins.

"Who in the world thinks this is acceptable?" I mutter aloud confronting a can of dog food smeared with remnants of lamb and beef parts.

There's no one around to hear, much less answer, my question. I find other examples of familial malaise. Mayonnaise containers dotted with mold. Soup cans contaminated by noodles.

"What's wrong?" René asks from the rear deck of our house. She's stepped outside into the warm December sunshine wearing her bathrobe.

"You people."

"What are you talking about?"

"Half this stuff can't be recycled," I remonstrate. "There's so much gunk stuck to the inside of these cans that the guy at the recycling shed will laugh at me if I try to give them to him."

"They're your sons."

Because I don't know who left the bits and pieces of food in the various containers, I've included my spouse in my admonition, an implication she ignores. She retreats into the house. I return to sorting.

Eventually, all of the items make it into the rear of my old Lumina van. There's so much stuff packed into the Chevrolet that I have a hard time finding the shift lever.

Thankfully, I've done a thorough job of sorting. I'm spared recriminations and haranguing at the recycling center. The old guy in charge is in a good mood and accepts all that my van carries. We have a nice chat about politics, as nice as can be expected given the present state of our democracy, before I head back home.

My second task of the day is more daunting. Sampson, our yellow Labrador retriever, passed away. I was in the Twin Cities at a judicial conference when he died. Christian had been nursing the old codger along, feeding him special food, sneaking him into the house over the course of the dog's collapse.

The yellow Lab started to lose appreciable weight during the summer. René took him to the veterinarian. The vet x-rayed the rail thin old dog, took blood tests, but made no diagnosis. Our family suspicion was cancer of some sort. The vet suggested doing an ultrasound with the possibility of exploratory surgery. René and I vetoed putting the dog through any intrusive procedures. He was nearly fourteen, an old age for any dog; older still for an outdoor Labrador. There would be no treatment, no intervention. We both knew our decision meant that Sam wouldn't make it through the winter.

What we never contemplated was the reality of dealing with a dead family pet in December.

"Dylan, move the dog out to the storage shed," I'd advised over the phone from the judicial conference when I was told of his passing.

"OK."

I approach the shed with trepidation. I don't know what to expect. Sam's been dead two weeks. It's taken that long for my schedule to clear so that I could deal with him. Or what used to be him. Despite the fact that I cherished his scraggly old face and white whiskers, I haven't cried for Sampson. I think it's because I've been grieving in bits and pieces throughout his steady decline. There's simply nothing left to shed tears over. He's been so sick for so long, the end was anticlimactic.

The dog's body is rigid and stiff and covered by an old quilt that Christian lovingly wrapped around him.

When I was eleven, growing up in Piedmont Heights in Duluth, I went out to feed my old black Labrador, Deuce, only to find the dog stone dead in his kennel. I know how hard losing a dog is on a boy. Chris tried to stave off the inevitable with love and a warm blanket. It simply wasn't enough.

I grab a shovel, a pick, and a sledgehammer in hopes of loosening enough soil under the compost pile behind our shed so that I can bury the old dog. My efforts to dent the earth are rebuffed: I make no headway against the ground. I return the tools to the shed and stand over the dead animal.

"Need some help?"

Matt appears behind me, his square shoulders framed by the shed's doorway.

"Grab one side of the blanket. We'll put him in the back of the van."

Though Sam is but a shadow of the dog he once was, he's still a load to carry. We struggle across frozen ground, the animal swaying between us on the quilt.

"Thanks."

323

I cover the dog with the quilt. Dignity, an attribute Sam displayed even in the depths of illness, remains important.

"What are you gonna do with him?"

I look away from my eldest son, a boy who has seen dogs, cats, and horses buried near the banks of the Cloquet River.

"I'll put him somewhere back in the woods on Grandpa's land."

"You sure? I don't think our other dogs will leave him alone."

I stare across the brown landscape.

"I'll cover him with trees and brush. I'll put him in the deep woods where they don't go."

Matt appears unconvinced. I open the driver's door, start the van, and head out. Matt's eyes follow the path of the Lumina as the vehicle descends the small hillock fronting our farmhouse. I know he thinks I should do more, that Sampson deserves a better end. It's all I can do to keep from crying as I drive away.

Bluefin Bay

We were invited to spend the weekend at Bluefin Bay Resort in Tofte, Minnesota, by our friends Jan and Bruce Larson. The winter was dismal in terms of cross-country skiing. There was no snow. Not just a lack of snow: literally, there was no snow in the woods around our home on the Cloquet River. In a normal winter, I'll ski the trails on our property several times a week for exercise. All told, I was only able to ski our trails twice. On both occasions, the snow cover was so meager that the bare ground scraped the wax off my skis before I was halfway through my two-mile loop.

When the Larsons found out that they weren't going to be able to go with our "gang" of high school classmates on a planned Caribbean cruise (derisively dubbed The Big Idea by some of our friends) Jan called René to invite us to share a weekend in Tofte. Jan had won the stay at the resort through a contest at work. The cost to us would be minimal. The economics of the invitation along with a promise of skiable snow convinced us to accept Jan's offer.

"There are only two bedrooms and a bathroom," Jan notes as we arrive in the second story condominium unit. "I pictured it to have a living room," she adds as Bruce deposits luggage on the floor of one of the bedrooms.

I poke my head around the corner and smile.

"We can all get cozy in our jammies and watch TV in your room."

"I don't want to see you in your jammies," Bruce moans.

I check out our bedroom. René is busy unpacking her suitcase. We're staying two nights. She brought enough clothing for a month.

"Why'd you pack all that stuff?"

"Never can have too many choices."

I climb a ladder leading to a small loft overlooking our bedroom.

"Cool."

The low height of the ceiling precludes me from standing. There's a skylight above my head. The floor of the loft is carpeted.

The perfect place to read.

It's Friday night. We're staying until Sunday. Whether we ski both Saturday and Sunday depends upon the weather. The four of us pile into René's Toyota RAV and drive to the resort's outdoor hot tub. The temperature has plummeted. It's below zero. There's no moon. Small shards of starlight interrupt the black sky as Bruce and I remove the canvas cover of the hot tub and climb in. Vapor hangs over the simmering water. Our wives join us. Wine is poured. No one disturbs us. After a long soak, we return to our rooms, dress, and wander over to the resort's restaurant. Following a wonderful meal, we head back to the condo for wine and contests. Boys against the Girls. Trivial Pursuit. The boys kick butt. It's a perfect evening.

The next morning we eat big breakfasts, drink pots of black coffee, and trade stories about our kids at a table in a restaurant overlooking Lake Superior. The window glass is interrupted by frost. Waves crash against the rocky shoreline and an old concrete pier extending into gray water. The mercury hasn't climbed. It's hovering at five below. The sky is open and displays a surreal blue canopy devoid of clouds.

We drive away from Lake Superior, climbing a high ridge in the Larsons' Ford Escape. Four sets of skis and poles rattle in the cargo area of the Ford. The roadway leads us from the shoreline of Lake Superior into the hardwood forests of the Sawtooth Mountains. I study a map of ski trails that the resort provides its guests. Bruce finds the parking lot for the trail we want to ski and parks the Ford.

A father and two children move ponderously on skis. We watch them struggle up a steep hill. The trail they are following is poorly defined. Aspen and alders interrupt the path. We clip our ski bindings into place and follow the kids. The family comes to rest at the top of the slope. We pass by. The track narrows. The woods thicken. We find ourselves encircled by trees.

"I don't think this is a ski trail," René says as we move through ankle deep powder.

It really doesn't matter to me whether we're lost or not. We've found enough snow to ski and ski smoothly, something that has been impossible to do all winter. I've missed the glide of cross-country skis against snow. I've missed the feeling of crisp below-zero air on my face.

"Maybe it just doesn't get used much."

"I dunno," Bruce adds, "I think René's on to something."

We continue on. The forest opens up ahead of us. We've found the trail that we were supposed to be on.

"Here we are," I say proudly, as if my wilderness skills have saved us. "I told you we'd find the trail."

My companions look at me but say nothing. I know what my wife is thinking. She's mulling over the myriad of times I've misread roadmaps on family trips leading us off our intended path. René must be in a very good mood. She doesn't remind me of those occasions.

My ski trail at home has a small stand of sugar maples at the top of what I call the Ridge Trail. Here, along a ridge parallel to Lake Superior, we ski through acre after acre of mature maple forest. Undergrowth is nonexistent. The openness of this hardwood forest is in stark contrast to the tight woodlands that border my property.

I ski past a beaver lodge protruding defiantly above pond ice. At the intersection of two trails, Bruce and I stop to wait for our wives. Two deer bound in front of René. Her head is down. Her concentration is fixed. She doesn't see the animals.

The snow cover peters out before we reach Highway 61. I cringe as my new skis traverse rocks and gravel. I give in and carry my skis the final few yards to the end of the trail.

Later that afternoon, the four of us soak in the outside hot tub. The sky remains clear. The air remains cold. A stiff breeze rustles the water of the spa. My hair freezes solid. A gorgeous young black woman joins us. A robust white male, his skin artificially tanned, enters the tub holding what looks to be a tumbler of scotch. He sits next to the woman. We learn that he's a photographer and that she's a model. They're in Tofte to shoot a cosmetic's commercial. It appears from the man's diction and mannerisms that he's gay.

327

What safer way to send a beautiful model out into the world than to entrust her to a companion who's totally disinterested in her.

The photographer takes a shine to Bruce, a point I'll likely use from time and time over the years when and if it's necessary. I theorize the man is attracted to Bruce's naturally curly hair. What else could it be?

Dinner at the historic Lutsen Lodge located on Highway 61 north of Tofte is wonderful. We laugh and reminisce, telling stories that we've all heard countless times before. Retelling old pearls of history is something good friends tolerate.

Back at the condo, we resume Trivial Pursuit. The girls win the first game. There's an upset in the making. I put down my wine glass and concentrate. Bruce and I pull out the second game. We also win the third game, and with it, the match, by the narrowest of margins. Both teams had gathered all their "pies" but we are able to answer a question selected by the girls. Victory is ours. The natural order of things is restored. I can drive home tomorrow satisfied.

In Search of Snow

"**South Dakota**?" the female attorney queried. "I've never heard of anyone going to South Dakota to downhill ski."

I was sitting behind my bench in the Duluth courthouse. I'd just finished a hearing and was shooting the breeze with the attorneys.

"Terry Peak," I explained. "It's in the Black Hills, about twelve hours from here. I wanted to find a place that was challenging but close. It's over a thousand vertical, making it steeper than anything around here."

The woman's skeptical look didn't abate.

"South Dakota?" my wife René posited as I explained my plan to her later that same evening, "who goes to South Dakota to downhill ski?"

I bit my lip.

"Well, I'm only going if they have snow. Right now their website shows that the hill is half open."

Our conversation took place in early January. At the time the ground around our home in the country was devoid of snow. Minnesota wasn't alone. Most of the northern United States, with the exception of New England and Up-State New York, remained barren of snow cover. Even Upper Peninsula Michigan, where residents normally tunnel their way from their front door to the street through drifts, lacked snow.

"I read about Terry Peak when I was a kid. It always looked like a nice place to try."

"Have a good time by yourself. I can't afford to take a week off from work. I need time off in March for our cruise."

We were planning to celebrate our twenty-fifth wedding anniversary in the Caribbean with seven other couples from high school. We were set to leave March first. In early January, while my long suffering spouse was looking forward to sun, beaches, and down time away from our four sons, I was thinking snow.

"If you go it'll be hard to get Jack to daycare by eight in the morning if I need to be at work in Biwabik by eight-thirty."

I stared at my corn flakes. I was sitting at the dining room table surrounded by another gray Minnesota winter day. It seemed like the sun hadn't presented itself for a lifetime. The trace snow covering the grass in our backyard was a reminder that my cross-country skis were accumulating dust in the garage. There was not enough snow to consider touring our property on my primitive trails. In truth, there was not enough snow to make a snowball.

"I'll take Jack and Chris with."

"Have a good time," my wife repeated, cognizant that driving twelve hours in a van across Minnesota and the entire State of South Dakota with quarreling siblings, ages five and fifteen, would be a true test of my patience.

I kept track of the snowfall in the Black Hills via the ski hill's website. Two weeks before our slated departure, after convincing Christian, my fifteen-year-old son that the trip would be an adventure (and a week off of school), I remained unconvinced that there would be enough snow in the Black Hills to make the journey worthwhile. I began planning alternative skiing scenarios: an overnight trip to Lutsen; a couple of days in Upper Peninsula Michigan. I made the mistake of sharing these possibilities with my teenaged son.

"I don't want to go to Lutsen. You said we were going to South Dakota."

I'd already made a reservation for a hotel room at the Deadwood Holiday Inn Express. Deadwood, a historic venue turned gambling destination by the South Dakota legislature to ensure a steady stream of revenue for the old mining town, is only five miles from Terry Peak. The price for a room in Deadwood was right: thirty-five bucks a night, breakfast included. Five nights for two hundred dollars. One night's lodging at Lutsen would cost as much or more than our entire trip.

Snow began to fall in the Black Hills. I watched the white powder accumulate via the Internet. Runs opened. Lifts began operating. By the last week of the month nearly all of the slopes were ready for use, but doubters persisted.

"I thought you were headed out west," an attorney commented at a dinner party the Saturday evening before we left for South Dakota.

"I thought you were going as soon as the trial ended," a female lawyer added referencing a murder case that had taken up an entire month of my judicial career.

There had been a danger that the jury, which had concluded its deliberations the day before, would need more time to decide the case, postponing our trip.

"Tomorrow. My two youngest sons and I leave tomorrow."

"Montana or Colorado?"

"South Dakota."

I watched shrouds of doubt color the lawyers' faces. Their reaction caused my stomach to rumble. An unpleasant premonition presented itself.

"I didn't know you could downhill ski in South Dakota."

Sunday morning. This is to be the last road trip for our tired 1995 Lumina van. I read the odometer as we pull onto I-35 in Midway Township south of Duluth. The vehicle has 210,000 miles on it. I'm hoping to squeeze at least 1,700 more miles out of the engine.

Chris sits in the passenger seat, his attention riveted on a book. Jack is sitting behind Chris, his imagination occupied by several Star Wars figurines. I've removed two rear seats to accommodate our ski gear and luggage.

"How many hours to Rapid City?" Chris asks.

"Twelve."

The teenager nods his head. Sounds of clashing light sabers erupt from the rear seat as the old van accelerates towards the promise of snow.

"The big building on the hillside is Gustavus."

I point out Gustavus Adolphus College to Chris as we cruise the main street of St. Peter, Minnesota.

"Why aren't there any trees?"

"A tornado wiped them out."

We follow the Minnesota River Valley out of town. The waterway's flood plain is fringed with oaks, cottonwoods, and low ridges. A light drizzle is falling. There's no snow. The Minnesota River is frozen, but only hesitantly so.

The highway we're on slices through the farms of southwestern Minnesota. The rain intensifies. To a native Minnesotan, encountering rain in early February, in any part of the state, is unnerving. The exposed black earth of the region is moist from rainfall. There are no snow banks, no drifts, not the slightest indication that it's winter. We pass lakes covered with meager ice, fisherman poised gingerly over holes in the mist, their trucks brazenly parked on the suspect surfaces of lakes. These ponds are prairie potholes sculpted by glaciers; the same glaciers that removed the rich topsoil from Canada and deposited it here to the eternal benefit of Minnesota farmers.

Even in small town America, one cannot escape the Golden Arches. I pull the beleaguered Lumina into a McDonald's in Windom, Minnesota for lunch. As we eat, I read a local tourist handout and discover all the reasons why one should visit, perhaps even move, to this small town on the cusp of Iowa. Downhill skiing, the purpose for our trip is not mentioned as an endearing attribute of Windom, Minnesota.

Near Worthington we connect with I-90. It rains in earnest. We enter Rock County, the southwestern-most county in Minnesota, the only county in the state without a natural lake.

"Are you sure there's snow out in the Black Hills?" Chris asks as he looks up from reading his book.

"The website said Terry Peak has plenty of snow."

"I hope so."

We pass through Sioux Falls, South Dakota. The sky remains gray. The van's windshield wipers contend with light rain. Mitchell, South Dakota, renowned departure point for pheasant hunters, retreats in the rearview mirror. Night falls. Traffic speeds west at a comfortable seventy-five miles per hour. At Chamberlain, the landscape folds into the valley of the Missouri River and the rain changes to sludge. Sleet cloaks the freeway. The night is so black it leaves the impression that we are entering a forest. It's an illusion. There are no trees out here on the prairie: only rolling hills giving way to incessant plains.

"I'm gonna slow down," I lament, the front end of the van feeling less than secure as we round corners. "I don't think we're gonna make it to Deadwood in twelve hours."

Jack is snoring loudly in the back seat. Chris is staring at the inky shroud enveloping our vehicle. Big flakes of white plaster the van's windshield. The snow intermingles with clean rain. The van's wipers thrash wildly at the mixture.

By the time we reach Wall, site of the famous drugstore, I'm wringing wet from sweat. My hands are sore from clenching the steering wheel. The roadway is a nightmare. Traffic is crawling along at twenty-five miles per hour. Truckers stop and put out flares, blocking the inside lane while they put chains on the tires of their rigs.

"This is a lot of fun," I moan as I pull off to refuel.

A local sheriff and a South Dakota State Trooper are chatting with the cashier in the truck stop as I approach to pay for my gas.

"I slid right through the stop sign on No. 14," the deputy admits. "Locked 'er up and slid right on through."

"It's plenty nasty out there, that's for sure."

"This is the first snow we've seen since northern Minnesota," I add.

"Where you from?" the deputy asks.

"Duluth."

"Long ways from home."

"Headed towards Deadwood to ski."

The officers refrain from further comment. I exit the station and confront a brisk wind. The weather doesn't let up until we are on the outskirts of Rapid City. It's nearly nine-thirty Mountain Time, ten-thirty Central time.

"Whatdoya think?" I ask Christian. "Should we stay overnight in Rapid City and try to make Deadwood tomorrow morning?"

"How far is it to the hotel in Deadwood?"

"I gotta go potty."

"In a minute, Jack, It's thirty miles to Deadwood."

"Let's go for it. I want to get to our hotel."

"OK."

We make a pit stop so Jack can do his business. When we reconnect with I-90, we find our path to the Black Hills blocked by two state patrol cars. The freeway north is closed due to the sleet.

"What do we do now?"

"Is there another way, a back way, to Deadwood from here?"

Chris studies a travel atlas.

"We can take 385 west, then north and come in the back way through Lead."

The drive through the canyon is harrowing. The road twists and turns behind the beginnings of the Black Hills. Spruce and lodge pole pine-covered ridges soar above us. We pass few homes.

"Look at all the snow."

The reports from Terry Peak have not been exaggerated. The roadway is lined with high banks of plowed powder.

"The road's under construction," I observe as we crawl through the storm. "There's no more pavement."

Huge mounds of snow-covered earth line the highway. The Lumina's tires spin on loose gravel. The climb seems endless.

And then, we are in Lead. The bright lights of the high school, the Burger King, and assorted other businesses greet us. We're five minutes from our hotel. It's ten-thirty, three hours past our anticipated arrival. As we check in at the Holiday Inn Express in Deadwood, the clerk smiles.

"Your wife's on the phone. She's worried about you."

I take the phone from the young woman.

"René?"

"You OK?"

"It was hell on the freeway. I'll tell you about it once we check in. I'll call you right back."

My kids sit on suitcases while I fill out paperwork. Tomorrow, we're going to find out if the trip to Terry Peak was worth the drive.

Morning comes. I roust Christian and Jack from bed. I've slept fitfully. Jack and I shared a queen-sized bed. My rest was disturbed because Jack has a tendency to spin like a top when he sleeps, which means his feet usually end up kicking me in the small of my back. Last night was no exception. I felt tiny toes prodding my spine on a number of occasions.

The hotel offers a nice continental breakfast. After we've cleaned up, we amble down to the lobby to eat. I eavesdrop as ranchers wander in and out of the dining area. The Rapid City newspaper I picked up at the front desk indicates there's a stock show in town. The local television news playing on a big screen in the lobby recounts the antics of little kids, boys and girls no bigger than Jack, attempting to ride bucking sheep as part of the stock event. Twelve hours from home, my sons and I are immersed in the American West, standing out in our downhill ski clothing amongst Stetsons and finely polished cowboy boots like proverbial sore thumbs.

"This sure is a long way up," Chris says as our van chugs through the winding terrain of the Black Hills.

We pass back through the town of Lead on our way to Terry Peak. Conifers lining the steep hills on either side of the two-lane highway are thick with snow. The sky is empty, high, and blue.

"That's the way to Deer Mountain," I say, pointing to a sign for another local downhill ski area. "Maybe we'll spend our third day there."

Jack is quiet. He's dressed in a black ski jacket, black snow pants, black mittens, Sorels, ski helmet, liner, and goggles. I can't see his eyes because of the goggles but I know from the inclination of his head that he's awake and considering his surroundings.

Chris maintains silence. He appears to be sleeping or perhaps unconsciously pondering whether or not this trip, a journey of fifteen hours, was worth the effort.

"There's the hill," I say as the road makes a sudden pitch upward.

Off to our left two high-speed chair lifts climb from the base of the ridge to the ski area's summit. The top of Terry Peak is essentially bare, topped by a cluster of radio antennas and little else. At 7,100 feet the hill is significant. With over 1,100 feet of vertical it should be challenging.

"Shouldn't we turn?" Chris asks as we pass the Nevada Gulch parking lot.

"We're going to the beginner area so I can work with Jack. You can get to this part of the hill from there."

"OK."

We park in front of the main chalet. The three of us put on our ski boots in the car before entering the building. I approach the only clerk at the ticket desk and hand her my credit card. The price is $35.00 for a full day for Chris and me. Jack is free. Spirit Mountain, back in our hometown of Duluth, Minnesota charges $35.00 for a half-day ticket. Given that Terry Peak boasts more vertical, $35.00 for a full day ticket is a bargain.

Outside, I help Jack into his bindings. Because I'm teaching Jack, I don't need ski poles. A tether will secure Jack to me. The connection will allow me to control his speed and teach him how to snowplow. You can buy a special harness for this purpose. I use a lunge line left over from when we owned horses. Jack doesn't know the difference and it works essentially the same. I used the same system to teach Chris. Before the lunge line, I used an old lead rope, again, from our horse barn, to teach Dylan, my second son, how to ski.

I taught my eldest son Matt by skiing with him between my legs. I also used this technique with my brother Dave and my sister Annie. Skiing with a kid between your legs isn't easy. It does a number on your knees and lower back. The tether is a vast improvement.

"By the end of this trip," I say to my youngest son, "you'll be skiing without my help."

Jack smiles. Chris remains silent. I sense the teenager doubts my prognostication.

The beginner's chairlift floats on steel cable through cool air. Jack, Chris, and I glide through early morning light surrounded by snow-covered pines and spruce reminiscent of iced Christmas cookies.

"Why don't you check out the harder runs?" I suggest to Chris when we reach the top of the beginner hill.

The teenager nods and slides towards Surprise, an easier run leading to one of the high-speed chairlifts. I watch Christian make graceful turns until the slope of the hill interrupts my view.

I loop the tether around Jack, secure the end of the line in my right glove, and urge him forward. His little skis pick up speed. My son makes no attempt to slow his descent or to turn as he roars down the hill.

"Put the fronts of your skis in a "v", like this," I demonstrate at the bottom of the slope. "That way you can turn and stop."

Jack smiles. On our next run, Jack resumes his quest to see how fast and how straight he can ski.

Towards the end of our first day, I convince Chris to watch Jack while I ski without a thirty-pound child attached to my wrist. I begin on the "blue" or "more difficult" runs. Kussy, the main hill running next to the Kussy Express lift, is a gem. Though listed as "more difficult" (as opposed to "black diamond" or "most difficult"), when I ski Kussy from top to bottom without stopping, my knees shake. That, in my view, is the mark of a real ski hill. After making a couple of runs on Kussy, Homestake, and Empress, I tackle the black diamonds. Holy Terror, Ben Hur, and lower Kussy all challenge my forty-eight-year-old knees and hips. I bounce. I twist. I turn. Finding a steady cadence to my descent, I have a whale of a good time. I remember why I love to ski.

"Forty-five minutes," Chris moaned at the end of the day as I encounter my sons at the bottom of the beginner hill. "You said you were going to take two runs."

I smile.

"I lied."

"Jack and I fell asleep on the benches in the chalet."

"Let's go back to the hotel for a swim."

Light powder snow greets us when we arrive at Terry Peak the next morning. It's 9:00am. Though the hill is coming to life, there are few skiers. A solid wall of clouds envelopes the summit. The antenna towers and guy wires disappear in gray. Our view of the surrounding peaks and valleys is obliterated. Standing at the top of Kussy with Jack once again safely controlled by the tether, I watch Chris plummet towards the base of the slope. A temporary lapse in the squall reveals blue sky. A hint of sun appears. The resulting view recalls another ski trip with my wife to the Green Mountains; though the spruce trees (which give the Black Hills their distinctive coloration) cannot be mistaken for the maples of Killington, Vermont.

Jack learns. By the end of our second day of skiing, he makes three consecutive runs down the beginner slope without a spill and without the aid of the tether.

"Wanna try Deer Mountain tomorrow?" I ask Chris. We're sitting on the edge of a precipice in the Lumina. Chris is videotaping the main face of Terry Peak through the open window of the van as we head back to Deadwood.

"Sure."

"Sounds good."

"I wanna go swimming," Jack laments, his head leaning heavily, the effort of two days of downhill skiing enticing him towards a nap.

"Pizza first."

Whining erupts from the rear seat. I put the vehicle in gear. The Chevrolet creeps forward. Contented snoring replaces my youngest son's objection. My eyes follow the blacktop as the vehicle negotiates the roadway into Lead, South Dakota. I'm mindful that one of my wild notions actually paid off.

Snow falls. Thick flakes drift through the silver sky adding a layer of fluff to sixteen inches of new snow already on the ground. My sons are bundled up in their ski clothing as our van pulls up to the base of Deer Mountain Ski Area.

We spent the past two days skiing Terry Peak, the best-known ski hill in the area. Until I saw the "Deer Mountain" sign along the highway just beyond the Terry Peak turn-off, I didn't even know there was another downhill ski area in South Dakota. I convinced Chris that we should spend our last day skiing at Deer Mountain. Jack wasn't consulted. He's pretty much just along for the ride.

"There's no one here," Chris says as I turn off the vehicle's engine.

338

A moderate slope rises above us as we exit the vehicle. Unlike Terry Peak, which has the attributes of a subtle mountain, Deer Mountain is reminiscent of ski areas in Minnesota, Wisconsin, and Upper Michigan; more a hill than peak.

"Looks OK to me."

After pulling on our ski boots and toting our poles and skis to the front of the chalet, we enter the building to purchase lift tickets. Inside, other than a smattering of employees, the only other people in the chalet are several dozen enthusiastic young Native American boys and girls under the supervision of five or six middle school teachers. It's clear the kids are here not to ski but to slide on Deer Mountain's inner tube hill.

I approach a counter and pay for our lift tickets. Once again the prices are reasonable. Jack skis free. Chris's ticket is $24.00. Mine is $27.00. I grab a trail map and study it. The diagram shows two hills connected by a tunnel. I'm encouraged that the area boasts more runs than Terry Peak.

"Let's go," I urge the boys as I rise from a picnic table and head towards the door.

The four-person chair lift is amazingly slow. Instead of being whisked through swirling white, past majestic lodge pole pines to the snow-enveloped top of the hill, we dally through the air at an agonizing pace.

By the time we arrive at the summit, the falling snow has completely eliminated our view. Still, there's a compensatory magnificence to the slow parade of the snowfall.

"Chris, lead us on."

I wrap the tether around Jack's waist. Despite the fact that Jack negotiated the beginner's slope without the safety rope by the end of our second day at Terry Peak, Deer Mountain doesn't offer a hill modest enough for Jack to ski without the tether.

"Here goes," Chris shouts, pushing off with his poles.

We ski an open bowl. There's a trail off the top of the bowl to the tunnel but its closed, effectively eliminating a good portion of Deer Mountain from use.

"Snow plow," I command as my youngest son and I head over the cusp of the ridge and fall into the natural hollow.

The snow is thigh deep and fluffy. Jack weaves and bobs like a prizefighter but does little to slow his speed. I dig the edges of my skis into the base of the snow pack to slow us down. The kid wants to go fast.

"Slow down."

Jack doesn't listen.

I yank on the tether, spilling the kid to the ground. Standing over him I emphasize that I'm the teacher and that he's the pupil.

"Every time you don't listen, I'll pull the rope and you'll sit on your butt. Understand?"

Jack looks up. I can't see his eyes because of his goggles but I know he's considering his options. It's an open question whether he'll acquiesce. He nods slightly. I nod back. The crisis passes.

After a quick lunch of room-temperature leftover Pizza Hut pizza and cold soda, I leave Chris in charge of Jack. I intend to take a couple of runs by myself. Exiting the warm building, I note that there are less than twenty patrons taking advantage of the beautiful snowfall. It's Wednesday, the first day of the week that Deer Mountain is open. The locals are probably working. Even so, you'd expect a few die-hard skiers from Rapid City, only a half hour away, to play hooky on a day like today.

My ski poles are missing. Actually, they're my wife René's poles. I'm using hers because they're in better shape than mine are. I search the perimeter of the chalet on the off chance that someone picked them up by mistake and set them down in a different spot. I don't find my wife's poles.

"Someone took my ski poles," I explain to a young woman at the ticket desk.

"I'll tell the lift operators to watch for them," she says after taking down a description of the stolen items.

"Seems odd anyone would take them today. There's no one here."

Even with Chris's help the poles are never found.

"I need to rent poles," I advise a kid in charge of rentals in the basement of the chalet. "Mine were stolen."

"Help yourself," the young man says. "We don't charge for poles."

"Thanks," I reply, wondering how a ski area with so few customers can afford to be so generous.

I hit the black diamonds and soon discover that, while the top half of the runs, the portions gentle enough for grooming, are fantastic, the middle portions, which are too steep to groom, are an ugly mix of powder and frozen ruts. Despite the deception, I take four or five runs on the toughest hills and manage to keep my nose out of the snow.

I ski with Jack for the remainder of the afternoon. Chris seems content to discover the runs of Deer Mountain on his own. By four o'clock I've had enough. Three days of skiing with a five-year-old have made my calves tight and my lower back sore. We leave Deer Mountain without René's ski poles.

The ride home is uneventful. Though it's only a few degrees above zero and the wind is whipping across the plains, the roads are clear and the sun is out. Just before Sioux Falls I swing north, take the freeway twenty miles or so up the road towards Brookings, and then head east again on a two lane towards Pipestone, Minnesota.

Music blares from the CD player. The Lumina purrs along. At Pipestone, we connect with Minnesota 23 and turn north. We skirt a metallic forest of windmills erected on the cold and desolate plateau of southeastern Minnesota. The blades of the giant pinwheels spin slowly, creating an elevated ballet.

North of Pipestone, we also encounter the first evidence of winter we've seen since leaving Rapid City. A regional storm pushed through the Minnesota River Valley near Granite Falls and deposited twelve inches of fresh snow on previously naked earth.

James McMurtry
Iris Dement
Neil Young
Brenda Weiler
The Grateful Dead
Leslie West and Mountain
Bruce Springsteen
Arlo Guthrie

341

Crosby, Stills, Nash, and Young.
Lynn Miles

I force my kids to listen to my music until night blankets the Minnesota countryside.

"Put on Pink Floyd."

We pass the Black Bear Casino in Carlton.

"Who's 'Pink Floyd?'" Chris asks.

I sing a line or two from "Money", one of the most famous songs on the album.

"OK, OK, stop with the singing already. I'll put it on."

Jack is asleep in the back seat. Green dashboard lights plague my tired eyes. Twelve hours of driving. Only a few more miles to go. There's not a star, much less the moon, visible in the sky. The first track on the album begins.

Breathe, breathe in the air...

It's been a perfect trip.

Another Hunting Story

Autumn has arrived. The first traces of snow litter the ground in stark contrast to the yellow stubble left after haying. I'm sitting in my Honda Passport SUV in the driveway outside my house, waiting for Jack and Christian.

The vehicle idles smoothly. The radio is off. The sun breaches the tree line. It's a lovely October day. As I sit waiting to drive my two youngest sons to school, a large cottontail dashes across the short grass bordering the blacktop drive. The rabbit's run is crazed: Zigging and zagging that seems to have no purpose behind it, at least not until I see the kestrel.

Over the past several years, a family of kestrels has taken up residence on our land. From time to time, adult birds of this diminutive branch of the hawk family sit on Jack's swing set contemplating the pasture surrounding our house, waiting for an errant mouse or mole to show itself. These birds of prey are smaller than a robin. A field mouse is a banquet for a kestrel. I watch in amazement as the frantic bird dips and flits above the rabbit.

The rabbit has every opportunity to simply disappear. Tangled weeds, shrubs, and scrub afford an easy retreat for the rabbit but it doesn't bolt for the woods. Instead, it sprints along the edge of our field tantalizing the overmatched hawk into attack after futile attack. Unlike other times I've witnessed similar encounters (usually between red tail hawks and cottontails) during which the frightened rabbit usually succumbs to sheer terror, this cottontail doesn't appear the least bit concerned about its fate.

The dance continues for a few minutes. The kestrel finally gives up. The rabbit skitters into the undergrowth. The boys climb into the car for the ride to school.

Christian has expressed an interest in hunting. After completing gun safety, I allowed him to use my grandfather's old Stevens Savage .410 side-by-side to hunt partridge and rabbits on our property. I'm not there to witness it but on one of his very first excursions into the woods with a shotgun and our Labrador, Copper, Chris nailed a partridge in mid-flight. The dog, after rousting the partridge from its hiding place, retrieved the downed bird despite having never carried anything in its mouth beyond the commonplace ball or stick. It's a story I'm certain deserves a more detailed telling than I've given it here but it's a tale for Christian to write.

Today is Sunday. Chris and I are exploring the backwoods near Wolf Lake in rural St. Louis County. Copper sleeps in the back of the Passport while I drive down a gravel road and read a map at the same time.

"Papoose Lake should be around here somewhere," I say, my eyes darting from page to windshield to prevent disaster. "There must be a trail somewhere off to the left."

A sign next to the road we're on indicates that a bridge that once spanned the Cloquet River no longer exists. The road ends at the river. I park on high ground. The forest looks grousy.

"This is as good a place as any. Load up the shotgun and let Copper go to work."

We walk a narrow trail paralleling the river. On a bank overlooking the Cloquet, I'm treated to a surprise.

"Chris."

"Ya."

"This is that sand bank where we saw the wood turtles. Remember, when we canoed down from Indian Lake?"

The knoll I'm standing on pitches sharply into the river. Indeed, it is the spot where we stopped our canoe to photograph rare and elusive wood turtles found only along this stretch of the Cloquet.

Chris walks up, stands besides me, nods, and then returns to the hunt.

We enter what was once pasture. Insistent jack pine interrupt the dormant hay field. The trees are intent upon returning forest to an open space created a century ago.

"This will work," I say as I walk behind the dog and my son.

Earlier, I'd pulled the Passport into a boat launch on Wolf Lake to study country depicted in my latest novel. The vacant field we traverse affords a similar opportunity. The waving grass and the decaying pine stumps fit the feel and emotion of the story I am writing, the story of Finnish immigration to northeastern Minnesota.

I'm searching for Papoose Lake so I can experience the shoreline of that insignificant pond, to smell the air, to listen to the wind rustling the vegetation surrounding the lake. I intend to include a Finnish homestead on the shores of Papoose Lake in my story. Though fiction doesn't require perfection, it does require honesty. One doesn't try to insert a lake where no lake could possibly exist. But one can take a vacant pasture and, using the time-traveling abilities of pen and paper, place a turn-of-the-century Finnish homestead on that field.

"This could be the farm in my story," I say, thinking aloud.

Chris pays me no mind. He follows the quickening stride of the retriever into a thick grove of jack pines. Two ruffed grouse burst from cover and flee to the other side of the river. No shots are fired.

We see no other birds. Chris and the dog hunt intently for two more hours. The sky darkens. We pack up and head for home. Along the highway, we pass deer nibbling grass located next to the pavement. We count forty deer in the span between Brimson and Island Lake. Only one of the animals has antlers.

I park the Honda in our garage and let Copper out. Chris unfolds his legs and exits the car with the cased shotgun in hand. Though my third son didn't shoot a partridge, I was able to bring authenticity to the narrative and dialogue crowding my mind. From that perspective it was a very productive hunt.

The Biggest Striker

It's not often that you get to share a tall tale about the game of soccer. The sport is so, shall we say, refined. Sure, soccer has a margin of mythology to it. But the sport's mystique, at least here in America, isn't on par with ice hockey, football, or baseball. Tall tales just don't abound in the soccer world. Pelé pointing down the field and calling a goal during the World Cup? Nope. Mia Hamm getting turned around and scoring on her own goaltender? Never happened. A father well over fifty years old coming back from retirement to play middle fielder with his sons? Impossible. But there is at least one true story that will forever be etched in Hermantown youth soccer lore. This is that story.

The U-16 Boys Hermantown Havoc traveling team takes the field, their white and black jerseys billowing in a warm summer breeze. A team from Blaine (a Twin Cities suburb) warms up at the north end of the field. Balls sail through the air. Goalies leap to snatch spheres out of the atmosphere or swat them to the ground with vengeance. The sun settles in the west over the rooftops of the Hermantown Community Church and its more liberal counterpart, Trinity Episcopal Church. Heavy commuter traffic zooms past the soccer complex. The parking lot at the Community Church is empty. There is a scarcity of movement across Maple Grove at the Deerfield Apartments. The sun descends. The air cools.

I'm sitting on a canvas camping chair. The wind switches and comes out of the east, from the Big Lake. Goose bumps form on exposed skin. I wrap myself in a blanket. I keep an eye on Jack, as he plays with another little boy on a gym set a good hundred feet or so away.

The game begins. I watch my son Christian, a middle fielder, a kid that I used to coach, miss an easy steal. He chases after a Blaine player advancing up the near sidelines. The west side of the field is lined with portable chairs like the one I'm using. Fans supporting their teams separate into camps: a necessity so that fistfights don't break out over insensitive comments or observations. The empty space between the parents, a soccer-No-Man's-Land, is crucial to preserving peace.

I hear Matt bellowing at his players. He stands across the field beneath a portable awning sheltering the reserve players for the Havoc. Matt's arms are crossed. His voice is clear and direct.

"Use your support," Matt yells to his players. "Short passes," he urges.

Chris moves the ball past a Blaine forward. Free of pressure he studies the field and launches a looping pass to Jake Sedor, one of the forwards, who is racing down the right sidelines towards the opposing goal. As I focus on Jake's run, a large black object appears in my peripheral vision across Maple Grove Road.

"Oh my Lord," I exclaim as my brain recognizes the intruding mass. "It's a moose."

Sure enough, a lanky, slender shouldered bull moose canters his way across the blacktop road between passing vehicles. The animal resembles a very ugly and overly tall draft horse. I watch the animal saunter onto a vacant soccer field next to where the boys are playing. The contest stops. No whistle is blown. The players are simply awestruck by the sight of a bull moose standing on mown grass. Play is suspended by silent accord.

"Wow," says a mother of one of the Blaine players. "I've never seen a moose before."

My bet is that most of the folks standing at the Stebner complex this day have never seen a moose. And even if they have, they've never seen one completely exposed; unprotected by swamp, trees, or other natural vegetation. I know I haven't. Not in all the canoe trips I've taken or in all the hours I've spent hunting. I've seen my share of the largest member of the deer family. But not like this. Not with an evangelical church, a day care center, a busy road, and an apartment complex as backdrops.

The bull's antlers are small and just beginning to come into velvet. Though he's young, his maleness, like that of a prize stallion, is visible and impressive. The animal lifts his head, staring down his funnel-like nose at us with seeming disdain, and studies the cluster of humans standing a few dozen yards away. Without a sound, the bull trots towards a thicket located at the south edge of the soccer complex.

"Jack," I shout to my youngest son as the moose glides majestically past the swing set, "see the moose?"

My son's small head, his hair newly clipped, his ears big and perky, emerges from the crow's nest at the top of the play set.

"Let's go see the moose," I hear Jack call to the little boy he's playing with.

Before I can intervene Jack is down the slide. My son plants his feet on the pea rock surrounding the playground and races across the U-6 soccer field towards the lumbering animal.

Mrs. Romano, the mom of one of the Hermantown players, retrieves a camera from her car. I inadvertently yell directly into her ear as she walks by. She doesn't say a word. Her attention is elsewhere.

"Jack, get back on the swing set."

My son hears my voice. His head rotates in my direction. He stops in his tracks.

"Get back up on that swing set!"

My son darts up the slide. His buddy follows suit. The moose shuffles its feet. Mrs. Romano snaps a few pictures before the animal decides he's had enough of humans and disappears into the brush behind the Community Church.

The crowd murmurs. The game resumes. It's obvious that the appearance of the moose (which the folks from Blaine probably believe is an everyday occurrence in Hermantown) is too much for the boys from the Twin Cities. The Hermantown Havoc wins the game going away, without having to call upon their secret weapon to take a penalty kick.

Getting Away

Dylan, my eighteen-year-old son, and I dip our canoe paddles in the inky water of Brule Lake. It's after eight o'clock in the evening. There's a hint of dusk remaining beyond the rolling hills surrounding the western shoreline of the lake. The sky is intermediate. Not high and distant. Not close and confining. There is no moon. The stars are masked.

We paddle in silence. Our eyes strain to identify the contours of the shoreline, islands, and reefs that disrupt the smooth plane of the water. Behind us my twenty-three-year-old son Matt and his friend Chris Oppel labor to keep up. Though both canoes are heavy with gear and the older boys are appreciably stronger than I am, Dylan and I make better time. I think our vessel's supremacy has something to do with my thirty-five years of manning the stern position in a canoe.

We float next to a large island. The air is calm; absent wind or rain. I study a Mackenzie map by headlamp. The lake is flat. No waves slap the gunwales of the canoe as I try to determine our location.

"You're welcome to pitch your tent with us," a woman calls out from the island.

By the texture of the voice, I'm guessing the speaker is in her early twenties. I hear other similar voices talking in low tones around her.

"We can't get our fire started," she adds.

It rained the prior evening. In reality, it was a deluge, the first significant storm since July. It's September, well beyond summer in northeastern Minnesota. But until yesterday's rain it had been hot, muggy, and Kansas-like in the north woods for the past three months. Tonight is more typical of early September weather: cool, with an abundance of gray clouds.

"Maybe we should take them up on their offer," Dylan suggests.

I can't see my son's face but I suspect he's grinning from ear to ear. Matt hears the offer and joins in.

"Sounds like a good place to camp."

I mull over the woman's offer. Finding a group of desperate women in need of assistance was one of my fondest fantasies when I started coming to the Boundary Waters Canoe Area Wilderness with my high school buddies thirty years ago. However, such fantasies hold certain unacceptable risks for a forty-eight-year-old married father of four. My response is swift yet polite.

"Thanks for the offer, Ma'am. I think we'll keep looking."

"We tried all the campsites on the other islands and across the bay," she responds in a pleading tone. "They're all taken."

I smile. I sense the younger men in my group are not happy with their guide.

"All the same, I think we'll keep moving."

I study the map. The boys remain silent. I think they're mulling over whether mutiny is still a capital crime.

"There's an island in the middle of the lake that has a campsite on it."

Dylan resumes paddling. I adjust myself on the plastic seat and join in. The other canoe catches up and glides alongside us.

"I think that's the island," I say, pointing to a small clump of balsam, spruce, and undergrowth surrounded by exposed boulders.

"I dunno, Dad," Dylan replies. "It looks too small."

"The map says there's a campsite here."

We circle the island looking for the telltale clearing of an improved campsite.

"I don't think this is it," Matt says.

I dock the canoe at the only accessible point on the island. I hand Dylan a flashlight. He exits the canoe and disappears into the brush. Within minutes he's stumbling over deadfall trying to make it back to my location.

"There's no campsite here," he advises.

We push off from shore and head towards Cone Bay. There's a distant glimmer visible across the water.

"That's a campsite," Dylan says, pointing to the flickering campfire.

"Looks like it's taken. There should be four more along the far shoreline. Hopefully one of them will be open."

Traveling at night across a lake as imposing as Brule in an open canoe is a spiritual experience, though I'm not so sure the boys share my sentimentality. We spend three hours exploring every inlet and nook of the northern shoreline of Brule Lake. It becomes clear that I'm wholly inept at coordinating the muted features of the landscape with the map on my lap.

"What about that bay?" I ask Matt as he and Chris negotiate a narrow passageway in the shoreline.

"Nothing there."

"Did you go to the end of it?"

"Nope."

Everyone's patience has worn thin. It's after eleven. We need to set up camp, make dinner, and turn in. Tomorrow we're going to portage into a brook trout lake that Matt fished in the past with great success. Oodles of fat speckled trout are known to reside in the lake. I long to feel one of those storied fish on the end of my spinning rod.

"Dyl, let's take a peek. From the location of the campsite on the island," I continue, looking out across Cone Bay at the flickering campfire we left behind, "there should be a campsite on the left side of this bay."

Matt and Oppel remain out on the main body of water, convinced that our errand is a waste of time. Dylan and I paddle quietly through night air. Fog settles over the placid surface of the bay. The only sound to be heard is the noise of water trickling off the blades of our paddles.

"What's over there?" Dylan asks, pointing at the marshy shoreline.

"Let's check it out."

The moon makes a brief appearance and illuminates the shoreline in yellow light. Thick clouds act as a reflective backdrop as we enter shallow water clogged with weeds.

Dylan leaps out of the canoe and threads his way through the undergrowth.

"It's a campsite."

"Matt."

"Ya?"

"We found it."

The older boys land their Coleman canoe next to our Old Town Discovery.

"You said there wasn't a campsite in here."

"I said we didn't go to the end of the bay," Matt replies defensively.

"Same thing."

"Hey Dad."

"Ya?" I say, swinging an overloaded Duluth Pack onto my shoulder.

"Tomorrow, let me carry the map."

Dawn comes early when you're sleeping on rock. Especially if you're middle-aged and bear the after affects of a spinal fusion. No matter how well designed a sleeping pad and sleeping bag you use, the fact is that the Canadian Shield, the rock which underlies all of the BWCA, is still rock. No amount of cushioning makes it any less so.

I awaken at dawn. The day is overcast but without threat of rain. I get dressed, open the cooking kit, and lumber to the shoreline where I fill a coffee pot and two big steel pots with water from the lake. I stretch the muscles of my lower back and scan the marsh around the small bay in front of me for signs of wildlife. Nothing stirs. I carry the water back to the campsite. I set up a single-burner propane stove. Gas hisses. I strike a match. Blue flame dances. I place the coffee pot on heat.

Snoring emanates from the nylon dome tent where the three boys remain asleep. I drop water purification tablets into a pot full of cold water, shake the pot, and allow the water to settle before adding another tablet to disguise the chemical taste. This water is for fruit drink. It won't be boiled and though the water in most BWCA lakes is potable, I'm not willing to take chances. I allow the tablets to dissolve before spooning heaps of instant fruit drink into the pot.

The coffee is ready. I pour myself a cup, put another large pot of water on the burner, and stroll down to the water's edge. I find a weathered stump that fits my rear end and sit contentedly to watch the sun climb. After a few minutes of silent reflection I hear stirrings from the tent and I return to the campsite to prepare breakfast.

After a meal of instant oatmeal, breakfast bars (did you know you can get Cocoa Puffs and milk in a bar?), juice, and coffee, we load the canoes with fishing gear and begin the long paddle to the western terminus of Brule Lake where high bluffs jut above conifers and broadleaf trees. Fall has lightly painted the sugar maples. The real show is several weeks away but there's no question that autumn is just around the bend.

"It's across from those two points," I say, looking at the map once again.

I point to a narrow opening in the landscape as Dylan and I drift in the Old Town.

"You sure?" Matt asks.

"I'm sure."

Matt and Oppel paddle up.

"Through that gap," I say, pointing to a narrow passageway.

"That's how I remember it," Matt agrees.

The canoes round the point and head north through another channel.

"That's where we portage," Matt says, pointing to a huge cliff. The base of the ledge is littered with boulders loosened by ice and time. "But I don't see the path."

We inch closer to land. Tucked neatly to one side, just below a dip in the adjacent hillside, the trail appears. Our canoes drift to shore. Dylan and Oppel toss gear on their backs and begin to climb. Matt flips the Coleman over, places a life jacket across his shoulders as a portage pad, lifts the canoe into place, and begins to trudge up the slope.

Despite back surgery I can still portage a canoe. Once Matt has a sufficient head start, I grab the gunwales of the Discovery, turn it over, and place the canoe on my shoulders in one motion. I begin trudging uphill. The portage trail winds up, up, and up through trees. I concentrate on placing one hiking boot in front of the other as I climb.

"Doesn't this thing ever go down?" I hear Matt ask rhetorically after a few hundred yards of ascending the rocky trail.

353

"It has to," I answer, though I know he isn't talking to me.

"I don't think so. Seems to me, the trout lake sits higher than Brule."

"Can't be. You must be remembering another lake."

Halfway up the slope, I find Matt and Oppel resting on a large balsam that was toppled by wind. The Coleman's prow rests on the tree completely blocking the path. Matt looks exhausted.

"Coming through."

It's not about strength. It's about stubbornness.

"Show off."

The trail is rough. It's clear that the United States Forest Service and the Minnesota Department of Natural Resources are not expending funds to maintain this portage. Boulders and rocks make for precarious footing. Downed balsams and spruce block the path at frequent intervals.

If we catch fish, it'll be worth it.

Through a break in the foliage I catch glints of black water. As I crest the hill, the weight of the canoe begins to inflame my shoulders. Dylan meets me on the trail.

"Matt's right. It only goes up," Dylan observes.

I refrain from answering.

We eat peanut butter and strawberry jam on pita bread while sitting on the rocky shore of the trout lake. We pass around a bag of beef jerky and drink orange Kool-Aid purified by iodine to quench our thirst. The clouds are high and unrelentingly pewter. The lake spreads out down a narrow valley between high bluffs. The shoreline is riddled with stones and boulders deposited by long departed glaciers.

"Someone caught trout," Oppel notes, pointing to the skins of several nice brookies submerged in the lake in front of us.

"The jerks could have put the evidence in the woods," I mumble.

Not that I'm a saint. Years back, when I first came to the wilderness, I too cleaned fish in the lakes and streams that I canoed. But no longer. The impact of leaving offal or garbage near campsites is adverse to other folks enjoying the wilderness.

Our wrappers and twist ties will be packed out with us. The innards of any fish we catch will be deposited away from the water, in the depths of the forest, where varmints can clean them up. Dishes are done in the same pots used for cooking and the gray water is spread on the ground so that our impact here is minimized.

"Matt, I thought you said there were fish in this lake," I say as I toss a worm and jig into deep water.

As we fish, I form a theory about the remains we saw lying on the bottom of the lake. A front moving through piqued the interest of the lake's brook trout, rallying them from the doldrums of summer. Now the front is gone and the only evidence of fish is one small speckled trout that darts after my Mepp's Spinner but does not strike.

"There were lots of 'em. Big ones. Maybe this is the wrong lake."

"Wrong lake? I don't think so. The portage was right where you said it should be."

"Still, I remember a big cliff. I don't see any cliffs."

We work our way to the western end of the lake. A bald eagle spreads its wings and leaves a dead white pine, its black and white coloring contrasting with the slate sky.

"Here's your cliff," I call out, landing the Discovery against the foot of a bluff, the majority of which is concealed behind a wall of cedars.

"Doesn't look like the place I remember."

We catch no fish. We portage back to Brule Lake. At least we didn't leave any garbage behind as evidence of our folly.

A new day arrives on the heels of a brilliantly vacant sky. The sun rises over trees to the east and quickly warms the day beyond normal September temperatures. It's the last day of our three-day trek. My eldest sons, Matt and Dylan, and Matt's pal Chris Oppel remain fast asleep in our tent. I'm an early riser: I usually work on my writing at 5:00am in the morning. Of course, I'm not writing anything in the woods. I'm making coffee over the hissing burner of a propane camp stove.

We came to Brule Lake in search of fish. The evening before, on our return from the "secret" trout lake we managed to run into oodles of small-mouthed bass along the craggy shoreline of the big lake.

"Look at that," Dylan had yelled out from the front seat of my Old Town Discovery canoe as a bass struck Dylan's spinner near the placid surface of Brule Lake.

Soon, both canoes were fighting churning, wheeling, darting bass of all shapes and sizes. I held a particularly large specimen landed by Dylan in my hands.

"This one will be great in the frying pan. Nice fish, Dyl."

As I reached for my stringer, a thought occurred to me. *I wonder what the limit is?*

I opened my tackle box, put the fish on the stringer, and tossed it over the gunwale of the canoe. I dug inside the box and found my DNR regulations and thumbed through the pamphlet until I found what I was looking for.

"Oh, oh."

I reached over the side and raised the stringer out of the water.

"What are you doing?" Matt yelled from out from the other canoe as I slid the big fish off the stringer into Brule Lake.

I ignored my son, hoping that common sense would take over.

"Why are you letting the fish go?"

Dylan understood what I was doing and placed an index finger to his lips. I could see the light bulb go on inside Matt's head as if he was a character in a Saturday morning cartoon.

"Oh. I get it."

"Season closed two days ago. We can catch 'em but we can't keep 'em."

There's no wind this morning. The air warms quickly. In summer, our campsite on this dead end bay would be swarming with mosquitoes and flies of every configuration. But because it's September, there are no bugs. Not one. My trek down to the lake to fill up assorted pots with water for breakfast is pleasantly devoid of insects.

The boys get up. Our breakfast of instant oatmeal, breakfast bars, hot coffee, cocoa, and Kool-Aid goes down quickly. By mid-morning our gear is stowed. I invert my water-repellent oilskin bush hat to haul water to douse the campfire. Hot embers sputter and spew steam as I extinguish the last remnants of flame. A quick reconnoiter of the campsite reveals that we have followed the guidelines of the BWCA. We're leaving the campsite cleaner than we found it.

We fish the calm waters of the lake and land bass after bass, releasing them as soon as they reach the canoes. Some of the fish are smaller than the lures they chase after. Some would be fine specimens for the frying pan. All of them seek the warm waters of Brule Lake upon release.

"Catchin' anything other than bass?" I ask two guys in a square stern aluminum canoe anchored off a rocky point.

"Nope. Just bass."

"Lookin' for a campsite?" I ask, recalling the difficulties we faced finding a place to set up.

"Just in for the day," the man's companion advises.

"Good luck," I say before paddling away.

We enter a large bay that, according to the map on my lap, should be near where we entered Brule Lake two days earlier.

"I think the landing is straight ahead."

An informal race begins. Unfortunately, we're headed in the wrong direction.

"I think we're supposed to follow that guy in the kayak," Matt says, pointing out yet again that I'm illiterate when it comes to reading a map.

The two older boys shoot ahead. Dylan and I come about. Matt is in the stern of the red canoe. He sets a straight line for an opening in the shoreline, an opening, which, upon closer inspection, is the boat landing.

"Dig in. We'll take them on the inside."

Using experience to out-fox my eldest son, I cut inside his canoe. Dylan pulls mightily. My left shoulder, a joint that has given me trouble since high school, aches as I dig paddle into lake.

"Gotcha," I exclaim as we pass Matt and his buddy and cut them off from shore.

The prow of the Discovery meets sand. Our brief stay in wilderness is over. I'm tired and bone weary as I help load the canoes and gear and, as I settle in behind the steering wheel of the Honda, it occurs to me that I might want to pick up some walleye fillets on the way home.

Jack's Swing Set

"**Jack** really needs a play gym," my wife announced as she surveyed the emptiness of our backyard.

When we sold the old Sears farmhouse, the play gym I'd constructed for our three oldest sons remained behind as part of the sale.

"Well, when are you going to get to it?"

I knew better than to utter a response.

"I was thinking maybe next Saturday you could put it up."

"I guess I'll be working on it next Saturday, then won't I?"

We had already selected the particular unit at Menard's that seemed to fit the bill. The package included a tower, two swings, a rock-climb-ing wall, and assorted other stations in one fairly compact structure. The cost for the hardware and all of the lumber was around $500.00.

René borrowed her dad's truck to pick up the wood and hardware. When she pulled onto our back lawn in the little red pickup, the rear bumper of the truck scraped ground. Treated lumber was piled in the box of the vehicle to the limits of the topper.

"Is all that for this project?"

"Yup."

"Lots to cut, eh Dad?" Christian chided through a smile.

I scanned the stack of lumber.

Lots indeed.

"The box says it only takes five to seven hours to put together."

I stared hard at the printed information on the cardboard carton.

"René, you didn't read the fine print."

"How's that?"

"The fine print underneath the '5-7 hours' says that's con-tractor time."

"Oh."

My wife offered no further commentary as she headed towards the house.

Standing in summer light, the wind still, the heat meager, I read the instructions.

"Here's what I'm gonna do," I said to Chris, who was kneeling next to me as Jack danced around the pile excited as all get out that his long-promised swing set was about to be constructed.

"What's that?"

"Donate a buck to the church for every time I swear building this thing."

Chris smiled.

"You don't have that much money."

The time estimate on the box was right, that is, if you're only counting the amount of time it takes to saw the lumber. The wood wasn't precut. I had to measure and trim every piece. After six hours of sawing, I'd created a pile of pieces ready to be bolted together. I didn't utter one swear word during the process. The church was in jeopardy of being impoverished.

Sunday after worship, I began to assemble the main structure, the posts, the sandbox and the roof for the center tower; where Jack would pretend he was King Richard the III defending his domain. By nightfall, I was only half way through the assembly process. The church was three dollars ahead of the game. Total time spent to that point: sixteen hours.

Monday and Tuesday evenings, instead of watching the magical swirl of the Cloquet River or trying my hand at walleye fishing on nearby Island Lake, I worked on the play gym. Two more dollars were donated to Trinity Episcopal Church when I found the first and only major glitch in the quality of my construction. A plastic piece meant to fit between two posts as a *faux* rock ladder couldn't be anchored. A few curse words, some heady thinking and the gap was bridged by another post, allowing the ladder to be secured.

As stars twinkled Tuesday evening, I poured bags of mason's sand into the sandbox at the base of the tower. The swings were attached. The climbing ropes, slide, and other accessories were secured. Remarkably, the play gym appeared level and plumb from every angle.

"It looks great," René admitted, expressing genuine awe at my newfound construction prowess.

I kept my thoughts to myself.

"That really wasn't so bad now was it?"

I gnawed the inside of my mouth.

"Twenty-three."

"What?"

"Twenty-three," I repeated, picking up tools scattered across dry grass.

"What are you talking about?"

"The box said 'five to seven hours'. It took me twenty-three hours to put up this...." I paused, not wishing to owe the church any more money, "blessed thing," I concluded.

Behind me, my youngest son squealed with joy as he clambered up the slide.

"How can you put a price on that?"

My wife's rhetorical question drew no reply from me.

Wild Minnesota

It seems that life compels me to rush. I never have the time, or perhaps, I'm so blinded by my obsessive nature, that I never take the time, to relax. It's kind of pointless to trout fish if your mind isn't on the river. Despite this flaw in my personality, I still like to get away up the North Shore of Lake Superior in search of brook trout.

There are four trout species, not counting hybrids, that one can catch in Minnesota. German brown trout, rainbow trout (called steelheads when they occupy Lake Superior and return to the coastal rivers to spawn), lake trout, and brook or speckled trout. Of the four, only brook trout and lake trout are native to Minnesota. Before 1900, brook trout were limited by geography to Lake Superior itself and to those stretches of rivers, streams, and creeks between the lake and the first natural barrier (falls or rapids) located inland from Lake Superior's shoreline. That there are now native populations of propagating brookies above the first barrier in nearly every trickle of black water flowing from the interior of northeastern Minnesota is due to man's intervention: the artificial planting of fish above the first barriers during the late 19th and early 20th centuries.

My Honda Passport, a small SUV that I bought used and curse often, bounces along a blacktop highway threading the backwoods. It's a Friday morning in July. The sun is beginning to rise above the green leaves of aspen and birch and the feathered crowns of second-growth pines and spruce. There's not a cloud in the sky. Given my schedule as a District Court Judge, a vacation day during the week is a rare treat. But this day, one that's clear of rain and clouds, selected months in advance, does not foreshadow success on the water.

I'm determined to find the upper reaches of the Beaver River, a place noted for solid, if not spectacular, brook trout fishing. As you know from reading other tales of my angling misadventures, I'm a worm dunker. On rare occasions (when overcome by shame) I will resort to using artificial flies to tempt fish. Not today. Today, a day of leisure crammed between days of work, I will use worms: I want to catch fish.

A tiny ribbon of asphalt-hued water courses beneath the logging road. To the left side of the road, the landscape opens into a marshy plain. The place has all the look and feel of a beaver pond. Beaver ponds can, during their early stages of existence (before the water warms and silts up) hold fat trout.

I park the car by the side of the primitive trail and open the vehicle's rear hatch. The air is warm. The sky is open and silver blue. Fishing will be problematic. I pull on my neoprene waders, rig my fly rod (a cheap eight footer) with a hook, some split shot sinkers, and a small portion of night crawler. I snug my battered Australian bush hat down on my head, the brim sloped in multiple directions from the abuse it's seen over the years, and head down the ditch bank towards the creek.

The streambed is solid. There's ample gravel to support my weight as I wade downstream. I toss and retrieve the worm. Here and there, small chubs break free of the water and clamp down hard on the free food, only to break off once I haul them into open air. I catch no trout. I don't feel the telltale strike of a game fish: Only the nibble, nibble, nibble of pesky minnows.

The country opens up. At the far end of the clearing, perhaps a hundred yards from my position, a beaver dam blocks the flow of the creek. A shimmering pool of dark water has collected behind the artificial obstacle. The going becomes difficult. Hummocks of marsh grass, undulating piles of soggy earth interspaced with holes of brackish backwater, lace the perimeter of the pond. I sweat. Deer flies buzz my head, but thanks to the oilskin hat, they can't bite.

After fifteen minutes of plunging, slipping, teetering, and nearly submerging, I claim a small point of land jutting into the pond. I gingerly probe the murky water with a stick. The pond bottom is silty but solid. I step into water. The streambed holds my weight. I begin casting towards trouty places. I catch no fish but for the first time since leaving home, I feel the weight of my job, of marriage, of fatherhood, of trying to be a writer in my spare time, lighten. It's as if someone has filled my soul with a whiff of helium.

Here and there songbirds flit and trill. I'm not much of an ornithologist. I can't identify more than a few of the birds that inhabit the woods and swamps of this part of the world. I know the call of the robin, the voice of the red-winged blackbird, the chatter of the kingfisher. Beyond that, I'm pretty much clueless. An osprey glides into view, its wings outstretched, its voice distinctive and clear. The sun climbs. Fragments of cloud drift across the aqua and blue vault: The inconsequential pieces of fluff high and fragile. I wish that weren't so. I wish they were rain clouds gathering to spill. That'd help the fishing. But there's no rain in the forecast and none in the sky.

Beyond the occasional birdcall, the woods are silent. There's no wind. I work the near shoreline of the pond, pulling my waders free of the oozy bottom, loosening clouds of brown silt with each step.

Crash.

The noise comes from the far side of the pond. My heart races. I hold my breath. I know this much from nearly fifty years of life and an almost equal time in the bush: There are only two animals in northeastern Minnesota capable of making that much noise in the forest.

She doesn't see me at first. Her spindly legs clamber over the beaver dam. She steps into the deepest part of the pond with a grace that defies her size. Though some would consider her face, her large snout and loose neck to be unattractive, a cow moose is an impressive and beautiful creature when she's standing twenty feet away chest deep in water. Her eyes focus on me. It's clear she knows I'm here. She doesn't seem concerned by the small human mired in the muck of the pond. In reality, if she chose to charge me, out of curiosity or fear, I'd be a sitting duck. She'd be able to cover the distance between us in two strides. With my boots buried in the pond bottom, she'd bowl me over like one of those sand filled inflatable punching bags we played with when we were kids. I watch her carefully. She lowers her head, flies circling the thick fir of her back and rear, and moves steadily away from me in search of food.

For fifteen minutes I watch the moose eat. She never looks back, never acknowledges my presence after that first furtive glance. When she finally clambers off into the thick brush on the far shore, there is no mistaking the sound of a moose in the woods.

Later, as I drive north on Highway 2 towards Isabella, a bull moose canters onto the road, nearly colliding with a southbound Toyota in what seems like an urgent rush to cross the highway. Despite the fact that the bull is only fifty yards in front of the oncoming car, the car never slows.

How can you not see a moose on a highway?

I turn off Highway 2 and follow a primitive logging trail in search of better water. As I round the bend in the gravel road, a large animal lopes onto the path, stops, and rears itself on its hind legs. The black bear stands fat and ominous in the middle of the road watching the Honda intently as I place the vehicle in park. Satisfied that the car poses no threat, the boar lowers itself onto all fours and lumbers into the undergrowth in a manner reminiscent of ball players disappearing into an Iowa cornfield.

When I've fished enough to satisfy my lust, I head home. I catch one brook trout, a six-inch gleaming gem of color right in front of the beaver dam that I landed just before the cow moose joined me in the pond. I let the fish go realizing that God did not intend for me to catch trout on this day; that there were other matters on His or Her agenda for me to consider.

A Rainy Day

"**Where's** Copper?" I ask my eldest son Matt as we sit at the kitchen table. "I haven't seen him in a while."

The question references our three-year-old yellow Labrador retriever. A big, friendly dog, Copper usually stays close to home unless drawn into an excursion by our other "outside" dog, a black Labrador mix named Daisy. The speculation in our family is that Daisy's motivation isn't altruistic: She's trying to get Copper lost so she has the place all to herself.

"I haven't seen him since Sunday. He followed Kelly and me up the river when we took a canoe out."

"Where did you last see him?"

"He was in the Kaases's yard."

Barb and Jim Kaas live next door to us, in the old Sears farmhouse we sold to them. It's plausible, given the collection of horses and dogs assembled at the Kaas place, that Copper is simply visiting our neighbors.

Christian wanders upstairs from his bedroom clad only in boxer shorts.

"Chris, have you seen Copper?"

"Not since Sunday."

"Matt says the dog followed him up the river when he and Kelly went canoeing. Daisy's home so he's not with her."

"I haven't seen him."

I walk to a window in the great room and watch drizzle fall on the lush green of our lawn. June has been a rainy month, the kind of June I recall from my youth. The past few years, June has brought little rain and stifling heat, meaning that the lakes fed by the Cloquet and Beaver Rivers have been low, causing year-round residents on the lakes to complain to Minnesota Power, the corporate entity controlling the water level, to cease releasing water into the river. This year, the summer skies have opened up to quiet the complainers.

"You'll need to post pictures and information about Copper at the Minno-ette," I say to Chris. I hold a hot cup of coffee in my hand as I stand in the front entry of our home and watch the rain through a screen door. "He probably wandered all the way up to Island Lake. Some family is keeping him until they figure out where he came from."

Chris grumbles as he pours milk over his Frosted Mini-Wheats. Knowing his connection to the lost dog, I'm certain he'll post the notices.

I leave for work. By the time I come home there are posters up in all the local bars and convenience stores. No one calls about the dog.

The rain continues through Wednesday. Given that we've heard nothing about the dog, I begin to suspect the worst. A few days back, Chris rode our battered old Yamaha four-wheeler along the south bank of the river, near where Matt last saw the dog, but found no evidence of the missing Labrador. When I come home from work on Wednesday, I decide to search for the dog myself. I'm not optimistic. The realization that Copper likely never made it further than the Taft Road, the road that passes in front of the Kaas place, hangs over me like a pall. I'm saddened by the thought. Copper has been a good companion to my boys, especially Chris. I remember back to the day Chris and I first saw Copper's yellow puppy face staring at us from the top of the riverbank as we paddled home from a trip down the Cloquet River. That pup grew into an affectionate, obedient, gentle giant. Lately, with the addition of Jimi, my wife's miniature dachshund, to our family, Copper has found a new playmate. Though he outweighs Jimi by seventy-five pounds, Copper allows the pesky wiener dog to bite his ears, nip at his loose skin, and generally be a pest. When Copper's had enough, the big dog simply slaps a paw on Jimi's head and pins him, gently holding the puppy still until the little dog gets the message. Copper, when all things that matter in a dog are measured, has become one of the best Labs we've ever owned.

I dress in old jeans and a sweatshirt before pulling rain pants and a matching green poncho over my clothes. The rain attacks the roof of the front porch of our house as I sit on an old rocking chair and tighten the laces of my hiking boots. I decide against using the four-wheeler, figuring I can cover more ground on foot than I can if I'm restricted to trails.

My heart is heavy as I start my quest to find the missing dog. The rain intensifies. A steady pulse of clean, warm water strikes my rain suit as I leave the porch. I find no dog tracks in the mud of the access road leading from our house. I see no evidence of Copper.

I pause at the intersection of our road, the Knutsen Road, and the Taft Road, the two-lane county road that's a major traffic artery through Fredenberg Township. Dollops of rain splash against warm tar as I cross Taft. I follow the same trail that Chris had driven a few days earlier. I climb a small knoll. My eyes scan the underbrush, the vegetation sparse due to the presence of large white and red pines: The canopy precludes the incursion of alder. I walk a few steps along the ridge before I find our missing dog.

At first, I do not recognize him. Two or three days of summer heat have made Copper bloat to the size of a St. Bernard. His collar isn't visible. The dog's neck is so swollen that his collar has disappeared. I stop. I want to cry but, for some inexplicable reason, I can't. It's a scene, living in the country that I've confronted all too often. Dead dogs. Dead cats. Dead horses. I've buried a Noah's ark of animals on our land. Copper is just the latest in a long list of four-legged companions to have met his end living along the banks of the Cloquet River.

I kneel next to Copper and stroke his fur. It's clear from the wounds on his flank that he was struck by a car when he tried to cross the road. Copper, his life leaving him quickly, managed to crawl to a place of sanctuary, a sheltered nest beneath a huge white pine, protected from the rain, nearly invisible from the trail. I sigh, but still, I do not cry.

When I walk up our driveway to get the four-wheeler and its trailer, Chris is standing beneath the roof of the front porch. From the slowness of my gait, he knows.

"You found him?"

"Yes."

"Where?"

"Next to the trail going up the river. Underneath the big pines."

"I drove by there."

"I know. He was a ways off the trail. Must have crawled there. You stay here. You don't want to see him like this."

Chris doesn't say a word as I hitch the trailer to the Yamaha and pull the starter rope on the four-wheeler. The Yamaha coughs, then dies. I pull the rope again, flutter the throttle. The engine catches, then idles.

The dog is heavy and wet as I gather him in my arms and place him in the bed of the trailer. I drive slowly, filled with reverence, not urgency, as I head home.

Parking the trailer on the driveway, I walk past Christian and enter the foyer of our house. My son braves the weather to see his dog. I can only surmise that tears mix with warm rain as Chris silently contemplates his dead friend.

"He's gone," I tell my wife René as she stands behind the kitchen island preparing dinner.

"Copper?"

"He must have tried to follow Matt up the river. He never made it past the road."

"He was a good dog."

I leave it to my wife to relay the news to our youngest boy, Jack. At seven years old, the dog's passing will likely hit him hard. Sexist as it might sound, a mother's sensitivity is warranted in breaking such news to someone so young.

I walk back to the trailer. Chris looks away from his pal. His slender torso shudders. He follows the four-wheeler to the place I've chosen for Copper's grave. I turn off the Yamaha, grab a No. 2 shovel, and begin to dig. My son stands next to me for a moment before turning to escape the sadness.

It's only after I've patted the last of the muddy soil over Copper with the shovel that I allow tears to finally come.

The Boys Are Back

6:30am. Saturday. October. I'm in my writing studio. Instead of working on my latest novel (my fifth) I find myself looking out a window and studying the Cloquet River, a wide (and due to drought) shallow slash of black water slowly making its way west, to its confluence with the source of Lake Superior and all the other Great Lakes. Golden light creeps across the short green grass of our lawn. The sun's tentacles stretch over a ridge of trees, bathing the old Sears farmhouse we once owned in clean yellow light. It's morning on the river.

Boom. Boom. Boom.

The report of shotguns being emptied echoes through the river valley.

Boom. Boom. Boom.

That's Chris and his buddies. Sounds like they've got plenty to shoot at.

Robbie, Becker, Rodlund, and Chris greeted morning at the Munger Farm a little later than they wanted to.

"You look sort of tired," I said to Chris when he and his three hunting buddies gathered for breakfast in the kitchen of our house, sunlight already gathering to the east, the boys' desire to make it onto the water before dawn thwarted by delay.

"Celebrated my boss' birthday last night," my son replies. "Too much celebrating."

I smile. I remember my own young adulthood and all the "celebrating" I did. I let the comment pass. Chris cooks eggs and bacon for his crew. The boys make a youthful attempt at cleaning up their mess before Becker sounds the alarm.

"There's a guy canoeing down the river. His canoe is full of decoys."

"We better haul ass," Robbie says, "or he'll take our spot."

The boys make it to their blinds. Shotguns bark and I imagine beautiful green-headed mallards and darting teal falling from the sky, the ducks retrieved not by a dog (for the group has no dog with it) but by canoe.

370

My guess at what took place isn't far from reality. When the boys come back to the house for lunch, Robbie hefts two Giant Canada geese aloft for me to admire.

"Nice geese. Who shot 'em?"

"Me."

"Chris get anything?"

"Nope."

It's a gorgeous early October day. The boys are hunting local ducks and geese, birds that were raised on or near the river. Manitoba waterfowl haven't been pushed south by weather as yet. And since the Cloquet isn't a major flyway (the potholes of the Dakotas having usurped the lakes and streams of Minnesota in that regard) even when the weather turns and bitter winds and rain blow in from Canada, few migrating ducks and geese will traverse the Cloquet on their journey to the Gulf of Mexico.

The boys hunt until 4:00pm, the time set for waterfowl hunting to end the first weekend of the season. They take four dandy mallards (elegantly colored greenheads that have been fattening up for the trip south) in addition to the geese.

That evening, Massie joins the group with his dog. Chris opens a jar of Rene's homemade spaghetti sauce (just canned from this year's crop of tomatoes and the best sauce you've ever tasted), boils a ton of noodles, and feeds his hungry crew. The hunters gather in front of a roaring fire a stone's throw from the black water to relive the day's exploits. The sun is gone. Evening, its ebony veil punctured by eerily shifting stars, descends. The night grows quiet. Conversation wanes. The last beer is finished and the boys tumble into the basement and find beds. They're soon fast asleep. They've vowed to get up before dawn, ready to hunt. And that they do.

By the time dusk falls on Sunday, the hunters have bagged six nice Giant Canada geese, six mallards, a pair of wood ducks, a hell diver, and a couple of wayward mergansers.

"You guys have fun?" I ask Robbie as he walks tiredly from the fire ring where they group assembled to clean birds.

I've spent Sunday afternoon pulling carrots, potatoes, and onions from our vegetable garden; trimming my precious black raspberry canes; cutting and baling cornstalks for our

371

church's harvest sale; and tilling the garden. I've listened intently for shotgun fire in the near distance, appreciating that, with every discharge, the boys are experiencing the very reason I love living where I do.

"You bet. Thanks for letting us stay overnight. And for letting us hunt here."

"No problem. That's what it's for."

Chris and Massie aren't back yet. Though waterfowl hunting is closed for the day, they're back on one of my trails with the dog, hunting grouse. They won't be home until dark.

I look up at the clear blue sky. I take a deep breath, inhaling the smell of aspen leaves and autumn.

There's no better place.

Ashley, North Dakota 2010

We've been here four days. My 83-year-old father, my sons Matt and Chris, my father's buddy (and serious eater) Bruce, and two dogs have staked out our claim to North Dakota's pheasants. Only Chris has been productive, hitting most of the birds he's shot at. I've been dismal behind the sights of my twelve gauge over-under. Matt has been worse. But his yellow Labrador, Lexi, and a little Springer, Windsor, a dog borrowed from Chris's buddy Massie (who's undergoing a kidney transplant back home) have been such a joy to hunt with, just watching the two dogs work is a reward unto itself.

Then there are the old guys, men who once couldn't wait to get out into the field before the sun; men who now sip a third cup of morning coffee and think about how nice another twenty minutes of sleep would be. They've shot a couple of roosters. Very stupid birds who walked out in front of my old man's Tahoe and stood like statues so that Bruce could pop them both off with a single shot. Two birds with one shot. That's a feat for anyone, let along a guy who spends more time over his cereal bowl than in the field.

The weather has been horrible. We're working a sixty-acre plot of wide-open conservation land adjacent to a cornfield. We hunted the same patch at dusk yesterday and kicked out a mother lode of roosters and hens only to miss most of them. Today we're facing torrential rains, sleet, snow, and wind coming out of Canada in gusts between thirty and forty miles per hour. Even migrating geese and ducks know better than to be moving around on a day like today.

"Those Huns might be on the far side of that rise," I say to the boys as we creep up a sharp change in elevation towards a boulder-strewn thicket. "We might get a shot at 'em."

The birds (not Hungarian partridge, but a covey of sharptail grouse) rise from the far side of the ridge long before we're in range.

"Shit".

Twelve round-bodied birds flutter furiously against the wind. It appears we'll have no shot. But then, the sharpies do the inexplicable: They turn to catch the wind. Ever so briefly, they're suspended in midair as they try to take advantage of the gale.

"They're coming back," Matt says.

We raise our shotguns. Three barrels bark. A single partridge falls. I hit one, about thirty yards out, as it stalled in the wind.

"Nice shot, Dad," Chris says.

"Crap."

"What's wrong, Matt?" I ask my eldest son.

"Gun's jammed."

To shorten this piece, we'll fast forward past all the swear words and machinations between Matt, Chris, me, regarding Matt's Remington 870. The long and the short of it is that Matt stomps off towards his Nissan pickup a quarter mile away with his shotgun in two parts; our meager knowledge of field stripping and reassembling a Remington thwarted by weather.

"He's not happy," I observe.

"Not at all."

As Matt makes the crest of a hillock on his way to retrieve another gun, the flock of sharptail we just shot at flushes from beneath Matt's feet like doves ascending before Jesus. The birds flap furiously in the wind. Their departure is the last straw: We watch Matt launch the pieces of his inert shotgun at the fluttering birds.

"Now that's funny," I say, holding my gut as Matt kicks furiously at wind-swept grass.

"It sure is," Chris agrees. "But I don't think we should bring it up later."

My eldest picks up the pieces of his gun and moves on. Chris and I go about the business of hunting. The wind howls. The dogs try to work but the gale is so strong, any scent that's around dissipates like fairy dust. We stop and watch Matt crest another rise. Again, the sharpies take wing from beneath his boots. This time, Matt controls his temper and simply watches as the birds catch the wind.

That night, the five of us sip beer and watch the World Series in the little white house we've rented in downtown Ashley. Outside, the wind continues to pummel the land. Snow continues to fall. Inside, the dogs sleep heavily, their exhausted bodies curled tight against the storm. It isn't long before the story of Matt throwing his shotgun at a covey of sharptail partridge becomes the topic of conversation.

Caribou

800. Eighty-plus. Fifty-two. Sixteen. A dozen. Ten. Eight. Eight again. Six. Five. Two. Two more. Those are some of the numbers associated with last week's trek into the hinterlands of the Ontario taiga. For you non-adventurous types, a definition is needed here:

taiga | ˈtīgə |
noun (often the taiga)
the sometimes swampy coniferous forest of high northern latitudes, esp. that between the tundra and steppes of Siberia and North America.
ORIGIN late 19th cent.: from Russian taĭga, from Mongolian.
(From *The Apple Dictionary*)

Having given you a short lesson in geography, let me explain the numbers. 800 is the longest "official" portage some members of Boy Scout Troop 106 of Hermantown, MN completed on our recent journey north to Woodland Caribou Provincial Park. I say "official" because one of the passages between two of the boreal lakes on our route marked as a shallow creek turned out to be virtually dry. Which necessitated nearly a mile of dragging canoes through saw grass, muck, Canadian Shield gray boulders and pink quartz. Understand; I didn't go on this part of our collective journey but I sure heard about it from the six brave explorers who made the trek. More on that later.

Eighty-plus is the number of walleyes that my group, five pairs of canoeists, caught in two days of fishing on a lake which, because I'd like to go back and fish it again, shall remain nameless. Sixteen is the number of adults and young folks who made portions of the overall trip. I say portions because, as indicated, ten of us stayed on the fishing lake while six intrepid explorers made a large loop totaling over fifty miles of canoeing and portaging from start to finish. The explorers caught few fish but saw a bull moose resplendent in lily pads, water dripping off its rack as if staged for a Molson commercial. The six explorers also viewed pictographs drawn by long-forgotten First Peoples and touched the edge of true taiga where the spindly white spruce and jack pine that cover this part of the Canadian Shield give way to a virtually treeless landscape. And the explorers crossed over an old burn where the spindly conifers were charred to charcoal. Within the burn, Julie Belden, the only adult woman on the trip, found wild blueberries ripe and ready for the picking.

Another digression. The number two is significant here for two reasons (cute, eh?): There were two females on the journey, including Julie Belden and Heidi Hummell a teenager who defied the pouting, complaining version of young women seen on television sitcoms. Julie went with the explorers while Heidi and her father stayed with the fishing group. Two females. Two groups.

Ten? That was the most portages done by the explorers group led by Jim Belden in one day. Eight? That's the most portages completed by the fishing group led by Bryan Von Arb in one day. Eight was also supposed to be the number of fishermen staying behind to catch walleye on the secret lake I told you about but Mark and Heidi Hummell decided they'd rather catch walleye than wade loon shit. Go figure. So the second number eight in my computation became ten. A dozen represents my approximation of the snaky, voraciously hungry northern pike the group landed over the six days we were in Woodland Caribou. Since we were after walleye and lake trout, I don't think anyone minded that we tossed every pike back into the tannin stained water of the park. Five represents the number of lake trout the group caught, beginning with my son Jack's very first laker.

For those of you who are thinking, *A week on the water in a park akin to the BWCA isn't so tough,* let me explain some facts about Woodland Caribou Provincial Park. First, the name. Yes, there are actual caribou in the park. We didn't see any, not even the group that went further north. But, as indicated, the explorers did see a resplendent bull moose up close and personal and, the following scene will flesh out what the fishing crew experienced.

Morning. Before breakfast. The mist is clearing off Secret Lake. I am sitting on the rock outcropping a few meters from our campsite, sipping hot morning coffee and marveling at my good fortune. Good fortune because I was able to convince my fifteen-year old son that this would be an unforgettable trip. Good fortune because, with the guiding abilities of Mr. Von Arb, we've found walleye. Good fortune because I am married to a beautiful and gracious woman who knows that, from time to time, I need to replenish my internal battery on wilderness.

Anyway, on Secret Lake there had been another group camping on a spit of rock a mile or so away. That group left with the onset of the sun. The lake is calm. There is no wind. And yet, as would hold true throughout the week, there are no bugs. No gnats. No accursed black flies. No mosquitoes. So I am sitting on granite, looking out over a quiet body of black water, listening to the cry of loons in the distance, when I see them.

At first, I'm not sure that what I am seeing are caribou. This is because the animals aren't prancing along distant shoreline. They are swimming, making a beeline from the campsite the folks have just left for the far shore.

"Caribou!" I guess.

Nick Mallett, one of the Scouts, emerges from the trees. "Where?"

"There, near the point. They're swimming."

"My dad has binoculars."

"Get them. And tell the others."

Very soon, Nick returns with the eight others in our party. We all stand on the stony shoulders of the Shield, in a ragged line of expectancy, watching the animals swim. Each of us takes a turn with the field glasses. I'm last in line. I have the benefit of watching the animals emerge from the water onto solid ground at the mouth of a tiny creek Jack and I had fished the day before.

"They're not caribou," I finally say when I see the distinctive lanky legs and snout of North America's largest ungulate. "It's a cow moose and twin calves."

So yes, if one counts moose as a commonality between Woodland Caribou and the BWCA, together with the omnipresent granite, thin soil, and coniferous forest, there are similarities between the provincial park and America's most beloved canoeing retreat. But that's about where the connections between the two places end.

First, the portages. The BWCA may have removed the wonderfully helpful portage signs (marked in rods) that announced each trail, along with the convenient portage rests on longer overland treks. But the portages one carries his or her canoe across in the BWCA (even the remotest of the remote) are generally maintained. Not so with even the most well used portages in Woodland Caribou. The trails are rugged, narrow, prone to have jack pine or white spruce blow-downs blocking them, and are generally unmarked. You have to be a woodland detective to find the trail from one lake to the next.

Then there is the traffic. The two parks are about the same size. Woodland Caribou is 1.2 million acres of prime wilderness. The BWCA (without the adjacent Quetico across the border) is 1 million acres, give or take. But whereas the BWCA sees 200,000 visitors a year, Woodland Caribou has less than 1,000 visitors a season. That's right. Less than 1,000. So while you may see fellow campers and canoeists on lakes that are known for their walleye fisheries (as our fishing group did), the more intrepid paddlers, like our explorers group, can pretty well be assured of seeing no other humans.

Then there are the campsites. On occasion, after massive straight-line winds or fires, campsites in the BWCA become unusable. But the beaveresque crews of the US Forest Service usually have them cleared and in fine shape before too long. And all the approved campsites in the BWCA have fire grates and latrines, making camping, while certainly more primitive than your typical state park, doable for even the sissy pants in your group. Caribou has no fire grates. No latrines. And most of the campsites are prone to being rendered unusable without the aid of a hatchet and saw. Every night, the creaking of white spruce and jack pines ready to tumble to the ground made for some interesting sleep given that our thinly skinned tents provided little shelter against the sudden descent of trees. This isn't to say that some of the sites weren't as picturesque or more so than their American counterparts.

Our tenting spot on the crown of a rocky shoulder on Jake Lake was everything you'd want in a campsite: A clearing in the trees to let the breeze waft through. Plenty of firewood. Spots to use for your daily deposits (remember, there are no latrines and you really can't dig into rock!). Fish (Jack caught a nice three pound laker we baked for breakfast on Jake). And even a sandy beach to clean off the dust and grime of the trail.

Secret Lake boasted not one, not two, but three BWCA-quality sites, two of which the separate squadrons of our group inhabited before splitting into the adventurers and the fishermen (and woman, sorry Heidi-you did your part too!). But then there were times where the campsites designated on the map either didn't exist or had been obliterated by storms.
Case in point: our first night, which we spent on East Lunch Lake, was essentially an experience in sleeping on bedrock.

Thank God for the weather. Other than a rainstorm our first day on the water, which repeated itself as we slept on the rocky outcropping on East Lunch, we never encountered rain, or even wind until our groups reunited, our time was done, and we were back on Leano Lake searching for the invisible portage to the parking lot. Every day was sunny, warm, pleasant, and, though it's repetitive to say so, bugless.

Paddling Leano Lake, I marveled at how tan and strong my adolescent son had become in one short week. Not that everything was always perfect in our canoe. Oh no, that would be a lie. We had our moments, like when Jack was grousing that I wasn't paddling in the stern while he was trying to fish. He was frustrated, I think, because everyone else seemed to be catching walleye but us. His tone hinted disrespect. I splashed water on him with my paddle. We were in danger of getting into a row in the middle of the lake where everyone in the fishing group would have a ringside seat. But then, a walleye hit Jack's jig. He set the hook like a pro. We began to catch fish and the storm passed. Funny how northern walleyes, which fight so much deeper and stronger than their warm water cousins, can change a kid's perspective on life.

Once we made the parking lot at Leano Lake, all that was left to do was secure our gear, tie down the canoes on the four vehicles in our caravan, and make the long, dusty trek back to Red Lake where pizza awaited. Rumors of a Pizza Hut proved false. But we lucked out. Antonio's, it turns out, a place that, from the outside, looks like a hole in the wall, but on the inside, rivals the finest Olive Garden, had big pizzas, hand-made, cooked to perfection, and at a price far less than one would pay at a chain. Troop 106's good fortune held even in town.

Then it was off to Pakwash Provincial Park for our last night of camping before the eight-hour drive home. Pakwash is akin to the Minnesota state parks you may be familiar with. It has spots for tenters (like us) and RVs, pop-up campers, and everything in-between all snugged along the shoreline of beautiful Pakwash Lake. I donned my swimming suit, gathered up my toothpaste and soap, and headed for the sand beach, foregoing the hot showers that Jack and everyone else went off to enjoy. I think I chose the lake over the showers because, well, I just didn't want the magic of the trip to end.

After scrubbing my near-naked body with a bar of Dove and cleaning a week's worth of gunk from my gums over a cold water tap, I wandered down a gravel lane to the beach. The shoreline was deserted. Alone, my aching back, hips, knees, and shoulders finally at ease, I waded into Pakwash and let the cold waters of Northwestern Ontario surround me. Threatening skies sped to the east after lobbing a few splats of rain on my newly muscled shoulders and arms but there would be no rain to ruin the evening.

Katherine Lake

If you study a map of northeastern Minnesota and follow the thin black fissure that denotes the Cloquet River with your index finger, you'll cover nearly all of southern St. Louis County; the largest county east of the Mississippi River. This imaginary journey will lead you through remnant white pine forest, maple savanna, incalculable marsh, and over occasional rapids and waterfalls to the river's place of beginning in the middle of Lake County. You'll wind up a bit north of Two Harbors and a few dozen miles east of Lake Superior's North Shore.

I've made this journey in person. But though I had visions of floating the upper Cloquet, from its meager birthing place as a tiny meander leaving Katherine Lake, to the river's stony conclusion near Brookston where its tannin-stained waters merge with the St. Louis River, my visit to the shores of Katherine Lake wasn't as romantic as my daydreams: I made my only trip to Katherine Lake by car.

It's easy to forget that many of the rivers we Minnesotans love and claim as our own descend from pools of quiet stillness. Lakes are to rivers as glaciers are to icebergs: places of conception, nourishment, and birth. Katherine Lake is such a place. A shallow, sixty-five acre pond of murkiness boasting one tumbled down cabin perched on a singular island in the middle of bulrush-defined water; Katherine isn't a shining jewel of a lake. She isn't the sort of aquatic poster child the State of Minnesota would display on the cover of one of its tourism brochures.

My vision of launching a cedar strip canoe in the rivulet that exits Katherine Lake to paddle through dense boreal forest past moose, bear, and timber wolves and to float contently beneath the wings of osprey and bald eagles is a flight of fancy far removed from reality.

Katherine Lake squats forlornly against a decimated landscape, her boundary defined by hundreds of square miles of swamp and clear-cut. Still, there is a calm, a peace to be found standing on the unsteady shoreline of that little lake. She is, after all, the mother of the river I call home.

About the Author

Mark Munger is a life-long resident of Northeastern Minnesota. Mark, his wife, René, and their youngest son live on the banks of the wild and scenic Cloquet River north of Duluth. When not writing fiction, Mark enjoys hunting, fishing, and working as a District Court Judge.

Other Works by the Author

The Legacy (eBook in all formats)
Set against the backdrop of WWII Yugoslavia and present-day Minnesota, this debut novel combines elements of military history, romance, thriller, and mystery. Rated 3 and 1/2 daggers out of 4 by *The Mystery Review Quarterly*.

Ordinary Lives (ISBN 97809792717517 and eBook in all formats)
Creative fiction from one of Northern Minnesota's newest writers, these stories touch upon all elements of the human condition and leave the reader asking for more.

Pigs, a Trial Lawyer's Story (eBook in all formats)
A story of a young trial attorney, a giant corporation, marital infidelity, moral conflict, and choices made, *Pigs* takes place against the backdrop of Western Minnesota's beautiful Smoky Hills. This tale is being compared by reviewers to Grisham's best.

Suomalaiset: People of the Marsh (ISBN 0972005064 and eBook in all formats)
A dockworker is found hanging from a rope in a city park. How is his death tied to the turbulence of the times? A masterful novel of compelling history and emotion, *Suomalaiset* has been hailed by reviewers as a "must read."

Esther's Race (eBook in all formats)
The story of an African American registered nurse who confronts race, religion, and tragedy in her quest for love, this novel is set against the stark and vivid beauty of Wisconsin's Apostle Islands, the pastoral landscape of Central Iowa, and the steel and glass of Minneapolis. A great read soon to be a favorite of book clubs across America.

Mr. Environment: The Willard Munger Story (ISBN 9780979217524: Trade paperback only)
A detailed and moving biography of Minnesota's leading environmental champion and longest serving member of the Minnesota House of Representatives, *Mr. Environment* is destined to become a book every Minnesotan has on his or her bookshelf

Laman's River
(ISBN 9780979217531 and eBook in all formats)

A beautiful newspaper reporter is found bound, gagged, and dead. A Duluth judge conceals secrets that may end her career. A reclusive community of religious zealots seeks to protect its view of the hereafter by unleashing an avenging angel upon the world. Mormons. Murder. Minnesota. Montana. Reprising two of your favorite characters from *The Legacy*, Deb Slater and Herb Whitefeather. Buy it now in print or on all major eBook platforms!

Sukulaiset: The Kindred

The long awaited sequel to Mark's masterpiece of historical fiction, *Suomalaiset: People of the Marsh*, this novel-in-progress was a finalist for the 2011 Pirate's Alley Faulkner Award. Due to be published on the 10th anniversary of the release of its predecessor, *Sukulaiset* follows Elin Gustafson Ellison Goldfarb, one of the main characters from *Suomalaiset* as she and her second husband leave America for Karelia during the height of Karelian Fever. A love story. A war story. A story of purges and the Holocaust. Above all, a complex tale of Karelia, Finland, and Estonia during the Great Depression and the Second World War, this book will be as cherished as Mark's previous historical novels. **Coming to a bookshelf or eReader near you in 2014!**

Visit us at www.cloquetriverpress.com

24706430R00226

Made in the USA
Charleston, SC
02 December 2013